TROUT HUNTING

Happiness is a life dedicated to occupations for which that individual feels a singular vocation. Immersed in them, he misses nothing; the whole present fills him completely, free from desire and nostalgia... For that reason we want them never to end...And really, once absorbed in a pleasurable occupation, we catch a starry glimpse of eternity.

Jose Ortega y Gasset
Meditations on Hunting
Lisbon 1942

TROUT HUNTING

The pursuit of happiness

BOB WYATT

SWAN·HILL
PRESS

To Margaret
after all.

Grateful acknowledgement is made to the following for permission to reprint excerpts from these books:

Simon and Schuster, Publishers, New York, and D A Ortega Klein, Herederos de J Ortega y Gasset, for the quotations from *Meditations On Hunting*, by Jose Ortega y Gasset, (1986 edition, Charles Scribners Sons NY).

HarperCollins, Publishers, New York, for the excerpt from Annie Dillard's *Pilgrim At Tinker Creek* (1998 Perennial Classics Edition)

Valerie Haig-Brown, executor of the Roderick Haig-Brown estate, for the closing quotation from *A River Never Sleeps*.

Copyright © 2004 Bob Wyatt

First published in the UK in 2004
by Swan Hill Press, an imprint of Quiller Publishing Ltd.

British Library Cataloguing-in-Publication Data
A catalogue record for this book
is available from the British Library

ISBN 1 904057 52 7

Printed in China

Swan Hill Press
an imprint of Quiller Publishing Ltd.
Wykey House, Wykey, Shrewsbury, SY4 1JA, England
Tel: 01939 261616 Fax: 01939 261606
E-mail: info@quillerbooks.com
Website: www.swanhillbooks.com

Contents

Introduction:
What is fly-fishing, really?

When one is hunting, the air has another, more exquisite feel as it glides over the skin and enters the lungs, the rocks acquire a more expressive physiognomy, the vegetation becomes loaded with meaning... the axis of the whole situation is that mystical union with the animal, a sensing and presentiment of it that automatically leads the hunter to perceive the environment from the point of view of the prey.

Jose Ortega y Gasset
Meditations on Hunting

Assynt, Scotland

The unexamined life is not worth living, said Socrates, but fly-fishing has undergone such an intense period of introspection recently we are reminded that the converse is also true. Compared to the time spent thinking, arguing, reading, tinkering with tackle, tying flies, planning or just day-dreaming about fly-fishing, our 'real-time' on the water is laughably short. Nevertheless, something about fly-fishing encourages this reflective attitude, and there is certainly more to it than baby-boomer fashion and nostalgia. If we were to be high-faluting about it, we might say that fly-fishing embodies one of the few western cultural narratives to have survived modernity intact. I stop short of using the phrase *grand narratives* because when describing one's enthusiasms it is too easy to slip into that type of hyperbole, and *grand* should probably be reserved for the major cultural narratives, like democracy and football.

Looking at it from my perspective as an art school lecturer, I don't think it is entirely unreasonable to compare the fly-fishing tradition to what cultural studies boffins call the 'master narratives' of art. I don't mean to compare fly-fishing to art in terms of its importance to a culture, but there are similarities. Like art, fly-fishing doesn't make much sense in practical terms; its aims are primarily aesthetic. And, you have to wonder just how large a part, if any, art plays in our daily lives. Some respected cultural authorities argue that contemporary art is losing, or has already lost, its capacity for meaningful engagement with popular culture. The art of painting, accused of elitist aestheticism, an artifact of the old regime, has been declared dead several times over the past century by academics who argue that its cultural narrative or thread of meaning has been severed, and there are many, including some inside the art world, who would say, 'who cares?' Several other art forms such as Elizabethan theatre and opera have been preserved, again considered by many to be no more than exclusive highbrow curiosities in the twenty-first century cultural theme park. Fly-fishing, meanwhile, neither art nor game, has developed aesthetically and as a significant cultural activity at an astonishing rate that cuts across social boundaries, and appears to be gathering momentum.

Usually referred to as an interest, sport, hobby or pastime (the word 'mere' is implied), to its insiders fly-fishing is 'my world', a complicated matrix of desire, experience and associations. It involves your finances, your emotional relationships, your taste and your children. It normally involves your closest friends. It's fun, but like art, it's *serious*, and like other serious pursuits it is integrated into our very concept of self. If not entirely a way of life, for many of us fly-fishing provides a strong thread of meaning to life, although there is always a droll outsider to suggest that we *get* a life.

Every few decades, there is a paradigm shift in our thinking, and we currently find ourselves in what is probably another of fly-fishing's golden ages. At some point, writers concerned with the history of fly-fishing usually of trot out Ælian, the third century Roman who described the Macedonian practice of catching fish with speckled skins on a lure made from red wool and the feathers from a cock's wattles (I just trotted him out myself). We all recognise the significance of that moment; fly-fishing had been invented. To be correct, the practice of fly-fishing had been documented, since it had obviously been practised for some time before Ælian brought it to public attention, the beginning of a narrative handed down through two millennia. Hunting with dogs, on foot or horseback, probably the only so-called blood sport that surpasses it in longevity and compares aesthetically, is to all appearances singing its swan song in Europe, after thousands of years of unbroken tradition.

That this rather quirky and addictive pursuit has a history so long lends some weight to our attempts to explain it, even if traditions so old don't usually need explaining. After all, you'd think it would be enough that fly-fishing has survived the great upheaval of modernism, not as some quaint relic of the *ancien regime*, but a vital and creative activity that is only now entering its golden age. The equipment is not just efficient but elegant, even exquisite. The codes of behaviour are self-regulating and progressive; who, fifty years ago, could have imagined the current enthusiasm for catch and release? The better heeled and fanatic among us are putting flies in the way of every species possible, in every conceivable type of water, all over the planet. It no longer seems exotic or strange to read a photo-essay on the sporting qualities of some unheard of fish in the swamps of New Guinea. Somebody says, 'Man, those Honduran bat-fish will spool you in ten seconds flat!' We go, 'Yeah? Sounds good. How much is the airfare to Honduras, anyway?' This is such a prevalent attitude that everyone I fish with, regardless of economic circumstances, feels that they will fish for tarpon and bonefish, sooner or later. We can all imagine ourselves punching a cast into the wind on a bleak Tierra Del Fuego sea-trout river. In our minds, at least, we have all become world travellers.

Time-out in the Kootenays

The literature has never been so philosophical. North American anglers in particular have embraced the new attitudes with evangelical fervour. With few truly ancient cultural narratives to worry about, Americans have never displayed the slightest hesitation toward making some up. But then, the re-invented life is as American as chicken-fried steak. The North American angler has been reconstructed, from a bucolic and somewhat puritanical Ted Trueblood character to a suave, athletic, articulate, well informed, politically aware, sympathetic and somewhat ironic world adventurer, and she looks *good*.

British anglers have always been a little more conservative. Perhaps, in terms of ancient traditions, they feel they have more to conserve, but things are changing there as well, and in more ways than just swapping the tweed deerstalker for a baseball cap. I fish with a group of guys every July in northwest Scotland. Last year we had an after-dinner poetry reading to commemorate the death of Ted Hughes, the British Poet Laureate, whose fishing imagery ranks among his most powerful and moving, and it didn't seem at all pretentious or embarrassing (well, maybe just a little). I think it is important to realise that these developments are not just the result of snobbery and status anxiety, as some complain, although *Forbes* magazine recently announced that fly-fishing has succeeded golf as the chosen leisure activity of a majority of company CEOs.

The maturity of the sport and its scope for broadening the experience were evident back in the sixties, in the popularity of the writings of Haig-Brown and others. Initially, a relatively stable cult following, but soon it was clear that a generation had embraced fly-fishing in a way that could not have been anticipated. The question is, which came first, *A River Runs Through It* (the movie) or the public readiness for it? Robert Redford's stylish and poignant mix of romance, nostalgia, and environmentalism, distilled so effectively from Norman MacLean's novella, didn't cause anything, except for a few boomer fashion victims who became instantly haunted by waters, and hung some dried flowers in an old wicker creel by the fireplace. We were not just ready for it; we were hungry for it. 'The movie', as it is often referred to in the angling press, was a marker for the way things had changed.

Like the day President Kennedy was shot, I remember what I was doing when I heard Roderick Haig-Brown had died. I was not prepared for the feeling of loss I experienced. I felt I knew him and might meet him one day on a river. This was always less than a real possibility, but when fishing Vancouver Island's Stamp, Gold, or Englishman, I was conscious of being on his water. He had conditioned my experience of those rivers, and of all rivers. I was fishing in a more self-conscious way, the correct way, with more care and restraint than I had on the rivers of my predatory youth.

The effect of fly-fishing's grand narrative (I've decided that it is pretty grand after all) is that reflexivity is built-in; we reflect as we do the thing, not only after the fact. We are not mere observers but participants in the order of things, shaping ourselves as we shape the experience, and we add that experience to the sum of a world of our own making. Contemporary psychologists refer to this as 'self-construction', philosophers would call it 'world-making'. We feel integrated with the real world as we wish it to be – a spacious world of fresh air, clear water, and free, wild creatures that we search for with our artfully created lure. Fly-fishing conditions our sense of beauty and proportion and gives us some purchase on what seem like true values. Sometimes, when things are really going well, we find ourselves in a pure and self-aware state of happiness.

In his final interview before his death, Ted Hughes, a keen fly-fisherman, described it as our search for the 'original lost condition, a place where you are one among the bears'. Fly-fishing is certainly that, but is not only the reification of our primitive *ur*-self. It is also a deep integration with aesthetic traditions that, as Haig-Brown put it, have their foundation in the first guy who sneaked away to the creek when the tribe did not really need fish. Another Hughes, Robert this time, art critic for *Time* magazine and again a serious life-long fly-fisherman, makes the claim in *A Jerk On One End*, that Ernest Hemingway was not obsessed with fishing because he was a killer, but because he was an aesthete, a stylist.

We fish for pleasure, and the aesthetic aspects of fly-fishing are a deep and reliable source of that pleasure. As well as being essentially non-competitive, fly-fishing is so quietly elegant that it is difficult and inaccurate to classify it as a sport, and it is certainly no game. Despite the commonplace attribution, it has never really attained the status of an art – until now, that is, when its purposes are truly nearing the condition of art. By definition, art has historically been a matter of purposeless aesthetic form, of no practical use. Now that we seldom kill a wild fish, the outcomes of a day's fishing are certainly not material, if not completely intangible and fugitive.

To carry on in this vein a bit further, if the thread of meaning in many traditions of art, religion and many other ethnic and cultural narratives has been broken, it is not surprising that a pursuit as coherent and beautiful as fly-fishing should be embraced by so many. Few arts and sports have unbroken traditions so long, a philosophy and literature so well developed, or roots so deep in our essential humanity. The more philosophical among us have described it as a pursuit of innocence. In his thought-provoking book, *What The Trout Said*, Datus Proper quotes from Annie Dillard's *Pilgrim at Tinker Creek*, and it's worth repeating... 'It is possible to pursue innocence as hounds pursue hares: single-mindedly, driven by a kind of love, crashing over creeks, keening and lost in fields and forests, vaulting all hedges and hills wide-eyed, giving loud tongue all unawares to the deepest, most incomprehensible longing, a root flame in the heart'.

Unfortunately, it is the human condition to be incapable of recouping lost innocence, but hunting – and fly-fishing is certainly a form of hunting – just maybe brings us closest to that original state. The appeal of fly-fishing is so self-evident and fast-growing that we can imagine a terrifying situation where there are just too many fly-fishers, like the desperate fishing scene in *On The Beach*. This is already the case on some of the highly publicised waters, including some that appear to be in danger of being loved to death, and there are almost no last good places left undiscovered. Places where one can be one among the bears are still out there, but the bears are getting pretty used to living on our leftovers. The world is changing fast, and there will always be those who want to get 'theirs' before it is all gone. The rest of us, who usually have to fish behind someone else, may find the experience of true wilderness unattainable and that the original lost condition is not a preserved patch of Eden accessible by wealth and helicopter, but is really a state of the mind and spirit.

* * * * *

1. Tradition

And this is what concerns us: what does a man do when, and in the extent that, he is free to do as he pleases?

Jose Ortega y Gasset
Meditations on Hunting

Evening, Assynt, Scotland

1. Form follows function

For some, the traditional approach simply means the correct way to fish. The orthodox view, it has as much to do with self-presentation as catching trout. If you are a fly-fisher then you already belong to this camp to some extent. Any fishing is good, but fly-fishing isn't just another way to catch fish. I mean, why fly-fish if not for the pleasures of the tradition, its aesthetics, elegance and style, of viewing yourself as part of a great code of practice extending back at least to early Roman times? It's hard to duck the accusation that we consider dry fly-fishing for trout to be somehow superior to soaking a stink-bait for catfish.

In terms of pleasure alone, fly-fishing is considered by its practitioners to be higher on the scale of experience than bait-fishing, just as most would likely agree that dining on a rare Aberdeen Angus steak with a good red wine in pleasant surroundings is more pleasurable than bolting a burger and a chocolate shake in a bus station. This invites the objection that it is a class thing, but it isn't just snobbery. Admittedly, one experience costs more than the other, but the important difference is that it is undeniably more interesting and pleasurable. Whether we can afford them or not, some experiences are just more enjoyable than others, and anyway, fly-fishing isn't necessarily more expensive. As difficult as it is, anyone who has actually tried fly-fishing usually likes it more than bait or spin fishing, especially if they get a few fish. By definition, bait-fishing means messing around with bait. It not only smells better but everything about fly-fishing is a source of pleasure and interest, even its difficulty. The beauty and function of a modern fly rod or reel is appreciated because we have a history and tradition to measure it against, a context. The techniques, strategies and ethics of fly-fishing are codified within a philosophy of aesthetic form and restraint.

And who is to say where tradition begins or ends? If fly-fishing were only tradition, of form over function so to speak, we might still be using brass reels and twelve-foot greenheart rods. As it is, a strong core of traditionalists regards the bamboo rod and the Catskill dry fly as the apotheosis of the art, like some exquisite beetle in amber. Their reason is the understanding and respect for hand crafted elegance and style in the tools, although there are plenty of 'boo' evangelists who will argue the case on grounds of performance alone. For example, my friend David McClennan owns a quiverful of creaky bamboo Hardys and worn Perfects, passed down to him by his father, and insists on referring to graphite rods as 'those chemical johnnies'. To David, I'm just another gimmick-obsessed tackle junkie who can't resist the increased performance and beauty of the new gear. Some people get quite exercised over this sort of thing. It just eats them up that anyone would spend that much on a fishing reel, as if we were spending the kids' shoe money, although in some cases we undoubtedly are. Others just feel it's not in the spirit of the thing to swagger around showing off the logo on your tackle, and they're probably right. While I agree that labels don't mean much to a trout, I don't throw in with the willow switch and bent pin brigade. All of my dozen or so trout rods (all absolutely essential, I hasten to add) are chemical johnnies, and my drawer-full of fly reels are as high-tech, or just as damned elegant, as I can afford.

This kind of thing, including the good-natured snobbery, is all part of the fun. Fly-fishing, for all its pretensions to being an art, if not a religion, is at the very least a broad church. On the other hand, we would not be enjoying the fabulous experiences we do today if it were only a matter of respect for tradition. Experiments in tackle and fly design have placed the next to impossible Permit and Yellowfin Tuna on the list of fly-fishing quarry. Bruisers like the tuna and marlin are now the focus of a specialist branch of the tradition, while fish such as the grayling, pike, even carp, historically considered vermin by trout anglers, have societies centred on their pursuit and protection, with their own emerging traditions within the larger one of fly-fishing. Fly-fishing is not only a tradition; it is a bonafide sub-culture with its own philosophical and ethical system, not to mention the inevitable branches, hierarchies, avantgardes and exclusive social elites.

It's not just the artificial nature of the bait that separates fly-fishing from bait fishing but the angler's attitude and approach to the quarry. Bait fishing is setting a trap for the fish, real food with a hook in it, and is comparatively passive. Fly-fishing is true hunting, active and seeking. Unlike bait fishing, despite the common misconception by those who do not fish, fly-fishing does not require patience.

A nice Rocky Mountain trout on the Deer Hair Sedge

These comments might enrage all those expert bait fishermen out there, and I practised it enough myself to know the difference between upstream worming and drowning maggots while snoozing in a lawn chair, but we're talking fundamentals here. It goes without saying that spinning falls somewhere in between. That said, not all fly-fishing is equal in terms of the quality of the experience. At one end of the fly-fishing spectrum is the dull game of pulling a lure past the nose of a benighted farm animal, a sort of wet chicken that has had no experience beyond competing for food pellets in a herd of identical fish. At the other end is the stylish, expensive and often exclusive world of wild fish, private water, restrictive rules and international destination angling. Between those two poles is a world of specialised and fascinating experience.

Although the art and craft have been thrust rapidly into their current state by passionate American anglers and tackle designers, the model for the worldwide philosophy of fair chase and the basic design of fly-fishing equipment is British, shaped by the highly ritualised protocols of nineteenth century England. Fly tackle embodies the idea of built-in restraint rather than efficiency, elegant and simple, combining superb craftsmanship with functional design. To many it sums up a preferred view of tweedy Englishness: cricket, warm beer and country pubs, although even the hexagonal bamboo rod is an American idea, and it is fair to say that it is in the American literature that the aesthetic and philosophical pulse beats strongest today. The quality of the experience, rather than the most effective means to catch the most fish, is the bedrock of the Anglo-American fly-fishing tradition. When one understands its ethos, the difference between fly-fishing and all other forms of fishing becomes clear. An aesthetic tradition, embodied in the tackle, theory and practice, is a large part of what makes the fly-fishing experience meaningful. While it is true that fly-fishing is often the most effective way to catch trout, with no understanding and appreciation of its traditions it is a less interesting and enjoyable pursuit, and rather pointless.

A deep source of pleasure for many fly-fishing enthusiasts in itself, tradition can narrow the creative and open-ended inquiry in favour of tried and tested methods, and crystallises into orthodoxy. Sometimes tradition can be so hide-bound that it seems like empty form, practised in an atmosphere of reactionary conservatism, style for its own sake. A good fly-fisher builds his or her strategies on sound traditional theory and practice, but with a creative and experimental attitude, keeping an eye peeled for opportunity. Tradition only becomes a problem if it stands in the way of your own pleasure or understanding, although many people get as much satisfaction as they want from the strictest codes of behaviour. It could be argued that it is ultimately a matter of style – you choose to limit your activities to a narrower and stricter code, or not. Despite the threnodies of a few recidivist Halfordians, the fly-fishing tradition is a progressive, generous and inclusive one, and it pays to be mindful that not everyone will be interested in the stipulations of your personal code.

2. The books

There is a lot of information available to the fly-fisher today, certainly more than we need for successful fishing, and it just keeps coming. All this how-to information might create the impression that fly-fishing's sole concern is the technology of pursuit, or worse, that it's just a game. The code, craft and ethos of fly-fishing is accessible to those who read the fly-fishing literature, and although some have come close no one book can present the thing in a piece. Any attempt to do so usually collapses into 'entry level' generalities or meanders into the bayous of specialist tactics. The best books outline a workable and effective approach to fly-fishing based on personal experience, and add some specialised wrinkles to the tradition. Rather than just another attempt to boil such a complex mass of information down, it seems to me that the best one can do for someone new to fly-fishing, and not bore the gravel guards off the old timers, is point to the great books of the past, mention some of the good recent ones, and maybe add a personal perspective on the expertise they contain.

There are hundreds of fly-fishing books in print, containing an unavoidable amount of repetition (as there is in this one) and conflicting advice. Some books are purely technical, objective analyses of the wild trout and its response to flies and tactics. The good technical books will help get your strategies organised. They often make up for their dryness by accurate observations of the fish, its prey, the tactics and flies that will work. Other books are beautiful accounts of experience in language that but for the subject would be considered art. Some are wise and reflective; some rather solemn, even pious; some pithy and ironic; a few are simply hilarious. The best have the clear ring of truth, forged on the anvil of success and failure.

Writer and publisher Nick Lyons considers Roderick Haig-Brown to be 'indispensable to the literate angler, through whom the mainstream of fly-fishing culture runs most clearly.' *A River Never Sleeps* and *The Western Angler* were my first serious fishing books as a teenager; it was

Deliberations on a high corrie loch, Scotland

thirty degrees below zero, and I found the books in the 'bookmobile', a converted bus-cum-mobile library that smelled richly of diesel fuel and prowled the winter suburbs of Calgary in an attempt to provide the rudiments of culture to the house-bound inhabitants, who had yet no concept of what it meant to be a TV addicted couch potato. Already crazed with the fly-fishing obsession, indulged by a father and uncles who believed it to be a wholesome and harmless pastime compared to doing the hand-jive to the *Shirelles*, I was astonished to discover such books existed. Epiphany is a word devalued by overuse these days, but I had one in the bookmobile on that cold prairie night

Although my grandfather was a fly-fishing Yorkshireman, I knew nothing of England, or for that matter British Columbia, a mythical place beyond the Rocky Mountains. Haig-Brown's prose conveyed pictures of places and events that were at once as fantastic and real as the ice patterns on the bookmobile windows, populated by cougar hunters and forty-pound Chinook salmon. The events involved silver bright summer steelhead running into a sea pool on the flooding tide, or Kamloops trout rising to travelling sedge on the big green lakes of the interior plateau. Other books followed; *Fisherman's Spring*, *Summer*, and *Fall* took me through the North American seasons in three wonderful volumes. *Fisherman's Winter*, a season in South America, was the first account of destination fly-fishing I ever read, which led to Zane Grey and Hemingway, and ruined any sensible career path before it had a snowball's chance in hell. Haig-Brown spoke, so immediate was his literary voice, of fish, tackle and methods in a way that put me *there*, the line curling out toward the cedar stump where the big cutthroat trout just showed himself, the gleam and solid live weight of the fish as it turned down with the fly. Well, I mean to say, that was me… gone.

Before encountering the great British fly-fishing literature, my main contact with tradition was through the American outdoor magazines, the egalitarian hook and bullet press. There were three big magazines, *Sports Afield*, *Outdoor Life*, and *Field and Stream*. *Field and Stream*, the New York based magazine, boasted names such as A. J. McClane and Ed Zern on the masthead and catered to what eventually became known as the international destination angler. One got the impression that one wanted one's comfortably frayed canvas fishing jacket to have an Abercrombie and Fitch label and that one should at least recognise Ernest Hemingway on sight. It wasn't Arnold Gingrich's *Esquire* but you suspected that the editors sipped their lunchtime martinis at the same Madison Avenue watering holes, and didn't order pump-action duck guns from the Sears catalogue.

Outdoor Life was a westerner's magazine and Joe Brooks was its most famous fishing editor. The illustrations always showed some guy in a cowboy hat, usually Brooks himself, holding enormous Montana brown trout, sometimes caught by his application of A. H. E. Wood's greased line technique, warmed up as the 'broadside float' for American readers. A western boy myself, these articles meant the most during my formative years, if they didn't quite have the je *ne ce quoi* of the *Field and Stream* pieces. *Sports Afield* was the bass fisherman's mag; Jason Lucas busting lunker largemouths on the mid-western farm ponds, good ol' boys spearing bayou bullfrogs by the beam of a miner's headlamp, and mail order kits for starting your own worm farm. It's clear that I was a fly-fishing snob from the get-go.

By the time I was at art school in London, I spent as much time in the Charing Cross second-hand bookshops as I did in my studio. I was getting a handle on the kind of fisherman I wanted to be, and although my bloodstock were farmers and tradesmen I knew it had something to do with an unreasonable allocation of time and effort to something that had no practical outcome. Essentially, this is the rationale for the appreciation of art but, characteristically, the English gentry decided to apply the aesthetic attitude to something more down to earth – fishing.

After a century, Skues' *The Way Of A Trout With A Fly* stands as a great monolith of rationality, humour, and it must be said, obsession. Few of trout fishing's problems were not pondered and solved by Skues, fewer have been resolved since. Mottram's ground-breaking *Fly Fishing: Some New Arts and Mysteries*; Eric Taverner's *Trout Fishing From All Angles* in the Lonsdale Library series; W. C. Stewart's, *The Practical Angler*; Chaytor's *Letters To A Salmon Fisher's Sons*; Jock Scott's *Greased Line Fishing For Salmon*; Courteney Williams' *A Dictionary of Trout Flies*; Harris' *An Angler's Entomology*; Viscount Grey's *Fly Fishing* (which, I'm convinced, was a major influence on Haig-Brown, the author's voice is too similar to be otherwise); these wonderful books, stuffed with information, provided much more than that. They opened a window into an unknown side of the Anglo-American sporting aesthetic. They also showed me the way originality works; that even the most revolutionary ideas sprout from the taproot of tradition.

The best writing is always the result of the author's close observation of a subject that they feel is as important as anything else in their lives. The essential works of Stewart, Halford, Mottram, Grey, Taverner, Skues and Sawyer provided me with a background for the rapidly developing North American fly-fishing culture. They are more or less contemporaneous with

The traditional wet fly on a highland burn

Gordon, La Branch and Hewitt in the States, and much of the tradition is the result of true cross-cultural discourse. In these seminal books, I found the original ideas on which current expertise and philosophy is based, much of it as fresh and relevant as any how-to video. British and Irish anglers weave distinctive threads into the expanding fabric of the literature. Fogg's *The Art of the Wet Fly*, a thorough and inspired tactical treatise, is among the best trout-fishing books ever written. After Mottram, W. H. Lawrie's, *Scottish Trout Flies* is one of the earliest to emphasise the design rather than the pattern of trout flies; Clarke and Goddard's *The Trout and the Fly* and John Roberts' *Grayling Fishing* are future classics; Brian Clarke's *Pursuit of Stillwater Trout* is the bible of contemporary British lake fishing.

Casting is at the heart of fly-fishing, it's importance can't be emphasised enough, and there are many books on that subject alone. I find it pretty hard to make sense of most of them, not helped by illustrations that are about as accessible as the wiring diagram for a 747. A diagram with more than one arrow in it trips a circuit breaker in my brain. Some writing on casting is riddled with technical neologisms and contains some bewildering or downright bad advice. The problem is usually the attempt to put incredibly complex physics and subjective sensations into language, but sometimes it's just wrong. Knowing how to do it and writing about it are two different things, and finding the words to describe the physics of casting a fly line makes modern art journalism read like a recipe for pancakes. This leads frustrated or intimidated beginners toward live tutorials by a professional casting instructor, a good idea since most instructors today have read Lefty Kreh's books. A short cut is to buy Lefty's little paperback *Advanced Fly Casting*, go to the park or local swimming pool, better yet, a river, and do exactly what he says. Get a handle on what Lefty means by the 'speed-up and stop' and you're away to the races. Mel Kreiger and Joan Wulff are among the best and clearest of writers on the subject.

Schweibert, Marinaro, Swisher and Richards, and Caucci and Nastasi fuelled our taste for the taxonomic system, the technical rationality that characterises the positivist approach. Their observations are presented as scientific findings, as opposed to the subjective musings of Grey and Haig-Brown. Belatedly, I read LaFontaine's *The Dry Fly – New Angles* and read Gary Borger's *Designing Trout Flies* as I was in the closing stages of writing this book. At about the same time I received a copy of the 'revisited' edition of Rob Sloane's *The Truth About Trout*. It was gratifying to read these books so late in life, to find that I had arrived at some of the same conclusions they had, on widely varied waters, especially regarding the reasons dry flies work. It always feels good to find yourself in agreement with acknowledged experts. I also found some points of divergence, which makes me feel good too, if a little nervous.

Lately, the technical aesthetic has given some ground to more subjective writing, concerned with fly-fishing's intangibles. Publisher Nick Lyons, a fine writer himself, almost single-handedly revolutionised American angling writing in the eighties, his books and edited selections have contributed enormously to the current literary taste among American fly-fishers. Following the pithy and intelligent books of Robert Traver (*aka* John Voelker, US Surpreme Court Judge and author of *Anatomy of a Murder*), authors such as Datus Proper, Seth Norman, James R. Babb and Ted Leeson work a secular moral philosophy into the pursuit of the cold-blooded and slimy, delivering existential self-analysis with hip irony and humour. John Gierach's deceptively effortless, shade-tree familiarity brings the satisfying feeling you find when you laugh at your own jokes. Tom McGuane's *The Longest Silence*, ranks, in my opinion, alongside Hemingway's *The Green Hills of Africa*, and contains the funniest and most succinct vignette of fishing versus domestic cohabitation I've read. These writers make me feel I could fish with them and enjoy it, although real fishing pals are not so easily acquired.

The military axiom that intensity breeds expertise can surely be applied to fly-fishing. The current level of expertise is almost frightening and appears to be predicated on the idea that fish are getting smarter. The tradition would be vastly poorer without the 'how-to' books, and just about any of the new ones will get one started. The best of them focus on specific situations, and are really excellent accounts by anglers who know their subject, but some just add to a growing body of quasi-scientific jargon and craft-shop minutiae. To venture yet another book on fly-fishing and hope to make it interesting is to walk a tightrope between cliché and iconoclasm, and any attempt to cover the entire range of situations an angler might encounter is doomed to the elephants' graveyard of general information guides. Trotting out the old workhorses of the genre will only bore or insult those who have put in a lot of time on the water, while to argue against expert opinion is to invite indignation, or worse, public embarrassment. There's a lot of pleasure to be found in the details, but as absorbing as its technicalities can be, fly-fishing is so much more than that, and simpler. You could get by nicely on Gary Borger's *Presentation*, but by skipping Skues, Grey, Traver, and Haig-Brown you would not get the feel for the tradition, its context, a consciousness of our debt to great angling thinkers of the past, and the understanding that fly-fishing, like hunting, is not a game but a form of happiness.

* * * * *

2. Where to Find Them

If game were superabundant there would not exist that peculiar animal behaviour which we distinguish from all others with the precise name 'hunting'.

Jose Ortega y Gasset
Meditations on Hunting

Fishing the 'lift' on a Scottish stream

1. A place known to contain trout

George Leonard Herter was an entrepreneurial type no longer common in corporate America. Herter's catalogue was the size of a phone book and offered an array of hunting and fishing gear that was clearly an extension of the proprietor's personality. Salted throughout the supporting text for the items in the catalogue were gems of lore, horse sense and pithy insight into the outdoor life. There was also a considerable amount of bullshit. The idea was that with the know-how, the correct political orientation and Herter's gear, success was guaranteed, a quintessentially American can-do attitude.

Herter knew the part that dumb luck plays in success, no matter how well tooled-up we are. For example, Herter's book on deer hunting, prosaically entitled *How To Hunt Deer* contains the instruction, 'Go to a place known to contain large numbers of deer.' This, by the way, is kin to the cookbook recipe for elephant stew that begins, 'Take one elephant....'. Herter's catalogues have gone the way of the tailfins on a Cadillac, but his principle that good fishing depends on reliable quantities of fish seems to withstand the test of time.

Confidence depends upon knowledge and skill, and it is essential to know that the water you intend to fish has trout in it. Put-and-take trout fisheries are founded on this insecurity, and trade on the clear and certain knowledge that the water not only contains fish but lots of them, and big ones to boot. Know-how for many anglers has been replaced simply and sadly by know-*where*. In the worst cases, the elegant techniques of fly-fishing have been dumbed down to a matter of chucking a lure into the path of a bemused farm animal whose last meal was served by shovel. That this is now the situation on some classic English chalkstreams, cradle of the most refined and stylish form of the fly-fishing tradition, is something to ponder.

Just to make worthwhile the inevitable indignation over elitism, snobbery, or differences in taste, I may as well add that in its worst cases put-and-take fishing is not only badly off-plumb, it's not really trout fishing at all. It just looks like trout fishing. The difference in required skill between catching a big, farmed trout and a small one is completely artificial and meaningless. If you applied the put-and-take model to some other domestic animal the point becomes pretty clear. It's rather like the difference between going out for a romantic evening with a woman whom you find interesting and attractive, and hiring a hooker. There may be superficial resemblances and a certain amount of fun involved, but the distinctions are important, and not only a matter of taste.

I know that seems hard on our stockie-bashing pals, and a bit like a Sunday paper rant on slipping standards, but we should really keep our eye on the ball here. The worst of these put-and-take places, holes in the ground euphemistically called 'small waters' in Britain, are a disgrace. The fish-farm trout is no different than a miserable battery hen, even if it's the size of a yearling pig. The stocked fish that has had a chance to adapt to natural feeding, the free-range trout, if you will, is certainly a different matter, but I feel strongly that catching freshly stocked trout, especially big ones, is a poor introduction to trout fishing. It distorts both our understanding of nature and fly-fishing's wonderful tradition. Apart from conditioning us to expect fish that are uniformly bigger than nature would normally provide, the ease with which they are caught does not teach us much about nature, the trout, or anything else for that matter. Anyway, all you need to assure yourself of the comparatively low level of skill required to catch tame trout is to spend some time fishing for spooky wild ones. It's certainly understandable for a city bound angler to want to get out and bend a rod now and then, but we shouldn't kid ourselves that put-and-take fishing has any meaningful relationship to the real thing.

The concept of 'wild' is itself an issue. By now, in Britain at least, almost all wild strains of trout have been genetically mixed through more than a hundred and fifty years of artificial stocking. In fact, the purest strain of British brown trout is likely to be found in New Zealand. So, rather than argue over wildness in terms of genetic purity, it's maybe more useful to think of wildness as a state rather than a trait. In natural conditions, trout will vary in size and a certain amount of experience and specialised know-how is required to catch a big one, but since it is real trout fishing that is precisely what makes it interesting. You have to match your ambitions to the potential of the water. If a wild water normally grows half-pounders, you are not disappointed if you do not catch any three-pounders. Finding a twelve-inch brookie in upstate

New York is just as challenging and satisfying as stalking a twenty-inch brown on Arthur's Lake in Tasmania. Unlike stockie-bashing, as you learn about the fish and its environment you gradually catch bigger fish, so you can swagger about and bore people at dinner parties with some justification. You get a purchase on what real trout fishing means.

2. The potential of the water – occasions for hope

In his fine book of essays, *Royal Coachman – the Lure and Legends of Fly-Fishing*, Paul Schullery characterises fly-fishing as a series of renewed occasions for hope. Something we all hope for is big trout. I've never met an angler who was not interested in the exceptional fish, the one that rises most often in our daydreams. Not all trout waters contain big fish, an observation that seems self-evident to the point of banality, but possibly the most important thing to understand if one is to find where the larger fish actually live. The next most important thing to know is what constitutes a big fish for a particular water. For instance, on most Scottish waters, a wild brownie of about twelve inches and three-quarters of a pound is a nice fish. With appropriately light tackle, you can spend a happy time catching nothing larger than this, secure in the knowledge that you have had excellent fishing.

Wyatt with a typical west-slope cutthroat from a special river

Most rivers and lochs have a few old trout swimming in them, but it can be a disheartening task to narrow your endeavours to the pursuit of these challenging but essentially un-catchable fish. After all, that's the reason they are still in there. From an early age they have become so spooky and specialised in their feeding habits that normal angling methods don't affect them. They may be nocturnal; they may be strictly fish-feeders; they may live in some inaccessible bit of cover. Usually all three. For the fly-fisher, practically speaking, these are impossible fish. A determined bait-fisher might catch one of these tough customers, but it would require some specialised and inelegant techniques to take one on a fly, defeating one of the main objectives of fly-fishing – to do the difficult thing well, to catch a good fish with grace and style. When it comes to taste and tactics, it's up to you where to draw the line.

A fly-fisher's perfect quarry is the big, young trout – the free-rising, fast-growing, insectivorous trout found on exceptional water. There are rivers and lakes with fish like this all over the world, but they have become very popular places. Eutrophic alkaline rivers like Alberta's Bow and Idaho's Henry's Fork are this type of water, as are some New Zealand rivers and Ireland's big loughs, fly-fishing's great destinations. Somewhere among Scotland's acid, moorland lochs, the food-rich basins of the Irish limestone country and the high Kamloops lakes of British Columbia's interior plateau are the simply good places on which we spend most of our time, our home waters. Home waters are usually a compromise, a place we can get to easily on a weekend, an evening after work or a week's fishing holiday, and which has a reasonable stock of trout.

If the water is a healthy one with no serious pollution or natural predator problems, only the food supply and the angling kill will affect the range of sizes. On hard-fished small streams where anything can be killed, the fish will be mostly small, with a very few old nocturnal bullies hidden beneath the banks. On medium-sized waters where catch and release is not practised, pot fishermen will relentlessly pick off most of the trout of eating size. Big rivers and lakes, with more places to hide and a wider range of abundant food, will always have more large fish, although many of them might be inaccessible to the fly-fisher.

Big is a relative term. On some lakes and streams a big trout might be a foot long, not a bad fish anywhere but possibly one of a very few old fish of that size. Many small moorland streams or Scottish 'burns' are like this, and while it is certainly a pleasant way to spend a day this is not really the type of water for the hunting of larger trout. The best type is the medium-sized stream that flows through alkaline country, rich with food and cover. In Europe, and increasingly in North America, waters like these are usually well preserved and expensive to fish.

A better bet is the large river, where fish may be fewer and harder to find, but where there is a chance of an occasional two-pounder. There is a lot of lightly fished water that falls into a kind of middle band in terms of quality. In Britain and Ireland, these are the medium to large rivers that may or may not have salmon fishing. Salmon rivers make good trout hunting grounds, even if they do not necessarily provide the best trout habitat. They have a lot of cheaply accessible association water because the owners do not think trout are important. A salmon river often has a lot of water that is not fished at all, by anyone. Salmon anglers stick to the known salmon lies and, these days, most British trout fishermen stick to the stocked reservoirs. This leaves a lot of water essentially undisturbed. I've been surprised by the quality of the fishing I've had on some very public water, not least because I have it to myself. I've seen hatches and rises of trout on popular British association water that would compare favourably to some so-called destination waters.

The big trout of the world's great destinations are typically young fish. A New Zealand ten-

Robbie McPhee with a 'top fish' from a South Island stream   *photo: Bruce Masson*

pounder may be the same age as a ten-incher in a European river, where, once trout reach a pound or so, they are probably beyond the skill of the average trout angler today. This is not an insult so much as a lament. Even in Scotland, where plenty of good, wild public trout water is available, more and more anglers are seduced by the instant gratification and leisure centre attractions of the put-and-take waters. This is too bad; it means regional river skills will atrophy and ultimately disappear, and with them the fascinating local traditions and style, the riverman's narrative. To stay alive, a song has to be sung.

For the stillwater angler seeking trout in wild or relatively natural conditions, a good rule of thumb is to locate waters that have neutral pH values, the more alkaline the better, up to a point. Alkaline water produces the rich feeding necessary for the production of good populations of larger trout. Very alkaline lakes can be full of big fish but they can also be very difficult. The feeding can be so rich, or so specialised, and the water so clear, that the fish are very resistant to conventional fly-fishing techniques. The best stillwaters have a wide range of food available at different times and the trout are forced to be more opportunistic. The Irish loughs are good examples; a broad range of *diptera, ephemeroptera* and *trychcoptera*, as well as big and varied baitfish populations, which make for active and opportunistic trout of an uncommonly large average size for their age.

Whether the fishing you can reach on an evening or weekend is a tiny moorland beck or a concrete-lined reservoir, it can provide all the satisfaction of a managed chalkstream. The important thing is to gauge your expectations to the potential of the water. Almost as important is to enjoy it without bragging about it. As much as I wish my fellow anglers well, you know, tight lines and everything, I get a little cagey when it comes to public bragging about my favourite waters. Not that they are especially hot – I doubt that Lefty Kreh would change out of his street shoes to fish my best spots – but they are places I can get to in an hour or so from home, and that means so can the entire trout fishing population of central Scotland. Frankly, the fact that they have any fish in them at all is a miracle. So, I like to keep these places dark. My local water may not be the Makarora, but it's still pretty good fishing, and more often than not my pals and I have it to ourselves. If I can help it, that's just the way I'd like to keep it. A little fish and tell is good for a water; the attention is actually protective, but it can go the other way, and fast.

As a young blood in western Canada I was always shooting my mouth off. I gave away good fishing spots as if they were old Neil Diamond albums. There were plenty of places to fish and few other fishermen to worry about. Incredibly, I often looked forward to meeting other anglers. The important thing was to get there first on the day. Well, that changed fast enough, as we've seen. By the seventies, a new kind of angler was evolving; tooled up, aggressive, and expert. Worse, they don't just brag to their buddies, they write about it in national magazines, with glossy photographs that make fly-fishing appear as *chic* as Formula One racing. If you haven't noticed the change, consider this, fishing clothes now actually look good. Worse yet, fly-fishing is now a thriving and very competitive commercial industry, so, open your cake-hole and your old fishin' hole is suddenly a destination.

If you have visited a North American 'blue-ribbon' trout water lately you will know what I'm talking about. Queues form on the famous stretches of the Henry's Fork, Firehole or the Bow when a hatch is in progress. Where such polite protocols do not obtain there are sometimes ugly confrontations, unimaginable thirty years ago. The Bow, one of my own home waters, is now a heavily used destination fishery. As far the welfare of the fish themselves is concerned there is no problem, so far. The trout are fine, increasingly wide-awake perhaps, but healthy and in substantial numbers. Speaking for myself and as good as the fishing is, it's not really what I have in mind when I think of a quality experience. Only yesterday it seems, western fly-fishing didn't involve being nearly run down by a jet-boat, the guide dead-eyeing you from under the brim of his outlaw bull-rider's Smithbilt, encouraging his somewhat nervous sport to fish a rod length away from where you stand. When it comes to the precise locations of your favourite spots, you might want to practise the art of dissembling, a polite word for bullshit. At the very least, take Patrick McManus' advice to always mention a bear in any report of good fishing.

* * * * *

3. Rivers I: Fishing the Water

So, leaving aside the magic of the primitives of the glacial period and their counterparts still living, the first task of all hunting is to find the prey, and to 'raise' it.

Jose Ortega y Gasset
Meditations on Hunting

The fast-water dry fly in the Alberta high country

1.The informed guess

A fine little book on chalk stream fishing, *The Angler and the Trout*, written in 1941 by Huish Edye, 'Distoffer' to his readership in *The Field*, introduced me to a term I haven't seen since; the 'master fish' – a specimen trout that approaches trophy proportions. Edye supplies a pretty sound outline for 'the living conditions to which a big trout aspires'. These he lists as:

1. A holt in deep water, with cover of bank, an undercut rock, or a dense patch of weed.

2. A feeding station, preferably shallow water, with line of retreat as easy as possible to (1) The shallowness probably gives a sense of security on the blind or under side.

3. A set of the current at (2) that brings concentrated food (especially surface food) within his reach.

4. And if he is elderly, spacious shallows accessible for the hunting down of minnows or other small fish.

Distoffer's next statement pretty well sums things up. '…quarters which provide all of these amenities are scarce, and are taken more or less in order of seniority. That is to say, they are taken by the most aggressive trout, which generally but not always means the biggest trout'. Find this set of conditions on any trout water and you are likely to have found the 'master fish' in that stretch. Depending on the carrying capacity of the water, this fish will be anything from a feisty ten-incher to a thuggish ten-pounder. My uncles in the Crowsnest Pass used to call this reading the water, and it's certain that, at least where fishing is concerned, it was the only reading they ever did.

I learned to read water by fishing an un-weighted worm or stonefly larva, which we called 'devil-scratchers', with a fly rod in the very early season between ice-out and runoff. It was a good school. The Alberta foothill rivers held lots of trout, so if you learned your lessons there was the intermittent reward of a thumping wild rainbow or cutthroat. It was a short step to the wet fly when the weather warmed up, although it did not go unnoticed that the size of the fish fell immediately.

My brothers and I had a tactic we called hole-hogging, basically a quick manoeuvre into the best spot on any pool before anyone else had a chance. Being 'hole-hog number one' meant that you selfishly put yourself into the best position for getting the biggest trout in the pool. There was no one else on those rivers to worry about, and eventually this primitive filial competition evolved into the accepted leapfrog *pas de deux* of proper stream etiquette, but we knew that the first cast into a pool often resulted in a better than average fish, right off the bat. With a brother or two breathing down your neck, you learned to evaluate a pool's amenities at a trot. When I reflect on those days, I realise to my horror that, despite its wholesome appearance, a small gang of motivated pre-pubescent boys with bait tackle represents the most intense predation a river will ever sustain.

Half a century later, my pal Bob Morton demonstrated Distoffer's principle of the master trout. We were in northern Scotland for our annual total-immersion trout therapy week. After the first few eighteen-hour days on the water, we tend to take it easy, the morning coffee runs to several pots and the map briefing collapses into reminiscence rather than strategy. On one of these mornings after a very wet night, Bob, Al Pyke and I were the last ones left in the lodge, a converted farmhouse. The other boys had set off for boats or stream inlets on several lochs in anticipation of good fishing after the spate. We decided to just fish the burn that runs behind the lodge, down to its inlet at the loch. We knew that the burn mouth fished well after a spate, sometimes bringing in a run of Atlantic salmon grilse and sea-trout. The plan was for Al to take a car to the inlet and we would fish down to him, then we would get a lift back to the lodge. Bob suited up and headed downstream well ahead of me, so, rather than just mopping-up behind him, I decided to take the car down to the loch head and fish upstream.

I started at the burn mouth; Al was nowhere to be seen. The sun was out, the stream was falling fast, and I began to pick up a few nice trout right away. I worked around the shore of the loch, hoping for a sea-trout or even a salmon, thinking of a wild day two years previous when

Bob Morton fishes a falling spate for foraging loch brown trout

we took five nice grilse from the surf, casting into the teeth of a hammering sou'wester. They weren't there this day, but at the tip of the sand spit, where the current dissipates into black loch water, I did get a thick-shouldered brownie of sixteen inches to the Veyatie Black. I fished my way back to the inlet and headed upstream to find the other boys.

After an hour, working up the stream with a Deer Hair Emerger, I met Al coming downstream. He looked pretty pleased with himself. I opened the lid of his creel to behold a beautiful basket of trout, maybe six fish of a pound or more. He had been picking them up on a team of dark wet flies, his usual claret bodied Bumbles. We looked upstream just as Morton hove into view. When he saw us, he reacted like a deer at the report of a rifle and bolted back upstream. We didn't see him again. Later at the lodge he said that when he spotted us he knew we would want to head back. No frigging way was he going home. When he did finally show up we understood his reluctance to quit. He had an amazing basket of trout, with several fish pushing the two-pound mark. One was a solid two-and-a-half pounds and it was clear that these were not resident burn trout. In an intense debriefing, Bob provided some fascinating information.

He took the biggest fish just below the lodge when he was still in sight of me at the gate. The fish was holding at the head of a short pool that has a deep run on one side. I knew the pool well, and the precise spot where the fish had taken Bob's fly is what the New Zealanders call the eye of the pool, the sweet-spot, where the current funnelled all the water-born food into a water column only three or four feet across. The trout only had to hold in the lower centre of this column to have first crack at any food entering the pool, and could easily guard it against any smaller fish. The pool's amenities met all of Distoffer's conditions for the lie of a master fish.

This trout had apparently run all the way up from the loch with the rising spate to take up this position, almost two miles from its usual haunts. This stream rises and falls in a matter of hours in a spate. These big trout reacted instantly to the flood and ran like sea-trout, taking up the best of the positions according to their size and aggressiveness. When Bob started out, the water was still coloured by peat run-off from the hills. He fished the first stretch of water with a team of size ten wets, but in consideration of the dark water he changed his point fly to a larger Black Pennell. On the first cast into the pool his fly was snatched sharply by something but the barb did not sink home. Two successive casts into the exact spot brought two more vicious pulls at the fly, the hook catching momentarily and coming free. On the fourth pass, Bob drove the hook home. He said it was certainly the same fish, the yellow-bellied two-and-a-half pounder. It impressed Bob that this fish was not about to let anything alive and small enough to eat get past him, and being repeatedly pricked by the hook didn't faze him in the slightest.

Something similar was repeated on each pool as Bob fished downstream. What also became clear was that the fishing deteriorated as the burn fell and cleared. By the time he got down to where he saw us, the big fish were simply no longer there. This makes sense, if they will run up the burn that quickly they'll surely return just as fast, as conditions revert to normal. A two-pound trout is at a severe disadvantage in that stream at normal height. The reason for being there in the first place – food – has disappeared, and security becomes job-one.

Our group had some excellent sport in similar conditions a year later, as a good spate was just beginning to clear. We were fishing where a substantial stream joins two lochs. We know that the fish from the lower loch will nose into the narrows below the mouth, and in really big water some will run well up the stream, right up to the top loch. The most effective way to fish it is to work down stream from the upper loch until you hit the big fish. In some pools they will be found in pods, the best fish usually in the eye of the pool and the others ordered by descending rank toward the tail. Sometimes a big trout is taken at the very tail of the pool, but this is probably a fish moving up from downstream. Once, I stood on a high bank and watched Al Pyke take six good trout from a shallow pocket only five yards long, which held only tiddlers the day before.

The interesting thing here is that Distoffer's conditions have all been met, but the trout's movements to feeding positions and escape routes have been extended in the spate conditions, in some cases a matter of miles. As soon as the spate falls away and the abundant food begins to thin out, the larger fish waste no time in retreating to the safety of the loch. The activities of trout are opportunistic and constantly changing with conditions; it's up to the angler to read the water and decide which conditions apply.

Trout have to eat, and big trout have to eat more. The fact that they are hard to catch does not mean that they are necessarily smarter. Once the conditions for optimum feeding and escape are met, the type and availability of the trout's food is the true reason behind its behaviour, not intelligence. Smart trout are simply those that have developed protective feeding habits, the main reason why they are big. Big trout may be wary, but they are also aggressive. If you find a way to present a fly that looks like familiar food without spooking them, it's likely that they'll take it.

Where we expect to find trout feeding is pretty clearly defined. We learn to look for changes in depth where the water shelves along rock and gravel bars, seams between fast and slow water, where the current eases in front of and beside rocks and other obstructions, and deep undercut banks. These are the classic stations for a feeding trout. On slow, deep water it is difficult to recognise feeding stations unless we see a trout rise. It is important to know that

Small but perfectly formed; a jewel-like highland brownie

these classic positions and food lanes are where we will normally find the average trout. During daylight hours, larger fish do not often take up a fixed feeding station in the open, except in a strong hatch situation.

Big trout are the neighbourhood bullies and roam around quite a bit in search of prey or just patrolling their territory against squatters. A study on Michigan's Au Sable River demonstrated that big brown trout will range as much as a mile or more from their security holt, usually during low light periods. On rivers with adequate and sustained insect hatches, these larger trout will take up a semi-permanent lie in a feeding lane, where a stream of food is carried to them, but generally, big trout tend to look for larger prey. If big trout were where we normally fish for them, and susceptible to our normal tactics, we would catch them more often. This means that if we are going to concentrate on the larger fish, as much thought should be put into our angling habits as into the trout's feeding habits.

2. River tactics: The sunk fly

Most urban anglers just don't have a chance to get out regularly to a wild river. In England the home water is usually a stocked reservoir, which at best provides a specialised experience. In the densely populated regions of North America it often means a stocked river with a few holdover resident trout, or a Great Lakes spawning feeder with specialised local techniques. Opportunities for the continental European angler are even fewer. Unless there is reasonable access to a large lake or reservoir where one can find wild or naturalised fish, fishing for wild trout is reserved for an extended annual holiday. If you are serious about your fly-fishing these days, you must expect to do some travelling. A travelling angler needs a flexible repertoire of flies and tactics that can be adapted to any situation, anywhere.

Since so many good books have been written on fly-fishing tactics, to begin at the beginning would just add to a crowded field of technical how-to books aimed at the novice angler. On the other hand, I know few anglers who have read all the books, so it never hurts to review the basics. A new fishing book should at least add something practical to the body of knowledge, even if it is just a few new wrinkles, or a slight difference of perspective, While they might fall short of a proper *vade mecum* and occasionally repeat what has been well documented elsewhere, my observations may help to get someone started, or just round off a well established trout hunting schema. As Edmonds and Lee say in *Brook and River Trouting*, for similar reasons, I'll just emphasise a few essential points, with the caveat that in fly-fishing for wild trout even the variables have variables.

In Britain and Ireland, trout fishing is essentially a stillwater pursuit. It is fairly common in the British Isles to meet anglers who have not developed much river technique, relying essentially on a simple downstream wet fly approach to running water. This is usually referred to as the traditional wet fly style, despite its being at complete odds with the classic upstream wet fly techniques of Stewart, Pritt, Edmonds and Lee, *et al*, not to mention Skues' arguments for its use on the southern English chalkstreams. Although the classic Scottish wet fly approach is distinctly upstream, most wet fly anglers I've met in recent years are of the across-and-down persuasion. On a river they'll invariably face downstream, fishing a line as taught as a bowstring. The intermittent reinforcement of an occasional fish and the positive feel of the tight line are what keep them from turning around and facing the current.

Mike Wyatt tries to concentrate in grizzly country

My pal Bob doesn't really believe in the upstream wet fly. He regards it as a myth perpetuated by angling writers mining worked-out rhetorical seams. He's tried it – doesn't work. Bob isn't afraid to take a position on things that matter (you don't want to get him going on the Marxist dialectic). There is something to his point. On the rivers Bob fishes, big ones such as the Tay and Tweed, the downstream wet fly is a proven and undisputed method to catch trout, especially in the spring. Not what you would call an enthusiastic downstream wet fly man, I protest that surely it can't be the case that all those who uphold the upstream wet fly tradition are talking through their hats. What would be the point in their adherence to a method if it didn't get results? Bob says, uh-huh, well, maybe it's a water thing. You know, it works on their water, for their trout.

This is the kind of discussion that takes place between fishing friends who know each other very well and respect each other's point of view, but I suspect that Bob is blowing some smoke here. In other words, I think he is being ideological about it, building his rationale around some established habits. You get the same thing among dry fly purists, although to a lesser extent these days. The average wet fly angler is an orthodox traditionalist, if not a reactionary fundamentalist, an accusation I take no small amount of pleasure in making to Bob over a pint. He argues that his method gets results, so he must be right...right? Maybe, but I can't help feeling that Bob is missing some opportunities. You naturally hesitate to critcise your pal's fishing technique, so, like most guy things, the subject must be approached delicately.

Short as it might be, a trout's memory depends on a context, as does ours. If the fly's appearance or behaviour is out of context, the fly will often be ignored. A trout is only concerned with territory, food and safety. When a trout rejects our fly it may not necessarily be frightened or suspicious; it just doesn't recognise the fly's appearance or behaviour as that of its usual food. As a prey-animal itself, wariness is part of a trout's daily life. On hard-fished waters the trout are constantly disturbed and the bigger trout will often spook at a perfectly cast fly, even if the angler is well concealed. A highly developed sensitivity to danger is how these fish grow old and stay alive. It may not understand the cause, but any unnatural disturbance will usually send a large trout to ground. Presentation is a matter of your fly operating within the normal parameters of the prey's appearance and behaviour, while you and your gear stay 'out of context'.

Despite our differences regarding presentation, Bob and I definitely agree on one thing; flies are important, and fly *design* is far more important than pattern. This goes as much for wets as it does for dries. To me, a traditional winged and hackled wet fly doesn't make a lot of sense. Bob, on the other hand, has worked out a rationale in which the wing still plays a meaningful role, something to do with its profile. His favourite early season fly is a winged Woodcock and Hare Lug, a great traditional pattern and I can't dispute that he gets fish on it, but I question the general usefulness of this type of fly and method – just where and when is it really effective? Despite its widespread use, particularly on the rough streams of Scotland and the north of England, I regard the downstream wet fly as a highly specialised technique, with a much narrower window of opportunity than is generally acknowledged.

Morton fishes hard, full on. He has enough Scottish Presbyterian in him that at least part of his approach is based on the old 'flee in the water' attitude. As any fishing guide will confirm, this counts a lot toward maximising one's chances. The fact that you are actually fishing when the trout begin to move, rather than just thinking about it, or worse, complaining about it, is possibly the most important of the things that you can control. By fishing, of course, I also mean watching and waiting, the biggest part of any hunt. Bob likes to do his watching and waiting while his line is in the water. As well as not disturbing the water unnecessarily, I think it's a good idea to stop casting and get some indication of what the trout are actually doing, if anything, and what you might do about it.

Another thing Bob does is select a 'sweet-spot' on the water he is working, water that fits his method. He knows from experience where he has taken trout before, the type of water where he is likely to encounter another one. He contrives to get his team of wets working just right as they pass through that spot. We both agree that as they enter the sweet-spot in any stretch of water, his flies are beginning their swing. Strictly speaking, a downstream wet fly swinging on a tight line does not provoke a normal interceptive response from the trout but stimulates a chase response. On the other hand, downstream fishing with a slack line drag-free presentation is effectively the same thing as the upstream wet fly and fits in with other dead-drift techniques.

Watching Bob, as I often do during one of my watch-and-wait periods, I can see that his sweet-spot presentation is largely a drag-free drift. His normal cast is directly across the current or slightly upstream, and he throws several upstream mends along his line as it drifts downstream. Bob expects a fish to take at the point where the drag-free period ends, when the flies begin to swing and rise on the tightening line. Several takes may have been missed throughout the drag-free period. His sweet-spot is actually a very short and narrow piece of water, and a lot of water has been lined unproductively in order to cover it.

The across-and-down swing is a reliable sea-trout and salmon approach. As we know, salmon and sea-run trout are not true feeders once they enter fresh water, but we exploit their hard-wired chase response to a prey stimulus. They have spent several years feeding at sea where all prey must be chased. Part of their response to the fast swinging fly is an instinctive and irresistible chase impulse, something like a kitten's reaction to a bit of yarn, and any savvy salmon and steelhead angler knows that fresh run fish are as innocent as kittens. They will

Searching the pocket water on Alberta's Oldman

commonly follow a swinging fly right to the bank. Salmon anglers know the importance of being the first to present a fly to a fresh fish. There are some unreliable techniques for catching stale fish, but most of the problems in catching fresh-run salmon revolve around giving them a sporting chance to get the hook in their mouths, once they decide to go on the take.

What we call play in a kitten is really an instinctive and adaptive hunting response. Like kittens, trout sometimes can't resist the escaping-fly stimulus, part of the reason for the effectiveness of the bob fly in traditional loch style fishing. A fly fished in this manner presents the aspect of vulnerability of a creature in trouble and trying to escape. The impulse to take the bob fly is also a factor in river fishing, but most experienced fly anglers agree that the larger river trout, experienced, territorial and wary, will usually spurn a dragging fly. It's rather like the old cat on the hearth that regards the teasing bit of yarn with no more than a twitch of its tail.

Looking again at Bob's view of the upstream wet fly, we no longer appear to be at odds. The difference is in the feel of the take, the source of his displeasure with the dead drifting upstream wet fly. It's not that it doesn't work, it's just that it is hard to *know* when it's working. During the drag-free drift, Bob can't feel the take, and in the fast dark streams of the rivers he fishes he can't see the take either, so he turns around and faces downstream. Now, he argues, he is fishing traditional across-and-down. I say he's fishing a version of the 'induced take', or the 'lift'.

In 1941, James Leisenring described a method to V.S. Hidy that he called 'the lift', in *The Art of the Wet Fly and Fishing the Flymph*. What the technique involves is a more or less upstream throw with a slack line and a drag-free drift, terminating in an intentional tightening of the line, not a pull, just ahead of a seen or suspected trout. The effect of the current on the tightening line results in what is normally regarded as a bad thing in dry fly fishing – drag. The sunk fly or flies begin a curving and accelerating ascent toward the surface. What we have here is a complex stimulus to the waiting trout, which by now has noticed the flies drifting toward it and has moved to intercept them. The lift stimulates the predatory attack.

For the sake of argument, we can divide a river trout's response into two types: interception, the relatively passive feeding response; and the chase, or aggressive hunting attack. Unlike a stillwater or marine fish, until a river trout reaches bragging size it has no need to hunt food, but merely intercepts it. It is interesting that even in running water the fish usually goes for the bob fly, the top dropper on a two or three wet fly rig, which indicates an attack response rather than simple interception, probably some complex reaction involving excitement. The fly employed has some influence on this, it appears. Bob has noticed that if he repositions his best pattern for that time of year, the Woodcock and Hare Lug, to the middle or tail position, offers to that position do increase. However, if he puts the hot fly on all three positions, the fish still tend to go for the bob fly, most of the time. It apparently has as much to do with the bob fly's position and its relationship to the other flies as it does with pattern

Czechoslovakian anglers developed a specialised version of the induced take, employing short lines and extra-heavy fly designs, known as 'Czech nymphing'. American anglers gather a collection of short-line presentations under the rubric of 'high-stick' or 'right angle' tactics, which include upstream indicator nymphing. All these tactics are based on the same principle, a drag-free drift to acquire depth, and an ascending fly at the end of the drift. In *Nymph Fishing for Larger Trout*, Charles E. Brooks described somewhat similar tactics for catching large trout in western North American streams in the early seventies.

Apart from a resemblance to some natural prey, the thing that distinguishes an artificial fly from other debris in the water column is its behaviour. Interestingly, while the heavy shrimp-like flies employed in Czech nymphing bear little resemblance to the natural fauna of the rivers where it is used, the technique is remarkably successful, indicating that it is primarily the action of the fly that stimulates the take. What really differentiates the various techniques are the weight of the fly employed and its direction of travel. With variations for specific situations, they all work, and for essentially the same reason, and the complete river angler will be able to employ all of them.

Tie on two or three soft-hackled wets and chuck them up and across the current, you have Stewart's classic upstream wet fly, the most difficult of all. The traditional northern wet fly methods, eloquently described by W.S. Roger Fogg in *The Art of the Wet Fly*, emphasise the natural movement of the fly. The great North England soft-hackle wet fly tradition incorporates the essential take-inducing lift as the fly moves on a tightening line. However you manage it, the dead drift and take-inducing ascent of the fly as the line tightens is the action to achieve.

The wet fly can be very effective when trout are feeding excitedly on the ascending nymph in the early stages of a hatch. This phase of the hatch is the real window of opportunity for the downstream wet. The bulging rise-form, actually the disturbance boil caused by the thrust of the trout's tail, is the telltale of this stage of the hatch, and it can be very frustrating for the angler who doesn't realise what is happening. Bulging trout move around very quickly, and a rise-form does not mean the fish will still be there by the time your fly has landed. A downstream wet fly is good medicine in this situation, rising and crossing in front of fish as it searches for the ascending nymphs.

The swinging across-and-down wet fly on a tight line has a tendency to attract mainly smaller fish. The fast-fished surface and mid-water wet fly will pull an endless stream of juvenile trout and parr as the fly swings into the shallow water near shore, where the little fish live to avoid the big ones. Even drag-free drifts with sensitively turned flies will get a response from a high percentage of small to medium-sized trout once the flies start to swing. Lots of action to be sure, but I am convinced that a dragging wet fly tends to discourage the older, bigger and more wary trout – except after dark, which is a real window of opportunity for the big downstream wet or surface fly.

Spring is a glorious time on the river for the fly fisherman; ranks of eager trout forming up to intercept endless flurries of hatching fly under a benign cobalt sky of sun and cloud, the streams bursting with life and promise. We all have this picture in our heads of a perfect fly-fishing day. Well, I reckon this has been the situation on no more than a dozen spring days in the last forty years. Spring, in Scotland at least, is usually a fairly miserable affair, with cold rain down your neck and stubborn trout that refuse to rise to niggardly hatches of olives. When they do show at all it is at noon for maybe fifteen minutes in a long cold day. After a few of these typically cold and almost fishless spring days, I began to wonder just what the fish are really doing if they aren't eating flies from the surface. One possibility, which many anglers may find hard to accept, is *nothing*. After all, if you've made the effort to get out on the river on a cold spring day, the least you expect of the trout is that they reciprocate. It's hard for us to reconcile the idea that the fish might be lying dormant on the bottom while you are searching the water so earnestly, but for much of the day that is precisely the case.

This disturbing fact was revealed to me in an old book, Murray and Pullar's *Bathymetrical Survey of the Freshwater Lochs of Scotland*, where I first encountered the idea that trout do not move until there is ample reason to do so. On the lochs of Scotland, where food is relatively scarce, brown trout spend long periods of time, *most* of it in fact, just lying doggo. The Scots have a word for these conditions, dour, and they should know. When an emergence of some insect such as lake olives or chironomids begins, the trout are roused from their torpor and feed

Bob Wyatt puts back a nice Red Deer River brownie during the PMD hatch

aggressively until the food is all eaten or otherwise disappears. The peak periods of predatory activity coincide with the peaks of insect activity, and those are nearly always associated with lowlight levels. If you think about this it makes sense. It conforms to what we know about predator/prey relationships and the conservation of energy, and explains the phenomenon of the rise on all waters, still or moving.

The chalkstream tradition of fishing only to trout that have shown themselves is not just a matter of style and orthodoxy, an example of empty form for its own sake. It is based in good old angler's pragmatism. Although we know that the nymphs of the prevailing hatch will be moving for a short period before they appear at the surface, what we call the 'pre-hatch' phase, generally this movement is of short enough duration. We can usually wait for fish to show on the surface before we present the fly. The reason we wait is not because no other method will work, it's just that we might just prefer to fish the dry fly. That said, the best time for a wet fly or nymph is also during the emergence, so it often makes little difference which method is chosen. Once the fish begin to move to the successive phases of the hatch, or the behavioural drift, fly-fishing works. It works all day if there is insect activity all day, or if food is intermittently available, keeping the trout in a feeding mode.

But what about the periods when there is no apparent insect activity? Many anglers carry on with nymphs and wet flies in the hope that the trout might be feeding subsurface. Except for the pre-emergence phase of a hatch, periods during or closely following massive invertebrate drift, or on high country streams where it pays for the fish to be round-the-clock opportunists, I no longer believe this. There are periods when the fish have just switched off, and you may as well have a snooze yourself. Big trout will generally not move to sparse or sporadic hatches. The question is whether they will take flies at all during those periods between hatches. During the prime period of spring and early summer, when insect activity is high and sustained, certainly. In the cold torrents of spring or autumn when food is scarce and sporadic, probably not.

Not, that is, unless you give them something worth going for. On the rivers I fish, salmon anglers take a lot of big trout on big, deeply sunk Waddington style lures and tube flies. This often happens on days when fly-fishing for trout is a dismal affair, frequently with no hatches at all. These trout, from two to four pounds and occasionally larger, are fish that are seldom if ever seen even during decent hatches of fly. What surprises me is how many of them there are. This tells me that these big fish are predominantly fish eaters. It also says something about the reaction of big trout to little fish generally. Being bullies, big trout will not tolerate smaller fish in their domain even if they are not actively feeding, so we can factor in the aggressive territorial response. I have also noticed that these big trout are taken during the normal spring salmon fisher's hours, between nine o'clock and five, possibly an indication of the times that baitfish are available but certainly an indication that fishing is not completely hopeless when there is no fly about. It's just pretty hopeless for fishing with tiny insect imitations.

Once trout reach a certain size they shift from eating insects to eating fish, unless there is an unusual supply of insect life available. American anglers have worked with this knowledge for years, some becoming big trout specialists using oversize streamers. Bob Linsenman and Kelly Galloup, authors of *Modern Streamers for Trophy Trout*, have worked out a set of tactics and baitfish designs that consistently produce big fish on hard-fished mid-western waters. In *The Truth About Trout*, Rob Sloane describes the Tasmanian tradition of hunting very big trout with baitfish flies. On British rivers this approach has not really taken root for some reason, maybe because of that conservative traditional attitude. Recently, some British anglers have been experimenting with baitfish imitations on their trout rivers and have made interesting findings, one being that British brown trout are the same animal as the American model, and streamers work as well here as they do in Michigan. It stands to reason that in terms of expended effort and nutritional value to a trout, one minnow is worth several hundred insects. A recent British study found that brown trout that fed on fish grew up to three times faster than trout that fed on insects. Just like when we eat a steak; we get the benefit of all that grass without the work or the monotony.

After the spring 'carnival' as the angling literature has it, and fly-fishing begins to tail off, we enter the dog days of summer. There are a few specialists who seem to get some pleasure, and some fish it has to be said, by crawling around in the nettles, casting flies the size of dust-mites at trout with the temperament of Jennifer Lopez. As interesting as this might seem in the

Bob Morton makes a careful approach on a highland stream

abstract, the realities of this kind of fishing have tended to discourage me, and I suspect most others, from becoming any good at it. Being on the water at daybreak always seems a bridge too far – summer dawn is at something like four am. This leaves the prospect of fishing at night.

Apart from spate fishing, the big sunk fly after dark is probably the most reliable way to catch the really big trout in a river. Some nights are perfect for the big dragging surface fly, but conditions have to be right; normally these are warm evenings with good cloud cover. Over the past few seasons, Bob Morton and I have been making a determined study of this summer evening thing. After sweating it out through the sullen afternoons, repeatedly disappointed by the failure of the classic evening rise to take place, we decided to wait them out until full dark. We re-awakened the boyhood delight of fishing while millions of responsible grown-ups are keeping sociable hours.

Now, the usual view of summer rivers is of depressingly low water, algae growth on the stones and choking weed in the runs, the ebullient riffles of spring now only 'frog-water'. While hopeless for the salmon angler, low water is actually an advantage for the nocturnal trout fisher, as long as oxygen levels remain adequate. It concentrates the flow and the fish into narrow channels, which makes it much easier to cover any feeders that show. Once the sun is down the moribund river begins to stir into life. The evening fishing develops by stages, beginning with an evening hatch of some sort if you're lucky, probably sulphurs or Pale Evening Duns in June and July, and Blue Winged Olives throughout the summer. This is a window for the dry fly, so we usually suspend our wet fly techniques to take advantage of some surface action. Some egg laying sedges may be flying about, but while the small trout and salmon parr will attack anything that hits the water, the larger fish usually ignore all this. The first serious phase of activity, if it happens at all, is the spinner fall at dusk. The spent flies will be invisible on the water and much smaller than you used for early season fishing. An eighteen is standard size for the BWO of mid and late summer, but you might have to consider going even smaller. Stateside anglers regularly go to size twenty to twenty-four to meet the summer hatches. I would too, if I could manage to tie one onto a leader.

Drag can really be a problem here, especially when reaching across the varying and deceptive currents in a larger river. While it might not spook the fish, any unnatural movement of the fly will cause it to be ignored completely, and counter to what Swisher and Richards claim, I believe this is much more important with small flies than large ones. Incidentally, when using small flies, dragging leader knots can put fish off as much as the fly itself. An across-and-down slack-line cast will simplify this to an extent, even if it shortens the overall length of the drift. Those fancy curve, reach, and slack-line casts that you see in the fishing book diagrams should be part of your late evening repertoire. Beyond a concern for size and silhouette, I don't bother with attempting accurate imitation of the naturals for this low light fishing. A simple, medium contrast hackle pattern like the Blue Upright with the underside hackles clipped so that the fly sits flat in the surface will do the job nicely. The sunk-spinner tactic, fishing a slim soft hackle wet fly just below the surface, is also a good one. Size, silhouette, and a drag-free drift are what matters.

The rise-forms are almost imperceptible in the gathering gloom, the fish barely exposing the tips of their noses as they quietly suck down the spinners. At a casual glance it is just the tiny rises of salmon parr, but if you watch closely you might see that much larger fish are at work in the glass-smooth slicks. The fish are normally out in midstream where the drift is concentrated, which on large rivers can make for long casts and problems with drag, but this is testing, totally absorbing, and intensely satisfying trout fishing. The places you see the trout are usually devoid of life in daylight. The big trout move into these stations only once the light goes. Something I've been surprised to discover in recent years is the distance large trout will travel to feed. They are nowhere near as stationary as I once thought, and have quite extensive foraging areas. If you suspect a stretch of river to hold larger specimens, it pays to station yourself at the most likely spot for interception, as in sea-trout fishing, then let the darkness develop. The fish will migrate to you on their feeding beat, and save you from some problematic wading.

One thing about night fishing – it's dark. Stumbling around in mid-current, at midnight with a flashlight in your mouth, whimpering in rage as you extract your dropper fly from both your waders and your landing net, while a squadron of midges sink their mandibles into your eyelids, is usually enough to knock sense into any but the hard-core enthusiast. On most rivers it's actually dangerous to life, limb, and tackle, and any riverbank is a real obstacle course in the dark. Recently, I managed to bash my knee, hole my waders and smash the tip of a pet dry fly rod, all in about two seconds of unseen but highly audible drama. The Scottish rivers I fish for trout are known primarily as salmon rivers, so they have considerable flows even in low water. Obviously, when you can't see the bottom, wading demands some extra care.

Once it's dark, and if the sky doesn't go clear and cold, the big sedges will appear. You will feel them on your hands and face before you see them. It's time to move upstream and start covering the streamy throat of the pool with a larger fly. The trout there will likely be keyed on to emergers, so a damp-dry emerger style or palmer is a good bet. There is no need to avoid drag here. A waking fly across the darkened stream can bring some very aggressive takes. When there is only the glimmer of the summer night sky to indicate the river's surface, the big trout move out into the open flats and shallow tail-outs, and into the edges of the stream. Morton usually fishes our favourite sea-trout pattern, the Smithy, and he does pretty well with it, including a few nice salmon at dusk. I usually use either a Smithy or a big Falkus-style Silver Blue, substituting a hair wing for the teal. I put the size eight or ten Smithy in the bob, or dropper, position and this accounts for a lot of the finnock (first-year sea-trout) and medium-sized brownies before midnight.

Depending on the air temperature, I'll use either a floating line or an intermediate double taper for this work, often 'lining-up' one size for the rod. I prefer the full belly of the double tapered line for rolling out casts and for increased feel. The fly, usually a big simple hair-winged wet pattern, size four or so, is fished on a fairly tight line but I keep an angle between rod tip and line to absorb the vicious takes. The big fly is a crude thing and I'm sure I could design a more sophisticated pattern for this work, but like Hugh Falkus, I take the 'ain't broke, don't fix it' attitude. These trout take the fly for something fishlike, no doubt. I have yet to fully investigate the use of a big surface fly for warm nights, maybe something like Mark Bowler's surface lure, but so far I haven't got around to it. Any big fly with a distinct shape in the water will pull the nocturnal brown trout. Dave Whitlock's highly evolved Muddler sculpins seem likely candidates, as are Kelly Galloup's Zoo Cougar and Kiwi Muddler, effective variants of Whitlock's designs. I tie a version of these things on big looped-eye salmon irons, mostly because I just like the kick-ass look of them, but also because it permits a good grinner/turle style leader knot, which I can tie in the dark. Rob Sloane's Fur Fly is another simple and proven design that has big trout written all over it.

Darkness seems to release these fish from their normal brown trout inhibitions; they don't take the fly so much as *nail* it. Fish are always solidly hooked on the big fly, and they jump wildly and run all over the shop, but the big hook usually gets a good hold. This last period is really quite intense as you concentrate totally on senses other than your eyes for information. One of the memorable sounds of night fishing is the distinctive whir of a big trout's fins as it jumps in the darkness. When it's over, the night will suddenly seem to descend into a deeper silence. You will feel that, from that point, whatever goes on out there doesn't include you. It's time to go home and disturb the slumber of your loved ones.

Depending on your code of values, the rewards of fishing at night may compensate for the inevitable deterioration in your social infrastructure. You might hope that your hunter's prowess will be appreciated, but don't kid yourself. The crime of dragging your cold, wet butt into bed at two in the morning is only compounded by the idiocy of leaving the gift of a couple of un-cleaned trout in the kitchen sink. When you find yourself investigating these marginal possibilities you realise that, as you suspected, fly-fishing is not a sport, it's a condition.

Dry fly

The excitement and delight in seeing a trout take your fly on the surface makes dry fly fishing, arguably, the most pleasurable of fly-fishing's experiences. Even so, the dry fly is not just an aesthetic preference but an exceedingly practical means to catch fish. Trout are surface feeders to a great extent, particularly in rivers. When food is plentiful on the surface, the trout are definitely looking up. The classic dry fly presentation is the upstream cast to a fish that has been sighted, but the standard method on rain-fed rivers of Britain and the snow-fed freestone rivers of North America is known as the prospecting or searching dry fly, also called fishing the water.

Hatches on rain or snow-fed rivers are often sporadic and unreliable, the trout eclectic and opportunistic feeders. Many of the world's best known fly patterns have been created for this type of fishing: the Royal Wulff, the Adams, the Elk Hair Caddis – impressionistic prospecting

A drag-free drift is essential on smooth pool tail-outs

flies that will pull fish on almost any water. Although they don't resemble any specific insect, they obviously present the necessary triggers to a predatory response.

Since so much of the fly-fishing literature over the past century or so has been devoted to the dry fly, there is little point in repeating its basic methods here, but we can touch on some essentials. For the reader new to the sport, the dry fly approach is based on one big thing; avoidance of *drag*. The importance of drag to dry fly-fishing cannot be overstated, but the trick is to know when it is actually happening, and how to control it. The speed and complexity of the current must be analysed or intuited before every cast, whether on the turbulent hill-country streams with steep gradients and rocky courses, or the deceptively smooth slicks of the spring creeks.

An upstream cast is usually the best way to avoid the current's influence on the line and leader. Fishing the upstream dry fly on fast, turbulent streams requires clever hands and line control, no job for the angler who likes to let the current fish the fly. The angler who can control drag will consistently take the best fish in any stretch of water. Placing your fly so that it covers the seams and edges of the current where trout expect their food to be delivered, keeping the fly line, leader and fly in water of the same speed, is the essence of the drag-free drift.

There have been some interesting experiments done on the effect of light or heavy leader tippets on trout. New Zealand anglers David Tasker and Andy Towbridge kept records of their results with heavy and light tippets for several years. The significant finding was that light leaders tended to break more often. What made a difference was the effect of the current on the heavy nylon; more surface area means more friction between the water and the tippet, increasing the incidence of drag. In itself, the visibility of the heavy tippet did not deter fish from taking the fly, even on spooky trout in the air-clear water of the South Island.

If the fly moves unnaturally, if imperceptible to our own eyes, big trout will often ignore it. 'Micro-drag' as it is called these days, imparted by the slightest friction on the tippet, usually causes a big trout to reject the fly. A light, flexible tippet lessens the effect of micro-drag, but there is almost always some resistance. Drag may not spook the fish; they just go 'nope' and resume watching for the next bite of food. Dragging knots are as noticeable as a dragging fly, so I stick with clear, knotless nylon or copolymer leaders of fifteen feet or more. I normally use store-bought, knotless tapered leaders and find them satisfactory in almost all circumstances. Even with some chopping and changing of butt diameters and tippets, it still adds up to fewer knots than a hand-made leader.

For pocket water, a shortish leader makes things a bit easier and it's worth making up some short, steep-taper leaders for this work. In a world where things float overhead continuously – grass, twigs, strands of weed – a trout has no idea of what a leader is and cannot associate it with the fly or to danger, unless it moves. The weight of tippet is essentially a compromise between reducing friction and break-offs. The exceptions, of course, are waters where the trout, repeatedly disturbed and hyper-sensitive to being lined, react to the shadow or flash of the thicker leader. This also applies to unfished back-country water, where anything out of the ordinary spooks the trout.

A dry fly fished from upstream of the trout would have got one banished from any English chalkstream not so long ago, and it's still the case on some pukka stretches. At best it has been considered a minor tactic for the exceptional situation – a brushy under-cut bank, a fish under a bridge, etc. At worst, it is regarded as a recidivist wet fly tactic, and by extension, poaching. Having misspent most of my youth in a kind of moral grey area when it comes to these behavioural distinctions, I didn't realise the downstream dry was non-U. On the rivers I fished it was just an obvious method of presenting a fly without drag.

The western Alberta freestone rivers are fast and full of pocket water, difficult water to effect a drag-free float. Not that what we considered drag was anything like the type of thing that would have worried Halford or Skues. To the gang I fished with, drag was not a subtle thing. In fact, we only noticed it when the fly was whipped downstream and threw up a roostertail of spray. We soon realised that when the fly did this we tended to catch fewer trout. The obvious way to counter this effect was to wade into the middle of the river and cast directly upstream. If that was impossible, the next obvious thing to do was wade out into the middle of the river and float the fly *down* to the trout. It wasn't brain surgery.

On most pocket water the target zone is so short that the current takes hold of the fly line almost immediately, and the fly is zipped away, no matter how deft your line handling. I learned early that, more often than not, I could get a better, if shorter, drag-free float with a slack-line downstream cast than an upstream throw. Fishing downstream, since all the line on the water is above the fly and slack when presented from upstream, provides less opportunity for drag. The only problem is that of being seen by the trout, but by wading deep and keeping relatively low, out of the trout's perceptual window, this is not too hard to avoid.

On the broad slicks of rivers like the Alberta's Bow, Idaho's Snake, New Zealand's Mataura or the Scottish Tay, a long quartering downstream cast is often essential for a drag-free float. It permits much more control than a long, quartering upstream throw. However, apart from the increased probability of the angler being seen by the trout, it does make for some difficult hooking problems, resulting in many pricked, or lipped, fish. These smooth looking slicks have subtly shifting surface currents and even the slightest drag will bring refusals. A lot of attention is paid to pattern in spinner-fall situations, but the fly is the least of our problems. A simple clipped-hackle dry fly of the right size will catch fish as long as there is no drag. A full repertoire of slack-line and curve casts is something to work toward. The importance of accurate casting cannot be over-emphasised, and is often what separates the good angler from the expert.

A tactic that might be thought of as a surface version of the induced take is Leonard M. Wright's 'sudden inch', first described it as a major tactic in *Fishing the Dry Fly as a Living Insect*. Basically, it is giving your fly a life-like twitch on a downstream cast, which Wright presents as 'heresy', with a wink. Wright's experiments, if I recall correctly, were made on stocked trout. He would throw chopped-up beef lungs, delicately referred to as 'lights', into the stream to condition his trout to floating food. It doesn't surprise me that his trout might attack a twitching dry fly or, frankly, if they produced the rise-form of a school of piranha. Despite Wright's engaging thesis, I've never found a moving dry fly to be consistently effective on anything but young fish.

Even on western cutthroat streams and the lochs of northern Scotland, where an active surface fly is a basic tactic, it is not the bigger trout that tend to go for it. On a smooth surface, the commotion caused by the moving tippet usually outweighs the potential attractions of the twitched fly. Trout, as we know, are highly sensitive to motion. It could be that when these tactics were developed, fishing pressure was so much less that the trout responded to the fly's movement as a sign of life rather than danger. These days, motion of any kind seems to frighten fish more often than it attracts them. The larger fish may just be getting too spooky, or at least have become inured to such tactics.

There's a place for the twitched dry fly in river fishing all right, but it doesn't pay to rely on it. LaFontaine regarded it as a reliable tactic, but I consider it a minor one, limited to rare occasions in broken water. It might work when trout are making the legendary 'slashing rise' to egg-laying caddis, but in my experience big trout seldom make slashing rises to anything but schools of baitfish. I've witnessed slashing rises by big trout on occasion, but usually only immature fish waste energy chasing flies that are taking wing. That much expended energy demands a big pay-off. The waking surface fly or lure is another matter, a good stillwater and night fishing tactic and a specific technique for big fish. Elsewhere in *The Dry Fly – New Angles*, LaFontaine says that drag discourages trout from taking because they have learned that a moving fly is often missed. This to me is a better explanation for refusals than the fish suspecting that the fly is a fake, but how LaFontaine reconciled that observation with his twitched fly tactic we will never know. I just put it down as another of fly-fishing's exceptions that prove the rule.

3. Lessons from western Canada – smart trout

I spent the last couple of summers on my old stamping grounds, the rivers where I cut my angling teeth in southern Alberta and British Columbia's Kootenays. I've got to say it was the best fishing I've had on those waters in over forty years. Several times I had to stop and reflect…what's going on here? There are more anglers and more river traffic than anyone could have dreamed of forty years ago, and the fishing just seems to get better every year. In fact, it has never been this good in living memory.

A lot of the good fishing for big trout is unarguably due to the no-kill regulations in place since1995. Devastating '100-year' floods in Alberta that year, caused by sudden heavy rain on a big snow-pack, scoured the rivers so badly that the fish and wildlife people slapped a no-kill regulation on a lot of streams in order to allow stocks to rebuild. Rebuild they did, and seem to be going from strength to strength. The number and average size of cutthroat trout in many east and west slope drainages has never been higher. While there is no doubt about the benefit of

Matching the hatch. Jim Wyatt wonders if his fly is maybe too big

leaving fish alive in the water, part of this success is possibly due to a rebound effect, suppressed populations responding to a good food supply, and may eventually plateau.

This is pretty well known now, by a lot of anglers, so I'm not giving anything away. At the time of writing, about fifty guides are operating out of Fernie alone, all beating the drum about the excellent fishing. The drift boat traffic on the Elk is, for want of a kinder word, relentless. One day, I waded a mile-long stretch between Sparwood and Fernie and for six hours was never out of sight of a guided boat. One thing is certain; this level of use is not going to get any lighter over the next few years. If you want solitude, it appears that North American fly-fishing does not offer the scope for solitary contemplation it once did – not on accessible rivers like the Elk and Bow, or Idaho's Henry's Fork at any rate.

You can't ignore the fact that North American wild fisheries are receiving heavy and increasing angling pressure, and many anglers worry that some streams are being loved to death. It is clear that trout are being caught and released several times over a season. This is especially true for the west and east slope cutthroat. A recent survey on a small west-slope cutthroat river showed that the fish were from four to eight years old, and almost all had been caught and released many times. One big trout had been caught and released three times in three days by the same angler. Over a long season this can result in trout tiring and losing condition, reducing their chances of surviving the winter.

This speaks highly of the hardiness of the trout, but on a couple of wilderness rivers in the Kootenays I landed several fish that had been caught previously and handled roughly, with torn maxillaries, split fins and other wounds. Some of us are still ripping lips, it seems. I know of guides who encourage clients to catch and release up to sixty and seventy trout in a day. In the Kootenays, I met one visiting angler who fished one roadside stretch of a small stream every day for three weeks, and bragged of an average of twenty trout per day. In the language of contemporary wildlife management, how can we present ourselves as sensitive 'users' of this wild resource if we are in such a competitive rush to get onto the next fish that we can't handle a trout gently and with a little more respect? After all, to ensure they are fully revived is only a matter of a few extra seconds. Besides, it's not an every day thing, what's the rush? It's rather pleasant to be in contact with the fish for that extra moment or two. Catch and release angling demands more care and restraint than catch to kill. The time is approaching when we should consider some self-imposed limits on even our no-kill angling.

I was working my way down a small east-slope Alberta stream one morning as the sun climbed in the cloudless sky. The trout were just getting going. One of my companions was

The average size of wild trout on western Canadian streams is twice what it was thirty years ago, while fishing pressure has increased a hundred fold

doing well with a nymph and indicator rig, but the fish were not responding well to the dry. It seemed like too perfect a day to bother with weighted nymphs and indicators, but I saw several trout drop back under my fly, nose-up, and flatly refuse my offerings right down to a size eighteen. At face value, this appeared to be nothing less than selective or suspicious feeding behaviour, the kind of thing that convinces anglers that the trout are wise to our fly patterns. I changed flies a few times, but reckoned finally that in those short turbulent pools I was probably getting some drag pretty early in my drifts, enough to put the fish off. I came onto another angler who was just getting out of his waders, turning them out on a shingle bar to dry in the sun. He watched as I worked on a fish that was rising regularly in an emerald green slot, tight against a limestone wall.

I had some trouble getting a drag-free drift, even from straight downstream, but after a dozen or so casts I finally got him, a plump fourteen-incher on a no-hackle Deer Hair Sedge. Not an exceptional fish by any means, but I had the satisfied feeling you get when you do the difficult thing in the way you think it should be done. As I turned the trout loose the guy on the bank, evidently a battle of wits type, said, 'They're too easy aren't they? It's fun, but I've had enough of the cutts for today. Going over to the Crowsnest for some rainbows. They're more interesting.'

I heard myself agreeing, laughing at the hare-brained naivety of these fish, but as I moved downstream I felt guilty, as if I'd betrayed something. Not only is a game of chess not the reason I fish for mountain cutthroats, but that morning had shown the fish to be wary of drag and to all appearances selective, the fishing quite technical. The guilty feeling went away soon enough. My companions stayed upstream and I had the stream to myself. The dry fly fishing picked up with the mid-day heat and the trout began concentrating on the surface. Soon I was enjoying one of those rare interludes in life when everything has conspired in my favour. Now, having regained their usual aggressive enthusiasm, the bright, thick-shouldered cutthroats were zeroing on my Deer Hair Sedge like it was their last meal, which until recently it undoubtedly would have been.

Every pocket bigger than a bathtub seemed to hold at least one fish of twelve to fourteen inches, and a couple of green-water slots produced trout over sixteen. On one deep run I saw a long dark shape charge out to intercept a fish I was playing, miss it, then retreat to a thin slice of shadow beneath the shale ledge opposite. My fish turned on the afterburners and stayed up in the head of the pool until I reached down to release him. To that fish I was no threat compared to that bull trout lurking downstream, demonstrating that evolution is a far stronger influence on behaviour than recent developments such as anglers. I also realised that I hadn't seen anything like that on this stream for over forty years.

Over the summer I heard many remarks of the kind that anglers made regarding the behaviour of the cutthroat trout as the air-head reactions of innocent dumb bunnies, beautiful no-brainers. By inference the rainbow is by comparison a rocket scientist, the brownie a quantum physicist. Since living in Scotland I've often found the brown trout to be as gullible and voracious as a mackerel, so I've begun to rethink this idea of trout intelligence. I'm not so sure of the reasoning behind the perception of the mountain cutthroat as a dumb-blonde.

If you compare the relative weight and structure of the brains in these types of trout, you don't get much in the way of measurable difference, if any. All of them have brains the size of a pea, and most of that is optical and olfactory; not much room in there for ratiocination I'm afraid. We won't get into discussing a theory of mind with regard to fish brains here, but we should at least note that that the brain of a trout does not have the structure to feel emotions like suspicion and fear, or experience pain – not as humans understand it at any rate. Anyway,

A good wild rainbow comes to hand on an Alberta foothills stream

who says fishing has to be a battle of wits?

The reason we think these wonderful cutthroats aren't playing with a full deck is their enthusiastic response to just about anything that floats, or so it sometimes seems. Wild rainbows do not do this, right? They are much more selective and clearly more intelligent. Brown trout, those sophisticated Europeans, are not only selective, they have taste, can read Latin and, as everyone knows, they can count. So, it stands to reason that if you are to catch one of these educated fish, you've got to tie in the correct number of tails on your size twenty-two, close-copy, colour system matched, turkey biot-abdomen, shaped poly-wing, genetic parachute hackled, thorax-style Paradun onto your 7x tippet or you are doomed to certain humiliation. Sociologists use the term 'received view' for the opinions that we get pre-packaged from the culture. We should maybe look a little more closely at some received views regarding trout intelligence.

G.E. M. Skues spoke affectionately of the trout as a 'rather stupid person', and that resolutely practical Scotsman, W. C. Stewart, declared, 'trout are not the profound philosophers as the notions of some would lead us to suppose'. Those guys knew a thing or two about trout. Stewart was a professional market fisherman, Skues a paid-up member of the English bourgeoisie. When not lawyering, Skues apparently spent *all* of his time fishing, or thinking about it. Good science tells us that what we are observing is not intelligence in the chalk stream brown and spring creek rainbow, and not stupidity in the freestone cutthroat. Fish may be capable of a certain degree of learning, as demonstrated by Mottram as early as 1920, but it is more accurate to think of it as conditioned behaviour rather than understanding. Putting it bluntly, the lack of a neocortex means a trout cannot think. When a trout rises we can be sure it's either responding to something that *might* be food or making a confident attack on something it is convinced is food. Once the big hatches begin to appear on the food-train slicks of rivers like the Henry's Fork or the Bow, the fish get in a groove, efficiently ignoring anything other than what's being served up regularly and in the largest quantities. To the trout anything that doesn't look and behave as expected just isn't food.

Selective trout

It's important to do what you can to take the voodoo out of fly choices. A good start is to match your fly as closely as possible to the prevailing hatch. In the new edition of their classic book, *Selective Trout*, Doug Swisher and Carl Richards emphatically reassert that a realistic imitation of the insect on the water is the most important factor in fly-fishing success, a statement not made truer through the force of its delivery, despite the invocation of scientific objectivity. They discount bad casting, drag, and other presentation problems as a bunch of anglers' 'excuses' for not catching fish, when all that is needed is a more realistic fly. Well, okay, but Swisher and Richards are expert anglers, for whom, presumably, flawless presentation skills are just part of a highly integrated approach. I've had trout ignore my offerings countless times and I can't say it was because my fly did not adequately imitate the natural. And what do we mean by realistic? To us, or to the trout? There is a presumption that the trout and we share the same values with regard to what looks real. With so many variables in play at the same time, especially when you consider the many aspects of presentation, especially drag, there is usually no way to ascertain the specific reason for a refusal, even if by changing the fly you finally manage to catch the trout. With the most scientific attitude, our perception of what is taking place on a trout stream is unavoidably a subjective interpretation.

Historically, the way of a trout with a fly has been treated as a sort of 'black-box' situation. We understand what we do and we observe how the fish responds, but what happens in between is a mystery. The popular concept of the selective trout is of a suspicious fish that is choosing between kinds of food for some reason. For all that has been written about how a fish responds to an artificial fly, including any number of supposedly scientific accounts, just *why* a fish should behave so fastidiously has been given surprisingly little attention. One thing is certain: feeding behaviour must be adaptive in some way or an organism will not survive. Beyond the natural wariness necessary for a predator, one that is also prey to other predators, what is adaptive about selective feeding behaviour? If you eat bugs for a living and something looks like a bug, why not eat it?

Some anglers go much further; they claim that trout remember and avoid certain patterns because they associate those flies with being caught. Gary Borger describes trout so anxious that even when they took a natural fly they raced away shaking their heads, as if expecting the bite of a hook. Now, it has been shown, in laboratory conditions, that goldfish can be conditioned to associate sounds with being fed, and have the ability to remember that association after an interval of several years. This means it's not impossible, but probably stretching things to say that wild trout learn to recognise and avoid specific fly patterns. As a case in point, in the summer of 2003, using a Stimulator, I caught a Crowsnest River rainbow that already had two

The larger trout in the Kootenay streams have usually been caught several times

Stimulators in its upper jaw, left by angers that struck too vigorously. You'd think two of those things in its lip would serve as a reminder to avoid any more. Trout have a memory, but it is doubtful if such specific memories can be established so quickly. The exception might be water that has been incessantly hammered with big attractor patterns and lures (such as Stimulators), the trout maybe conditioned to ignore such unnatural and disturbing items, but that's not quite the same thing. It remains the case that many anglers believe it's important to change fly patterns simply in order to give the trout something that they haven't seen before. Whatever; novelty seems to be the least important of the factors to be considered in fly design.

Swisher and Richards often use the more accurate term 'keying' in preference to 'selection', so it is evident that they are well aware of the semantic problems raised by the term 'selective'. This intriguing and perplexing behaviour has been described for well over a century by most of the great angling authorities. In almost every case, the observations of highly selective feeding behaviour have been made on chalkstreams and spring creeks, associated with large and sustained hatches of specific insects. Occasionally, when more than one species of fly is on the water at the same time, the trout are observed to select only one of them, ignoring the others even if the one they ignore is a better deal nutritionally. One old theory for such preference for one insect over another is that trout have taste buds, like we do, and simply prefer the flavour of one species to another. The trout's enthusiasm for flying ants has been explained by the taste-bud theory, as has the rejection of several species of fly, from the Grannom to the March Brown.

Faced with such insouciance, several authors have suggested that trout become sickened by a particular insect, or, on the other hand, sated. Having witnessed many times the extent to which trout will glut themselves on everything from snails to field mice when they are available, I'm pretty sceptical of that interpretation, too. When the going is good, the trout usually keep going. One New Zealand study found twenty-three mice in the stomach of one trout, a fish still greedy enough to be caught on a size ten nymph. Trout have often been observed to ignore the thanksgiving turkey of mayflies, the Green Drake dun, behaviour that has had experts scratching their heads for centuries. Fear of the big duns has even been suggested. There is a simpler explanation, one that accords with predatory behaviour throughout the animal kingdom. It's called the search-image.

In waters where the prey is varied or scarce, the lochs of northern Scotland or the freestone streams of western Canada and New Zealand, the wily brownie has to be just as 'dumb' as the mountain cutthroat, an opportunistic predator that tests and eats food as it is encountered. To the mountain cutthroat, anything carried down the stream that is small enough to eat just *might* be food, so it gives almost anything a try. Call it stupidity if you want, but in fast water, anything that looks like it might be food has to be tried quickly by mouth, so this puts the trout at a bit of a disadvantage when there are anglers around. When a specific prey is superabundant even the cutthroat will key on it and ignore anything that doesn't resemble it, displaying what we call selectivity. As a working principle, what we are observing is not true selectivity but the preoccupation of a very simple predatory brain.

In a sustained hatch the brown trout may display the fastidious behaviour that made its reputation, but outside of these windows of specificity it can be as rapacious as a pike, a ravenous glutton on the lookout for anything small enough, vulnerable enough or plentiful enough to eat with no danger to itself. For this reason, the traditional 'pulled' attractor wet fly, which looks and moves like nothing that flies or swims, still does business on Scottish lochs and Irish stillwaters, and fools thousands of brown trout every year. For example, over the past few seasons and defying all reason, a fast-stripped Octopus, a sort of bright golden yellow Carey Special with a fluorescent chartreuse tag, is the lure of choice on the famous drifts of Ireland's Lough Corrib. There is nothing in the ecology of the Corrib that looks or moves like the Octopus, but while there are days when you might conclude that the fish were 'selecting' the Octopus exclusively over other flies, you would be hard pressed to discover what prey it imitated.

The same goes for the wild rainbow trout. On Alberta's Bow, by all accounts an increasingly technical river, the pattern of choice these days is a big, wire-bodied San Juan Worm – a hook wrapped with red thread, trundled along the bottom below an indicator. In theory, this stiff, rather crudely fashioned lure is supposed to imitate a chironomid larva, or bloodworm, and though it is often ten times larger than the natural and has a clearly visible hook, it probably resembles a bloodworm more than anything else. It works, often spectacularly. When hatches are sparse and the fish stiff it is sometimes the only thing on the river catching trout. With so many anglers using the San Juan Worm, it makes you wonder just how many of these things the Bow River trout have seen over a season. Considering the amount of catch and release practised on that river, this does not speak highly of the rainbow's superior intelligence and memory. What it does illustrate is that, as long as the fish are not spooked, they will repeatedly accept a fly that presents a rough impression of familiar food, because they have to.

Big trout have two characteristics that auger against being caught; (1) they are wary of any kind of disturbance, whether they understand it or not; (2) they are only moved to feed when there is a plentiful supply of familiar food. LaFontaine described a study that indicated a trout had to see an unfamiliar food form a thousand times or so before it reacted to it as food. Biologists have observed introduced populations of trout reach near extinction levels because they didn't recognise an abundant source of prey, and starved to death. This makes you wonder about the tactic of showing jaded trout a fly they haven't seen before. It's unlikely that a trout can remember the details of a fly pattern after such relatively few encounters. In fact, if we haven't scared the fish into inactivity, we only have to present a passable imitation of familiar prey to the trout, in a way that familiar prey normally behaves. Of course, we all know it doesn't take much to make our fly look unfamiliar or behave unfood-like, but what we have going for us is it also doesn't take much to make our fly fit the parameters of what biologists call the trout's search-image. A good thing too. If trout were as rational as they are cracked up to be, by now they would be so wised-up we wouldn't stand a chance.

Cutthroats are great dry fly fish in bright, sizzling weather, unlike brown trout or even rainbows, which prefer to feed in low light levels. I love them because they are so wild. Like the Pinnated Grouse and the Mule Deer they don't really belong in this century. Some might say they are stupid, but I prefer to think of it as innocence. John Gierach wrote that he too liked cutthroats for this reason, and that he fished for them in the hope that their innocence might rub off on him. Even so, in my experience they can at times be as preoccupied and difficult as any chalk stream brown trout.

As the summer wore on, I often had to go down to size eighteen no-hackle emergers to match the Pale Morning Dun emergence (it usually hatches in the late afternoon in that region). Absolutely drag-free presentations, only an inch or less from snags and overhanging brush, were the only way to convince the bigger trout, the fish over twenty inches. Earlier in the season, with a wider range of food available, these same fish would have charged across the pool to smash a big, dragging Elk Hair Caddis or even a huge foam bodied Chernobyl Ant as soon as they laid eyes on it. I admit that I prefer to fish small natural looking flies, rather than foam bodied monstrosities like the Chernobyl Ant, no matter how well they work at times. Frankly, I resist tying anything onto my leader that resembles a baby's bath toy. Had these fish become educated and suspicious of artificial flies over the preceding three weeks? It certainly appears so, but maybe that's jumping too quickly to the old smart trout conclusion.

In late summer, these bigger fish often don't move until after sundown, at odds with the popular assumption that cutthroats are primarily mid-afternoon fish. Most guided trips end long before the better trout have even begun to feed, so many visiting anglers miss the best of it. Although I had several good trout to large deer hair, and rubber-legged floaters during the day, nearly all my best fish came late to small flies, usually the sunk-abdomen Deer Hair Emerger. I found that a small semi-dry, no-hackle Deer Hair Sedge or DHE made the difference, time after time. By my own subjective account, although other anglers were certainly getting what they regarded as plenty of fish, I got more and larger cutthroats by fishing smaller, roughly suggestive, no-hackle patterns that presented a stimulating prey-image. Most importantly, in the ultra low and clear water, presentation had to be perfect and drag-free, something normally associated with small flies and light tippets. Those cutthroats, pressured by anglers, increasingly wary in the low water, and keyed to the size and behaviour of the only available food, still had to eat.

Big rubber-legged floaters are good medicine on western rivers, most of the time

Now, it might be argued that it makes no difference whether one calls it selectivity or preoccupation, but it affects your whole approach if you believe your quarry is capable of suspicion and ratiocination. A suspicious mind implies a degree of self-awareness a trout can't possibly possess because it lacks the necessary brain structure for cognitive thought. Once we believe that trout are capable of reason and cunning, we are down the road of anthropomorphism and Brer Rabbit – we interpret the trout's actions as being similar to ours in the same situation. It just doesn't add up that a trout, as indiscriminate as a bluefish in July, is a suspicious and choosy connoisseur two weeks later. Nevertheless, I know many good anglers who attribute high levels of cunning to trout, rejecting flies because they recognise the hook for what it is, etc. On streams where pressure is extreme, and fish have been caught and released many times, this seems logical, but there are too many examples of trout being caught almost daily for weeks on end for this idea to hold water. The fact that trout simply do not have the necessary neocortex in their brains to do all that reasoning doesn't faze someone who wants to believe in the intelligence of their quarry.

In *The Dry Fly – New Angles*, LaFontaine makes a case for trout intelligence based on his idea that a trout's responses to stimuli are essentially like ours, in kind if not quality. He says that the simple decisions trout make are a low-level version of the same things we do, including play. Since a trout's brain has so little in common with ours, I don't think fish play, ever. What LaFontaine interpreted as playful responses are more likely confused or truncated predatory attacks. The appearance or behaviour of the fly, or a sudden awareness of danger, might conflict with the attack impulse. The fly is maybe perceived as prey that is hard to catch, such as wind-blown duns, or is not recognised as food at all – a kind of 'noise' like all the other waterborne debris that does not fit the trout's established search-image. Also, despite what some experts claim, sometimes trout just miss the target. If the angler has remained out of context, and the fly is a reasonable impression of the prevailing food, nine times out of ten it will be the fly's behaviour that will decide the issue.

Recently, on Ireland's Lough Carra, I killed a beautiful leopard-spotted September brown trout of nearly three pounds. When I inspected its stomach contents I was astonished to find it absolutely stuffed with corixa. The trout's stomach was so full it resembled a thick sausage. There were literally hundreds of light tan-yellow corixa and absolutely nothing else. No olives, caddis, shrimp, bloodworm, terrestrials – nothing. I've seen few better examples of a selective trout. The only trout I caught that day, it took a size fourteen, golden olive wet Bumble, unlike a corixa in almost every way but body colour. The most significant resemblance was in the fly's movement; short fast pulls after being allowed to sink on a long leader. Big Carra trout are notoriously difficult. The general impression of colour and movement – close enough, in other words – induced a take from a big, selectively feeding trout in shallow, gin-clear water and bright sunshine. During such a hatch, trout display what biologists call area search behaviour, very aggressively searching for successive prey opportunities while the getting is good. Even if it exhibits only one triggering feature, such as size or colour, anything in the trout's feeding zone that roughly accords with its search-image will be attacked. By the way, speaking of predatory behaviour, poached lightly and eaten with boiled new potatoes and fresh peas, that was the best tasting trout I've had in years.

In *The Truth About Trout*, Rob Sloane presents a good case against the received view of selective behaviour that has informed fly-fishing discourse for over a century. Fly-fishing's central mystery is that a trout will select an artificial fly out of hundreds of available naturals on the water. That they do this there is no doubt; why is still an open question for most anglers, especially when, for generalised predators such as trout, opportunistic feeding is a primary genetic trait. Former Commissioner of the Tasmanian Inland Fisheries and a trout biologist with a lot of fly-fishing experience, Sloane claims that trout display what we call selectivity only when a specific food is super-abundant, in other words, preoccupation with a single food source. Even in those situations it does not necessarily mean that striving for a perfect imitation of the natural should be our main objective. Even if it were possible, is it necessarily the best strategy to add another perfect natural to a plethora of perfect naturals?

One shot deal. For Bruce Masson, stealth and presentation are everything   *photo: Keith Mitchell*

Concerning the relationship of selectivity to spookiness, Sloane provides an interesting anecdote on the extreme preoccupation of trout feeding on amphipods in a shallow Tasmanian lagoon. These normally spooky trout were so absorbed in their feeding that they could be approached and prodded with a rod tip before they woke up to the fact that you were looking over their shoulder. Rob's example is more instructive than it may seem at first glance. Preoccupied with finding prey, the trout had put an equally important aspect of their existence out of their heads – safety. Even taking into account the limitations of the trout's vision in shallow water, Rob's story indicates that its brain is capable of processing only so much information at one time, and that its window of understanding is pretty narrow, or, more likely, non-existent. When the trout's attention is focused on a particular prey there is simply not much room for anything else. Limited attention characterises the formation of a predatory search-image, which partly answers the old question of a related behaviour; why trout are sometimes observed to prefer one species of prey to another that appears to be as good or better. Such narrowly focused behaviour is just the most efficient way for the trout to capitalise on a specific food source. It's not selectivity we're observing, it's tunnel vision.

Studies on predatory behaviour indicate that having to respond to different food-types causes a lowering of a predator's detection rate. In other words, a trout that has to feed on several types of prey becomes less efficient at recognising any particular type. This means where food is scarce and varied, trout will be opportunistic, non-selective, and not very efficient. They sample just about anything that looks food-like, which explains the mountain trout's catholic taste in trout flies.

There's more to this search-image thing. Where food is abundant and restricted to one type of prey, trout are very efficient at detecting and catching that one type but may not recognise any other type of prey as food. After a long period of feeding on one particular type of prey, the predator's memory of other prey types begins to fade. Worse, after a trout has been feeding on one type of prey for an extended period, it may take some time for it to recognise and switch to another type of food, even when it is abundant. Here we have the basis for what appears to us as suspicious behaviour, and an explanation for all those ignored Green Drake duns. This finding casts some doubt on the widely held idea that trout remember and avoid specific fly patterns.

The Darwinian principle of 'survival of the fittest' has been popularised as the predator's rather altruistic selection of only the crippled or old from a herd, as if it was judiciously pruning a garden for the benefit of the commonweal. By presenting this sentimental fiction as objective science, Farley Mowat's book, *Never Cry Wolf*, which Disney turned into a very popular movie, has done as much to reinforce this anthropomorphic nonsense in young minds as anything Beatrix Potter dreamed up. In reality, the crippled deer stands out from the herd through some difference in appearance or behaviour and the wolf locks on to it. It's just a matter of the best chance of getting a meal.

Any gunner knows that flock shooting is a good way to miss everything. The successful wing shot always selects an individual target from a covey of partridge or flock of duck. Cheethas and wild African hunting dogs have been observed to do this when hunting zebras and wildebeest among large herds. Franklin Russell gives a fascinating observation of prey-selection behaviour by African predators in *The Hunting Animal*. If large-brained predators do it instinctively, something like it is probably a significant factor in what we call selectivity by simple-brained creatures like trout. Charging blindly into a herd of caribou is the equivalent of flock-shooting. Like any predator, trout have to zero-in on one target in order to not become confused by many available targets. Abnormal appearance or behaviour is just bad luck for a prey animal. Once a wolf, or even worse, a pack of wolves has noticed it, that particular caribou is lunch. If there is no crippled animal we can be sure that the hungry wolf will select a healthy one from the herd, but without some distinguishing feature to focus on, the chances of success go down. You don't have to think long on this to see that it is an accurate description of predatory behaviour in trout. This suggests that an effective fly design should incorporate some exaggerated visual stimuli, or triggers, so our fly is noticed among the many naturals on the water.

Gary LaFontaine was on the right track with his theory of attraction. His assertion that an unfamiliar food-form had to be seen by a trout many times before it was recognised as food fits accepted search-image theory. His idea that a good trout fly has to stand out from the naturals

It's important to hustle-in trout in warm weather to avoid exhausting them

accords with what we understand about predatory behaviour. He designed flies to contain some exaggerated features, what behavioural ecologists term supernormal stimuli and which are well documented in scientific literature. For fly-fishers, the search-image idea means that if you haven't alerted a trout to your presence and haven't frightened it by your casting, a well-presented fly that is roughly the size and shape of some familiar food is usually not refused, if it gets noticed.

Fly-fishers have known since the earliest times that a rough impression of an insect is more reliable than an attempt at close-copy of the natural. To my adolescent dismay, my grandfather used to rough up my newly tied flies, turning the beautifully positioned wings into a scruffy, frayed mess before they even touched the water. He believed that slavish attention to detail and neatness actually worked against the fly's effectiveness. Whether they know it or not, the majority of experienced trout anglers tend to be of the general impression and primary trigger camp, putting the emphasis on basic design rather than details of pattern. The problems of delicacy, translucency and a convincing impression of vitality make exact imitation practically impossible anyway. The great trout flies of the world are invariably of the impressionist type, and for every Grey Duster, Adams, or Elk Hair Caddis there are a thousand forgotten 'realistic' patterns. True, this may be partly due to the comparative ease of tying the old favourites, but it certainly isn't the whole story.

Some hatches are famous for the extreme selectivity shown by the trout, usually on the type of water known as eutrophic, typified by spring creeks and chalkstreams. The North American *Tricorythodes* hatch is among the most difficult of these and is regarded as a situation where true expert anglers earn their stripes. The *Trico* hatch has its own lore, some of it approaching mythic proportions, with accounts of trout scrutinising and selecting only the females from the midst of a mixed fall of both males and female spinners – a claim that has been met with a certain amount of scepticism by knowledgeable anglers. For one thing, the male spinner is normally on the water at different times, and anyway, just how does one ascertain the sex of the size twenty-six insect that has just been eaten by a trout? The answer is that after spurning all else the trout has eaten that angler's meticulously tied female *Trico* spinner pattern. This is accepted as proof of the trout's extraordinary intelligence, and by extension, the angler's outstanding skill.

The range of variables makes such a claim impossible to prove or refute, but it should be kept in mind that the experience of many top anglers on the same rivers varies widely. Most of them have their own special and often quite distinctive designs for the same situation, including flying ant imitations, and, interestingly, 'sunk spinner' patterns tied on relatively large and heavy hooks to be fished sub-surface. The last thing I'd want to do is diminish a brother angler's triumphs, but speaking for myself, the real reasons for success is preferable to an ego-boosting interpretation. Incidentally, when the dry fly is proving especially difficult, those who fish the sunk spinner and flying ant have sometimes found the same super-selective fish to be downright enthusiastic.

Many presentationists fish a fly larger than the natural simply because it's easier for them to see on the water. It makes it easier for the trout too, a tactic often employed by British fly-fishers for the very difficult *caenis* hatch, referred to as the 'angler's curse'. Incidentally, English biologist and wild trout expert Malcolm Greenhalgh has shown that dark, floating CDC and deer hair snail patterns have proven remarkably effective for trout feeding exclusively on the tiny *caenis* emergers, similar in size to the *Trico*, supporting my argument that interrupting the attention of a preoccupied trout without spooking it is more than half the battle. Some very successful anglers maintain that colour and detail are relatively unimportant; if the size and basic shape of your fly are near enough, and you make repeated and accurate presentations to specific fish, the trout will eventually lock onto it and take it. Prey size is known to be a predominant feature of a trout's search-image. Size, shape and posture are the primary aspects of what I call, accurately I hope, a fly's prey-image.

Although we often treat spookiness and selectivity as interdependent and inseparable aspects of the same suspicious behaviour, a trout that is feeding hard is actually not that easy to spook, an observation backed up by anglers' experience and science. Biologists have established that when a predator is in hunting mode its search-image does not leave that much room for anything else in its brain, including its own security, making itself vulnerable to attack. It's also important to remember that a trout 'on the fin' near the surface has a very narrow perceptual window. This makes it easy for the angler to stay outside of the trout's cone of vision, but also for the fly to be out of sight. Savvy anglers move up close behind such a preoccupied feeder and repeatedly put their fly in its window until it is seen, recognised and eaten – or drag or a sloppy cast finally puts down the fish. The idea is to anticipate the trout's feeding rhythm and to re-present the fly until it is noticed among the hundreds of naturals. The fact that the fish will often take the artificial in preference to available naturals is proof that there is more to good fly design than precision mimicry. These accounts support the prey/search-image and presentation model rather than the belief in the perspicacity of a suspicious mind.

* * * * *

4.Rivers II: Sight fishing

There is one of the hunter's senses that must work indefatigably at all times. That is the sense of sight. Look, look, and look again; at all times, in all directions, and in all circumstances.

Jose Ortega y Gasset
Meditations on Hunting

A nice early season brownie to the DHE during an olive emergence

1. Looking vs. seeing

My pal Al Pyke called, wanting to get in a day's fishing somewhere, anywhere, with the stipulation that it be wild, close by and easy to access. We discussed the options, narrowed it down to a couple of association waters, and decided to run up the Tay. We knew these things: it is a big river; it is by all accounts over-fished; its trout are scarce, wild, and impossible to catch; access is easy and cheap. It sounded perfect for a pleasant day on the river with no serious expectations of success.

It was a brilliant, lazy, cloudless Sunday morning. After a full-cholesterol truck-stop breakfast, we tackled up as we looked out on the broad expanse of the river, running low in the dazzling sunshine. The estate gillies had their shirts off and were desultorily painting the boats. A long holiday weekend and not an angler in sight. There were a few caddis and what looked like some Pale Wateries about, but just a few salmon parr rising for them. In the first hour I coaxed up two pan-sized brownies and a foot-long grayling on a dry Blue Upright and felt, all things considered, pretty good. The first flotillas of canoeists paddled by and Al managed to catch an eel on a Hare's Ear nymph, which bit him on the knuckle as he tried to unhook it. So far, apart from the eel attack, things were turning out better than expected.

We strolled upstream along the high bank, remarking at the beauty of the river and watching for rising trout. It was now noon and the sun was straight overhead. There seemed to be a rise or two so we walked down to a pool and split up. I worked upstream to a beautiful area of boulders and trouty looking water. Wading out into the strong current as far as I dared, I began to search the pockets and riffles with a dry Grey Duster. The few caddis had now become a substantial hatch and it quickly grew into a blizzard of flies, drifting upriver in clouds. A trout began to rise twenty feet in front of me, and after a dozen accurate casts rather pointedly ignored my fly.

So, I said to the trout, it's like *that* is it?

I worked my way up the stretch and saw my Duster sucked under in a small eddy behind a boulder. My line suddenly twitched forward. I struck and a two-pound Brownie flung itself straight up into the air and tore off downstream for maybe twenty yards. This was a hell of a trout. It was five minutes before I got the fish to hand and carefully lifted it from the water. A still green two-pound trout is hard to hold and it twisted out of my grasp, popping the light tippet.

Okay, I said to the river. I've had my wake-up call. Time to go to work.

The caddis hatch was now so thick that the river downstream seemed to be steaming in the sunlight. Here was a major food form on the move. Several trout were now up and feeding and to my eye they all looked big. The fish were not taking the adult flies; they ignored my Grey Duster and dry caddis patterns, and everything else I tried. Waiting for the correct synapses to fire, I had the paranoid suspicion that the caddis blizzard was masking another hatch. Too much theory will do this to you. After an hour of neurotic fly changing, I had still not cracked it, and the trout rose steadily.

Only then did I notice the shucks, thousands of transparent shucks. In the fast water they were only visible from directly above. The fish were obviously fixed on to the emerging pupae. I felt like an idiot for wasting so much time in such a hatch – I may have even slapped my forehead. What had been going on *under* the surface all this time doesn't bear thinking about.

I quickly knotted on a size sixteen, Dark Hare's Ear Emerger, touched the thorax with floatant and covered a fish. It took instantly. As it felt the hook the trout blew up and tore off downstream, just like the first one. I promised to be a better person and praised out loud the disc drag on my reel – not usually a concern with river trout – but the light tippet held. This fish was smaller, maybe only a pound and a half, but I managed to fumble it, so it too was soon back with its people. I was excited now and beginning to whimper. There was a pod of big feeding trout occupying the riffle, but I noticed anxiously that the hatch was thinning out. I could feel a great opportunity slipping by. Story of my life. Honey, won't you give me just one more chance?

On went another emerger and within five casts I was into another fish, a hot sixteen-incher. With the sun behind my shoulder, I saw the fish take perfectly – the long tan shape of the fish in the dark water and the yellow gleam when it turned down with the fly. After a wild fight and another spectacular round of one-handed fish juggling, I managed to get hold of this fish. I decided to whack this one to quell any doubt of my masculinity and expertise, and confirm that it was not all just a bad dream. I also made a mental note regarding the widely recognised virtues of the landing net.

I finally got a look at what the fish were keyed to. It was all over my hands after handling the trout. It was, of course, the pupa of *Brachycentrus*, the small daytime caddis we call the grannom (so you can all put your hands down), which had only been hatching in astronomical numbers for two bleeding hours. Blindingly obvious, and yet another warning of incipient senility, if one was needed. The fly's body penetrating the surface spelled the difference between success and failure. I hooked one more trout of the same size, which I gallantly released at long distance. I snatched the fly away from another much bigger one, spooking it and denouncing it roundly as a coward and a bastard. Then it was finished.

I was reminded, for the hundredth time, of the importance of actually seeing what is before my eyes. In that situation I was blinded by a combination of overwhelming evidence and conventional thinking. In fact, I wasn't thinking at all, I was panicking. That experience drove home the importance of fly design, and is one of the clearest examples of the importance of an appropriate prey-image in a trout fly. If I'd stopped to analyse what was happening, matched my fly to the correct *phase* of the hatch instead of frantically changing dry fly patterns, I'm sure I would have had one of the better afternoons of my fishing life. I've been watching for another big grannom hatch for years since, but I've either missed it or it hasn't occurred. Meanwhile, in anticipation of a return bout, I've been concentrating on emergers.

In fact, for many seasons now, I have seldom tied on a conventional hackled dry fly. My reason is that I am no longer sure that trout eat as many perfect 'dry' duns as I once thought. What I *am* sure they eat a lot of are nymphs, emergers, cripples and spinners. When I reflected on how many times I have flogged away during a heavy spring hatch of olive duns, with rising trout all over the place, and getting only an occasional sniff at my exquisitely tied dry olives, perfect in size, shape and colour, I realise that I've been an idiot for a large part of my life. Most of the rises were probably not to the duns at all, but to the emergers, cripples, and the so-called stillborn duns – the sitting ducks.

2. Reconnaissance

Driving down from our annual pilgrimage to Assynt in northern Scotland, which the boys have come to refer to as the 'holy land', my pal Bob Morton was in a reflective mood.

'I have to examine the way I fish', he said.

'How's that?' I responded, 'You fish hard, put in more rod time than anyone I know. Catch a lot of fish'.

'I mean, I fish harder, but you usually catch more big fish'.

'Oh, I dunno,' I said, demurely, 'probably evens out'.

Bob fishes hard, and I mean *all* day. You'll know someone like him; everyone is ready to quit and head for the pub, it's like, where's Bob? He has that remarkable quality that a lot of good anglers have, he's relentless. Flee's in the water, so to speak. Pays off. I tend to hang back a bit, mostly because I prefer the dry fly and I've learned to wait for the fish to show before going after them. Pays off too. Bob's point was that by hanging back I target the larger fish, so it appears that I sometimes get larger than average fish, if fewer of them, over the day. I tend to agree or I wouldn't stick with it.

Logically, by specifically targeting individual and bigger trout you will tend to catch a higher percentage of them. You might call it a no-brainer. If sometimes I do get a higher proportion of bigger fish, I believe it is simply because I'm fishing more selectively and I'm fishing upstream. This approach will usually lead to a few more of the larger fish than 'fishing the water'. For one thing, big fish are spookier; it's how they got big in the first place. On hard fished public water, where we do most of our fishing, that's important. The water may have lots of big fish, but they are intolerant of random presentation and don't make up much of a day's bag.

There are a couple of good reasons for a restrained and focused approach. The first one is the larger trout's inherent shyness. On public water, but really on any water, the big trout is a cautious animal with peculiar feeding habits. Anything out of the ordinary will spook it. One thing that is sure to put a big fish down is a fly line passing overhead, although the fish has no idea what it is. Another reliable frightener to a big fish is small fish being caught around it. Fishing the water can always pick up a good fish, especially if you're the first rod on a pool or run, but if your swinging wet fly or broadcast dry fly does not get the bigger fish on its first pass, it's likely that fish will go to ground.

Experience tells many anglers that their best chance is the first pass through the pool, and they're right. This is the basis for some unseemly efforts to always be first down the water, which can be pretty dispiriting if one is forced to follow guys like that. It's not that they catch all the fish, but if they don't, and they never do, they put the rest down for themselves and anyone following behind them. This is why bank angling etiquette was invented, basically a polite leapfrog *pas de deux*. If observed, everyone relaxes and has a good day, having been given adequate room and time to explore the water any way he or she wishes, reducing to some extent the greedy anxiety that someone else might be catching 'your' fish.

Where waiting and watching pays off is during a hatch or an evening rise to a fall of spinners. This is nothing new, being the basis for the whole dry fly tradition. The beauty and pleasure of it is in the long periods of contemplation that attend the waiting for fish to show. You get the full floor show of river life; birdsong, deer moving through the woods, the scent of wildflowers and hay fields, light effects on the water, if you're sensitive to that sort of thing.

Often, reacting only to these environmental phenomena, I will find myself going in to action only moments before fish begin to show. This has happened so many times in my life that it makes me think we respond to some of the same stimuli that the fish do, and this is the source of that 'I *knew* I was going to get that fish' feeling. The best description of this phenomenon is in Kingsmill-Moore's, *A Man May Fish*. After a depressingly dour and fishless period, he finds himself singing as his mood changes with a change in atmospheric conditions, and immediately hooks a fish.

Once you have located your fish, or water that you think holds a fish, maybe even a big fish, you have a decision to make. If you are a traditional across-and-down ideologue you already know what you will do – go to the top of the pool and start fishing. You will do this whatever

photo: Bruce Masson

the type of water and whatever the time of year. All you have to decide is what patterns to fish and what size. Who knows? As long as you don't spook the fish this might work, but right off, even a good across-and-down wet fly fisher has significantly reduced the chances of taking a big fish. The reason, you'd think, is obvious – trout face up stream.

On exceptionally smooth and clear waters, British chalkstreams and North American spring creeks, and many low gradient New Zealand rivers, a downstream approach is considered anathema, although in many cases a careful downstream presentation makes a lot of sense in avoiding the lining of a spooky fish. Trout have pretty good peripheral vision as well, at least as far as movement is concerned. In my mind's eye, I can still clearly see a pod of large Ahuriri trout ghosting away from their shallow water lies as I approached casting range from downstream. They had begun to move to deep water long before I ever saw them, as soon as my head and shoulders entered their perceptual window. Why should it be any different on our northern hemisphere rivers? The reason we don't pay as much attention to stalking trout on our rivers is because we can't see them. We therefore and incorrectly assume that the trout can't see us.

One popular tactic to offset the disadvantage of a downstream approach is to fish a long line, but by doing so we have reduced our chances even further. Although the downstream cast-step-cast metronome does not actually sweep all the fish from the pool, the effect is similar. It has been proven to work on small fish, and the occasional good one, on the first pass, otherwise no one would do it, but it will certainly reduce the chances of connecting with the larger fish in the pool. If a large fish does not go for your swinging fly on the first pass, your fun is done. Apart from night fishing, the best opportunity for the downstream wet is a spate. Big aggressive fish, taking up the prime ambush spot, what New Zealanders call the eye of the pool, will often chase and grab anything that looks like food in spate conditions. The best fly in this case as in night fishing is usually a big one; a Black Pennell, a silver-bodied fry imitation like a Medicine, or the cheeseburger of trout flies, the Woolly Bugger.

If you have a larger technical repertoire you will prepare to fish the water according to its particulars. These range from the time of day, the quality of light, colour of the water, the depth and speed of the current, to the most important of all, the phase of the prevailing hatch, if any. If your primary aim is to catch a trout on the fly by any means, it is these particulars that will govern your approach, not whether you are a traditional wet fly angler or a Halfordian dry fly man.

Preparations will include your leader type, the rigging of the flies and the type or design of the fly. You must also decide whether to stalk your fish from shore or wade, big considerations in themselves, worth a moment or two before charging ahead. The British caveat against wading is another bit of traditional ideology. On chalkstreams, due to soft bottoms and weed growth, it makes sense to stay out of the water, but in my experience it is the shore-based approach that is more likely to spook fish. While the sweeping downstream wet fly has one good chance at the better fish, the upstream approach keeps you in business until you hook or otherwise spook the fish by a bad cast or clumsy movement.

Quiet wading in a moderate current, approaching from downstream as deeply as possible without splashing or creating waves, does not usually bother fish at all. However, trout are remarkably sensitive to vibration as well as movement, so in quiet flows a water-based attack requires caution. Those pressure waves radiating outwards as you wade in placid pools are in fact vibrations that can signal danger to the trout as clearly as throwing a rock at them. With careful wading, once up to your waist in the river you often discover good fish rising within a rod tip's distance from you. The reason is the trout's perceptual cone of vision, or window. Casting from shore, where they expect danger to appear, and from within the trout's perceptual window is far more likely to spook them. When stalking from shore it pays to be mindful of background cover, and only where a silt or weed bottom might be disturbed, or pressure waves created, should deep wading be ruled out.

Once you are in position, normally downstream of the fish or targeted piece of water, it's important to take time to observe any insect activity and watch for any movements by the fish.

Bob Morton nets a Tay brownie

During your waiting and watching period, you have also been analysing the currents to get some idea of how your fly will behave once you have made your cast. An angled approach avoids the leader falling across them. You will have worked out the required length of line while you wade or creep up on the target, careful that you have obscured your outline against a backdrop of shaded bank or trees (remember that a trout's eyes are so placed that it can see pretty well behind as well as forward). False casting is a very bad habit, especially over the target area. Line can be worked beyond the rod tip any number of ways, and a simple downstream water-haul will load the rod for the forward throw. If we paid heed to the natural wariness of their quarry, worried less about magic fly patterns and more about presentation, we would discover that our home waters held more and better fish than we imagined.

3. Fishing the hatch

This, to your hard-core dry fly man, is what it's all about, the classic situation; to have approached the water stealthily, taken up a comfortable observation post somewhere on the bank, and wait for the rise to commence, in effect like a deer hunter taking up a tree-stand, or a duck hunter in his blind. In itself, river watching is a source of deep pleasure, but it goes without saying that it is best practised on water that you have to yourself. The usual situation these days is, unfortunately, to have at least one other angler pounding his way up the stream behind you. The new etiquette, such as it is, probably demands that you either let the other angler through or urgently get to it yourself. Use it or lose it. If not a complete barbarian, the other angler will politely walk around and leave that particular stretch to you, but you can't count on such etiquette anymore, even among fly-fishers.

If you have the place to yourself, you can learn more in an hour of watching than in a week of just fishing the water. If there are no obvious rising fish, the first thing to look for is the telltale flash of a trout's side as it works sub-surface on ascending nymphs. Surprisingly, this is not as rare or unlikely as it might sound. In fact, I couldn't count the number of times I have spotted feeding trout in just this way, when there was no other sign of life on the water. It is your first and best indication of the pre-hatch phase of the feeding period, or the massive movement of nymphs and larvae that biologists call the invertebrate drift. A dry fly or emerger is a poor second choice for this phase of the hatch, the ideal situation for the upstream wet fly or nymph.

The induced-take tactic was developed for fish seen to be feeding subsurface. It is a specific method for imitating the action of a nymph or pupa as it rises toward the surface. The angler may be able to watch the fly as it sinks and drifts toward the trout, but usually what he watches are the actions of the fish. Any movement, it is certain, will be some kind of response to the fly – fight or flight. The trout may suddenly appear to 'stiffen', move forward or fall back with the current, or just bugger off. A quick movement to either side is almost certainly an indication that the trout has taken the fly, and should be struck immediately. Several good trout hunters I know judge the time to strike solely by the trout's movements. Needless to say, it depends on our being able to see the fish.

Other tell-tales are Skues' 'cunning brown wink', an almost imperceptible flicker of colour as the light catches the trout's movement, or the white flash of its mouth as it opens and closes on the fly. It maybe doesn't sound like much to rely on, but it is surprising how good you get at spotting these subtle indicators. In fact, over time, your response to a take becomes almost semi-conscious. You find yourself reacting to fish you didn't quite see, or didn't realise that you saw. Athletes describe this heightened state of awareness and performance as being in the 'zone', and it's not a skill developed by reading books like this.

There is no doubt that a nymph or soft hackle wet fly can be fished throughout a hatch, but that would mean missing out on one of the finest experiences in fly-fishing; a rise to the surface fly. I usually switch over to the semi-dry emerger as soon as I see good trout showing on the surface. If I think the place holds a big trout, I will sometimes forego fishing through the pre-hatch period and wait until the fish shows itself on the surface. The chance of putting a big trout down outweighs the pleasure of picking up a couple of smaller fish. The thing to reconcile here is that you might miss some fishing if you intend to fish only the surface fly. The hatch may not really develop, and a well fished wet fly or nymph might pick up a trout or two and save a blank day. This kind of risk taking is just part of it, but at the prime time of the season a surface rise is fairly reliable and worth the wait.

In the early season, better than average trout will feed in the shallow, rocky riffles

The main reason for waiting is that it gives the bigger fish a chance to take up their feeding positions as the hatch develops. If you are already fishing the water they may not do this at all. Once the fish are settled and feeding it is possible to approach them quite closely from downstream, eliminating the need for long casts and the risk of lining the fish. It is always tempting to try a dry fly straight off, but it pays to look closely at those rise-forms. Much has been written on the study of the rise-forms of trout and some of it is still viable today. Vincent Marinaro's, *In the Ring of the Rise* is still an excellent source for anyone fishing the smooth currents of the spring creeks and chalkstreams. Swisher and Richards' *Selective Trout* contains enough information on trout feeding behaviour to be considered the contemporary bible on the subject. The best of recent British books include Goddard and Clarke's *The Trout and the Fly*, and John Roberts' *To Rise a Trout*. The only reservation I have toward these books is with regard to their emphasis on imitating the fully emerged dun.

If I had taken a moment to observe things a little more closely on the day of that colossal River Tay grannom hatch described earlier, I would have caught several big trout. Those browns were head-and-tailing specifically for the emerging pupa. The rise-form should have tipped me off that it wasn't the adult they were keyed to. A porpoising trout is often a preoccupied trout, one usually concentrating on emerging insects. The trout can only process so much sensory information in that little brain and if you don't get the correct phase of the hatch right, your exquisitely tied dry fly will float by like so much stream debris. Call it intelligence and selectivity if you wish, but a fish keyed-in to the emerger or spent fly isn't being suspicious, just efficient. It just doesn't register your exquisitely hackled, high-riding dry fly as food.

Rob Sloane also emphasises the dun phase of the mayfly in *The Truth About Trout*. It is revealing that his old never-fail 'dun' imitation, Rob's Dry, is a simple palmered hackle pattern with the underside hackle clipped off. In fact, all of Sloane's favourite dry flies appear to be clipped hackle or flush-floating designs, no matter what they are intended to resemble. A fly with the underside hackle trimmed is going to fish flat in the surface film, like an emerger, a trapped still-born dun, or a spinner, so even Rob's Dry isn't a dun imitation at all. Like many expert anglers, Rob puts presentation ahead of the particulars of fly pattern in terms of importance. Sloane claims that with good presentation you can often convince a trout to eat what it doesn't really want, and I tend to agree.

Combine good presentation with a reasonably good prey-image that incorporates one or more of the primary stimuli, or triggers, and you have a combination that is nearly irresistible. This approach may seem a bit too simplistic for some, and maybe in some situations it is. There may even be a degree of learning that could influence a trout's reactions, but the popular selective trout model just attributes too many inexplicable preferences and too much fishy ratiocination for me to accept. I subscribe to the prey/search-image model because it not only accords with the findings of behavioural ecology, it provides some workable rules of thumb and some avenues for further investigation, maybe even a better understanding of our quarry.

4. Lessons from New Zealand

I've been fortunate enough, if at considerable risk to my retirement plans, to make several trips to the South Island of New Zealand, a real trout hunter's country. The rivers typically hold low numbers of large, insectivorous, exceedingly spooky brown trout. My visits are usually made in early April, near the end of the trout season. The lateness makes for less than ideal conditions, according to most of the locals, but has the advantage that there are almost no other anglers on the rivers. On my last two visits, I arrived to the late stages of a six-week drought. The rivers were down to their bones, the water absolutely transparent under a drilling sun, conditions in which I would expect poor brown trout fishing in Scotland, if not downright impossible.

The country of Central and South Otago exerts a strong emotional pull on me. It is visually similar to the landscape of my youth, but in a way that existed long before I ever laid eyes on a foothills river valley. With some notable differences, it looks like southern Alberta or Montana must have looked a hundred years ago. Drought or not, when my partner Margaret and I crossed the bridge at Omarama and I saw the Ahuriri valley, I pulled into the first motel we saw and we didn't move again for five days.

The motel office had a small fly-fishing shop, so I reckoned I had chosen the right place to set up headquarters. The proprietor, David, was submitted to intense questioning as I filled out the guest register. He said the fishing had been poor recently because of the drought, that the dry fly fishing was finished for the season. He said that a small weighted nymph was the only way to go and showed me a tray of local favourites. I had about a thousand flies with me on this trip, but I bought a few for diplomatic reasons. What I noticed about the flies on sale was their design. Most of them looked like conventional attractors to me. Trout flies used in New Zealand and dry flies in particular tend toward the general attractor type, the Royal Wulff and Hare and Copper being ubiquitous examples.

David's chunky nymphs had names that suggested caddis larvae, etc, but to me they looked more like all-round bugs, similar to the North American Zug Bug and Prince Nymph. Many of the effective New Zealand nymphs are extremely heavily weighted, a necessity in the fast currents, resulting in football-shaped bugs quite unlike any natural nymph. In effect, the typical

Veteran trout hunter Bruce Masson hefts another cracking South Island brown   *photo: Keith Mitchell*

Wyatt hooks up during a Deleatidium *emergence*   *photo: Margaret Mitchell*

New Zealand nymph is an impressionistic attractor. They work so well because the trout on these unstable rivers have to be opportunistic feeders, anything that looks remotely like food has to be checked out. This opportunism works in the angler's favour, and almost offsets the South Island trout's remarkable sensitivity to danger.

We can theorise about the reasons a trout takes an artificial fly, but in the end we are left with subjective experience and many questions. My own conclusion, after nearly fifty years of what you might call empirical experimentation, is that when it comes to fly fishing theory even the variables have variables. But, one way or another, to some degree, attraction is based on *mimesis*, simulation of the trout's natural prey. You could say that my fly boxes are of the reductive kind, as opposed to a broad variety of realistic imitations and attractors. With so many variables to consider, a few basic designs help make choices possible.

I can't say I've ever felt handicapped by this relatively limited selection, which means in most situations my few designs meet the trout's criteria, anywhere I have fished. Either that or I have been forced to compensate for any inadequacy in fly design by fishing harder and better. I may sometimes think I have the answer, but it's impossible to say where one aspect of my approach overlaps the other – skill and dumb luck. Even when perfectly matched in terms of fishing skill, the number of variables in any two anglers' performance on any day, on any stream, is too great to make conclusive judgements on the specific reasons they caught trout, or not. This amounts to taking a fork in the road. I took the one indicated by Thoreau's maxim for daily life…*simplify*. The way you choose to fish has as much to do with your choice of pleasures as it does with the chances of hooking fish. Usually, however, your choice of pleasures has something to do with a history of success. Understandably, the more successful your methods, the more you tend to trust your own theories - a proof of the pudding deal.

As far back as 1921, J. C. Mottram wrote about his experience with the dry fly in New Zealand. In *Some New Arts and Mysteries*, there is a telling passage on how presumption can skew the perceptions of even the most observant of anglers. One day, Mottram was faced with a river full of furiously rising trout that he could not catch on his Halfordian dun patterns. Throughout the rise, he did not see even one floating dun taken by a trout, and he made the logical conclusion that they weren't interested in the dun. He reckoned that the fish were eating only the emerging nymph, but he went further, jumping to the conclusion that rainbow trout preferred nymphs to duns, period. By extension, if it had been brown trout in the river, they would have eaten his dun patterns and provided 'proper' dry fly fishing. It is clear to us today that those crass New Zealand rainbows were displaying the very same selectivity that his posh chalkstream brownies did back home. They just weren't playing by old Halford's rules and were keying on the emergers, not the duns. Incidentally, the famous 'wet rise' on New Zealand's Mataura, notorious for the selectivity displayed by the fish, is another instance of the trout keying to emergers and ascending nymphs, a situation that used to frustrate dry fly anglers until the true nature of the trout's behaviour was understood.

New Zealanders have their own traditions and theories based on the opportunistic feeding habits of their quarry, similar to the trout of the western North American freestone streams. Unlike most British and North American anglers, the Kiwis took to heart the importance of stealth and observation. You never see a South Island angler striding up to the water the way we do. New Zealand trout fishing is all hunt, the attention to circumspection often extreme. The Kiwis tone down and camouflage their garments, even their fly lines, which they dye to a dull olive or grey. They use very long leaders, up to twenty feet with a single fly. Most importantly, they stalk their fish as if they were hunting deer or wild turkeys, moving slowly upstream only when they know they are out of sight of a possible fish. Mind you, those Kiwi trout aren't far off the size of deer and wild turkeys.

I've heard visiting anglers conclude, like old Mottram, that the New Zealand trout just aren't as sophisticated as their northern hemisphere cousins. What they mean, I gather, is that the trout are not normally 'selective'. Maybe not, but they make up for that by being the spookiest trout on the planet. The value the Kiwis put on stealth and presentation compensates for what a North American hatch-matcher might consider conventional fly design. Having said that, the fly most visiting American anglers use on New Zealand rivers is the Royal Wulff, possibly the best example of a general attractor in existence. South Island fly patterns aren't all that realistic because they usually don't have to be. For the most part, they are standard British style patterns that have been used for half a century. The mayfly patterns, such as Dad's Favourite and Kakahi Queen, are based on the standard Halfordian or Catskill model, and the nymphs are usually uncomplicated variations on the Hare's Ear, like the Hare and Copper. The Wee Muddler, a favourite Cicada pattern tied by Keith Mitchell and Robbie McPhee is very similar to my own simplified version of the Deer Hair Sedge, and an excellent all-rounder on South Island streams.

I had travelled to the other side of the world to catch trout on the dry fly because that's the way I like to do it. Flies like the Royal Wulff and Humpy weren't pulling fish, and the fact that the big hatches were finished meant that the standard mayfly and attractor patterns were likely to draw little response from those big browns. It takes a sustained and reliable source of surface food to get big fish looking up. Drought conditions meant poor hatches, if any. I was prepared to fish weighted nymphs if I had to, but I was still hoping to get a fish or two on dries. To hear that there was no dry fly fishing was a disappointment to say the least, but I had a wishful hunch that the reason David thought the dry fly season was over was simply the fact that the usual dry flies weren't working this late in the season.

Keith Mitchell in hard late season conditions on an unforgiving back-country stream

David had directed me to a section of river upstream of a big sheep station (ranch). Margaret and I walked across the big open pasture to the river to find it running clear and fast down the middle of a wide shingle channel. It was obvious that it was going to be tough. The sun was blazing although the air was cool. There were no flies at all and few terrestrials, the drought had dried those up as well. The river was obviously shrunk to a third its normal size and I reckoned the fish would be holding in the few remaining deep pools. Mag set up her beach chair out of the rapidly increasing wind and got out her book. I walked upstream until I came onto a wide exposed pool. Almost immediately, as I strolled slowly up the shingle bank, my eye caught a movement in the shallows to my left. Through polarised sunglasses, I saw the unmistakeable shadow of a big fish moving toward deep water. I stopped cold and backed-up a few yards. I had already blown my first chance.

I collected myself and resumed my slow progress up the beach. In no time I saw four more trout in a pod, but they had already seen me and were drifting away to the emerald green centre of the pool. Even with the polarised glasses the angle of the light made it impossible to see the fish before I had come about even with them. Too late, I walked away from the river and circled wide through the scrub to the broken water at the head of the pool. Keeping low, I crouched along to where I could see the bottom of the river. It was a sand bottom and I could see every foot of it. I slowly straightened up as I scanned the amazing green water, then froze in mid-crouch when I saw the vague tan shape of a big trout laying just at the edge of a sand shelf at the throat of the pool. I had on a size sixteen DHE, tied with a slim tan/grey dubbed body to imitate the *Deleatidium* mayfly common to these waters, although there was absolutely nothing on the water.

I worked out enough line by rolling it downstream along the shore. I reckoned I had only one shot at this fish. When I thought I had enough line out I used a water-haul to load the rod, rather than an aerial false-cast. Luckily, there was a momentary wind riffle, so the surface was not completely smooth above the fish, and the sixteen foot leader rolled out perfectly, dropping the little emerger about ten feet upstream. I couldn't take my eyes off the trout, expecting it to bolt for cover at any moment. I saw the big fish stiffen and begin to drift back under the fly. Then, unbelievably, it started to come up. The trout was in deep water, maybe six feet or so, and the time it took to rise dreamlike and nearly unbearable. Clearly locked onto the tiny DHE, the fish drifted downstream with the current as it rose deliberately through all that water, keeping pace with the fly. Then, as if in slow motion, the trout stuck its nose through the surface, and with a 'clip' sound, ate the fly.

As a demonstration of a big trout's reaction to a dry fly it was the most remarkable sequence I have ever witnessed. I could imagine the way the trout's stimulus/response mechanism was working, the fly's positive stimuli triggering the attack response, over-riding any 'not-food' input.

We have to keep in mind that a trout is actively *trying* to see food among the things that are floating down the river. To survive, a trout is programmed, so to speak, to test things that might be food. Once its brain recognised and confirmed 'prey', that big trout was locked into what

photo: Margaret Mitchell

biologists call its functional response. By the time it reached the surface, the fish was straight across from me and I must have been in full view. No matter, he was zeroed-in and locked-on like a surface to air missile. The only thing that was in that trout's head was my fly, as long as I didn't disrupt its attention or spook it by sudden movements or drag. I lifted the rod and he was hooked.

At the feel of the hook the fish boiled on the surface and surged back to its holding spot. My old RPL 590 hooped alarmingly as it absorbed the live weight of the fish. I had tied on a five-pound tippet, with respect for the possibility of big trout and with an eye toward the sunken snags on this flood-scoured river, but it suddenly seemed ridiculously light. This trout weighed at least five pounds, and after a moment of ponderous head shaking in clear view at the bottom of the pool it turned downstream in a heart-stopping rush.

Margaret arrived with the camera to find me trotting downstream, trying to pressure the trout away from a big sunken tree in mid-pool. The fish made one jump, clearing the water by a couple of feet, and came down with a crash like someone smacking the water with a cricket bat, sending waves to both banks of the pool. Then it charged for the snag. I held on tight, but as the trout reached the snag I palmed the spool, the light wire hook straightened and pulled free.

I caught one more trout before the wind blew us off the river, a nice four-pounder, again on the little sixteen DHE, not bad results for hopeless conditions. The next morning I was out again as the sun came up over the hills, fully expecting the wind to rise with it. The emerald pool looked empty, a common enough situation on these New Zealand waters for a day or so after being fished, but pretty discouraging when you can see every pebble on the bottom. On subsequent trips I learned that these big trout can disappear in such water like a snake in a brush pile; a thin sliver of shadow can hide a ten pounder.

Crossing the river, I sneaked up on a snye of the river that looked deep and protected by a big wall of willows and reeds. Staying low, I crept up to the tail of the pool from directly downstream, raising my head by inches until I could see most of the bottom of the narrow channel. As the surface welled up in a smooth boil, I saw a big tan shape near the head of the pool. It was lying in exactly the same posture as the previous morning's fish, with its nose at the edge of a gravel bar. To disappear, all it had to do was drift back into the shade of the far bank.

I ducked down and made one careful cast to the head of the pool. The DHE drifted with no perceptible drag over the trout's position. Nope. Another two casts to the right and the left. Still nope. I reckoned I'd spooked him somehow, so I moved cautiously upstream to take another look. The fish was still there; at least I hadn't driven him from his station. I decided to give him a rest and come back in half an hour. On the next run downstream I raised a fish of two or three pounds to the emerger, missing him. Then, unable to suppress my excitement, I returned to the little reed-fringed snye.

I set up a size sixteen gold-head Hare's Ear Nymph, four feet below a tiny white yarn indicator on a very long leader. I didn't look to see if the fish was there, but waded into waist-deep water to stay low and worked out enough line downstream for a water-haul, to lob the rig well above him without false casting. The extra long leader ensured that the end of the fly line did not come into the trout's window, even with the trout lying deep. The gentle current carried the little indicator toward the drop off, and suddenly it was no longer there. It took a moment for the relevant synapses to fire, but I eventually reacted and stripped hard with my line-hand. The rod tip was jerked almost to the surface as the trout blew up.

It was a big trout, six or seven pounds. It threw itself out of the water several times, level with my head, coming down each time with a terrific crash. It bolted for the willow roots under the bank and I held as tight as I could. The hook straightened and everything went slack. I chalked it up as another long-distance release and made a mental note regarding these light wire hooks and big fish. By now, the wind was fairly roaring down the river, so I packed up and headed upstream to find Margaret, get some lunch and do some reflecting.

Mag and I returned to the river that evening as the wind began to slacken a bit. As soon as we reached the bank I noticed a fish rising only feet from the edge. I got well downstream and watched it for a while. The trout was working in water so thin its tail and dorsal fin were showing in perfect silhouette against the setting sun. I strained to see what it was eating and noticed a small dun pop straight out of the riffle at my feet. The hatch was just beginning. There were no duns floating on the water, they were getting airborne immediately upon emerging. Jettisoning their shucks immediately, they seemed to pop out of the water fully formed. More flies appeared in the air and I saw that it was the tiny, late season *Deleatidium*. Since a previous visit to the Mataura further south, I had tied up a box full of imitations of this mayfly. The situation looked perfect for the DHE, so I put on a size sixteen with a slim dun-grey abdomen.

The first few casts had no apparent effect on the trout, but at least I hadn't spooked it. I realised that in such shallow water the trout's perceptual window was very small, so it couldn't see my fly at all unless I floated it right onto its nose. In the wind I had some trouble placing the fly at a nice angle, so I lined up the fish's tail and dorsal fin like the sights on a rifle and put the fly a foot upstream of them. That big nose just tipped up and he was on. The fish threw water for yards as he ploughed across the shallow for open water like a bonefish, and came off on the first jump. I was shaking a little with excitement, exacerbated by the sight of a pod of trout working on the far side of the shallow pool tail. I waded across and stalked to within range of the fish. The extremely shallow water permitted me to get very close to each fish without spooking it. All of them were feeding in about six to ten inches of water, their dorsal fins and tails were sticking up like little sails. I hooked three more beautiful trout out of that shallow, popping another one off on the strike.

Those spooky South Island browns confirmed again for me that observation, stealth, and presentation are the primary concern if one expects to catch exceptional trout, wherever they live. They were textbook examples. I've since applied what I've learned to Scotland's difficult rivers, where stalking fish is practically unheard of; the lesson is just as valid on the tea-coloured water of the Tay as it is on the crystalline slicks of the Ahuriri. Another thing it confirmed is the necessity to sometimes disregard conventional wisdom, even on unfamiliar water. Although the dry fly season was considered to be finished and conditions were tough for any method, that evening's dry fly fishing was simply superb.

On a recent trip with Bruce Masson and Keith Mitchell to their favourite river, one they rate among the best small streams in the world, I had the importance of stealth and presentation driven home, big time. Bruce and Keith are veteran Kiwi style trout hunters and are convinced that, as good as it is, this stream cannot sustain any pressure. The fish are big, but unbelievably spooky. Once it has been fished it must be left for several days, possibly weeks, to return to normal. On this trip, the boys were frustrated by the extreme jumpiness of the trout, which they had no trouble spotting but proved almost impossible to approach. Time after time we blew our chances through a clumsy approach, a bad cast, or a contrary gust of wind at the critical moment. The trout forgave no such blunders and rocketed up and down the pools, spooking everyone else for a hundred yards. Even when to all appearances we got things right, they spooked. We even observed trout spooking each other, with no help from us. This went on for three days. Bruce and Keith were beside themselves.

Late one day, a fish was spotted rising at the tail of a deep run with good cover. The boys generously called to me to come up and have at him. I crept carefully into position and Keith pointed out a trout of six or seven pounds, lying in shallow water under a thin line of foam and stream debris and occasionally tipping up to take something out of the scum line. Finally, we thought, after a full day of failure, a real chance to hook a fish. The pressure was on and I was shaking. We couldn't make out what the fish was eating and, having lost all confidence in my own choices, I asked Bruce what fly to try. He suggested I try Robbie McPhee's Wee Muddler. I had tied some the day before at his kitchen table; sparse, size sixteen, no-hackle jobs with a dark hare's mask body. On it went, but I worried that my tippet was a bit heavy for this situation and might cause drag. With great relief, I made a perfect cast, putting the fly just upstream of the trout with the leader nicely off to the side. We watched, frozen in anticipation as the great fish angled slowly up to the surface, hesitated under the fly, and sank quietly to the bottom. A classic refusal. I cast once more, another good throw, but the fish had disappeared. We couldn't believe our eyes.

What went wrong I still don't know, but we have had plenty of time to reflect. The presentation had seemed perfect. Was it the fly, the tippet, unseen drag, a flicker of movement that caught the trout's attention at the last moment? Who knows? All we had to go on was our individual interpretation of the behaviour of the fish. We all had a good look at what happened, and we all came up with different explanations. To Bruce, it looked like a classic case of suspicion or selectivity. There weren't enough insects on the water to suggest a preoccupied feeder, so he thought it must have been the fly. He reckoned these big resident fish have seen enough artificial flies to be suspicious. I'm sceptical of that interpretation myself, and suspect that just as the fish was about to eat my fly it was distracted and made uneasy for some reason; maybe some micro-drag, a moving tippet knot or scum collecting on the fly, movement by me or a flash of my line or rod tip in its perceptual window.

We all agreed that the fish were abnormally skittish, and the owner of the property gave us an explanation on the way home. Unknown to us, a guided party had fished the river just before our arrival. We were surprised to hear that they had seen no trout at all. Having spotted plenty of big trout ourselves, we suspected that the previous party had approached the water carelessly, driving the fish into hiding before they even laid eyes on them. These trout are territorial residents that know every inch of their domain. In the prevailing drought conditions, when just raising your head above the bank would cause a feeding fish to stiffen, a casual stroll up the bank would scare the daylights out of them. We just had the bad luck to fish behind somebody.

Painful as it was for my friends to experience a three-day skunk on their favourite river, I regard it as a valuable learning experience. What it confirmed for me once more was that we shouldn't jump to conclusions. Our interpretation of the behaviour of these jumpy trout caused us to lose faith in our flies when they probably had nothing to do with it. The flies were good patterns that had always worked on this stream. We didn't get very many chances but we might have made good on some of them if we hadn't had to fight a bad downstream wind that made clean presentations almost impossible. Normally, you can expect things to work out at least some of the time, a matter of percentages, but we had few good chances and just couldn't get a break. For me, the over-riding factor was the trout's extreme nervousness. There was just no room for slip-ups or carelessness. Anything out of the ordinary sent them packing – those trout were just too spooky to catch. It is too easy to say that the New Zealand experience is special somehow, that the same issues don't obtain back on our home waters, but I believe that trout are trout, wherever they swim.

* * * * *

5. Stillwaters I: Bank and Boat

If we are to enter into the moods of Nature, we must bring with us some vigour and elasticity and spirit. A feeble mind looking upon fair scenes with a languid eye will not feel the joy of them, and it is with nature as it is with friendship – we cannot take all and bring nothing.

Viscount Grey of Fallodon
Fly Fishing

Bob Morton invokes some bob-fly voodoo on a western Ireland lough

1. Loch-style

It was a commonplace among the old time writers to treat loch fishing with contempt. For them, drifting helplessly in a boat at the mercy of the wind and rain, the midges, mindlessly repeating the same short cast, boating an infinite number of identical three to the pound brownies to meet the impleadable objectives of some dour highland gillie ... well, it must have been pretty hellish. Especially wielding an eleven-foot cane or greenheart rod all week long. It is easy to see why whisky played such an important part in these proceedings.

Judging from descriptions by some of its enthusiasts, I think the effect of three days or more of it tended to distort reality to the point of hallucination. Some early accounts of heroic battles with half-pound trout are clearly the product of an over-stimulated imagination, undoubtedly fired by no small amount of the *uisge beatha*. You can still have this, but if you've a bent toward mortification of the flesh and psyche you could really achieve the same sort of penance by other means. If you're disposed toward the pleasurable aspects of fly-fishing, even if you prefer the more conservative approach, there is no need to conform to nineteenth century conventions quite that rigorously.

In the British Isles, there are situations where a guide is appropriate and even necessary, on the big English reservoirs and Irish loughs, for instance. There are some good guides operating in the Hebridean islands, but for the most part you can forget about being guided for trout. Most of the hotel and estate keepers in Scotland these days are concerned mainly with salmon, grouse and deer, anyway, usually lumping trout with mink, raptors and other vermin. They often lump trout anglers right along there with them. That's not just a joke. One Tay gillie said he'd like to poison all the trout in his water just to discourage the trout fishermen. He was serious! As far as upland gamekeepers are concerned, trout fishermen just spook the deer.

Anyway, it's so much more satisfying to figure it out for yourself. If heading for the lochs of Scotland all you really need is a permit, a map and compass, and Bruce Sandison's *Rivers and Lochs of Scotland*. You'll also need to do some sleuthing – Bruce's map co-ordinates are spot on but his descriptions are pretty general as far as the actual fishing is concerned, and sometimes, I suspect, purposefully vague. Fair enough. I'm not big on giving away my best spots either. A close reading will produce clues to some very good lochs. You will find that there is a great variety among the thousands of trout lochs and the quality of the trout they contain. This detective work, the first phase of the hunt, is part of the fun.

The British fly-fishing tradition known to the world, that of Stewart, Halford, Mottram, Sawyer and Skues, is a riverman's history. However, the growth of twentieth century fly-fishing in Britain has been on stocked reservoirs. It's safe to say that trout fishing in Britain is predominantly a stillwater activity. Because some of these waters are large and provide good natural food sources, the fishing has often little to distinguish it from wild fishing. The trout are healthy and 'naturalised', and a big grown-on fish is genuinely something to brag about. Many of the new techniques employed in the pursuit of truly wild fish have been developed on Rutland and other semi-natural waters. On recent trips to Ireland's Lough Corrib, it was clear that the prevailing methods owe a lot to modern reservoir techniques developed by competition angling on English reservoirs.

Faced with a featureless expanse of water, the first thought in the mind of anyone new to stillwater trout fishing is, 'Where do I start?' A good question, and the right one. To ask it implies the realisation that there are probably good spots and bad spots out there. In truth, if one knew how little of the total water available actually contained catchable trout, one would think of a lake as little different than a stream. The stock of trout accessible to fly-fishing reduces the problem to manageable proportions.

The fly fisher's principal quarry is the young, insectivorous trout of the shallows

Fly-fishing is primarily a shallow water method. Even the new sinking line technology is limited to relatively shallow water. Luckily for us, the practical limits of fly tackle closely approximate the limits of the food bearing water in most lakes, the *littoral zone*. Most of the bugs and small fish live their lives in the littoral zone, and so do the things that feed on them, including trout. The trout is at the top of the food chain, sharing it with other predators like pike. Big trout are pretty pike-like themselves, and if one is serious about big trout the tactics should reflect that similarity.

Truly large trout require special tactics that involve trolling and deep water techniques. The real fly-fisher's quarry is the primarily insectivorous trout of one to three pounds, that has not yet turned exclusively to fish eating, and is still 'looking up' for a significant part of its foraging. These young fish will react almost instantly to a hatch of fly, unlike big trout that need a sustained hatch over a period of days to get them to expend the energy on surface feeding. The extended and prolific hatches of the western loughs of Ireland are known for bringing up large trout. The hatches mirror those of North America with some regional differences in timing due to climate. The early chironomid or 'duck fly' of March and April overlaps the lake olive hatch, which in turn *segues* into the famous Green Drake hatch. Then, it is understood, the trout go off the fly and turn to summer fry feeding, returning to the surface during big caddis hatches, blow-downs of heather beetle or 'Bibio' and the crane fly, the 'daddies' of late summer and autumn, when conditions permit.

Normally, trout over three pounds or so expend their off-peak energy sparingly, saving it for productive attacks on massed minnow and perch fry. Once a hatch has been ongoing for a while, maybe weeks, sometimes a really big fish gets into a surface feeding habit. A consistent supply of insects in large quantity will get even double figure fish looking up. This is often the case on waters with a big fall of 'spent gnat', the Green Drake spinner. On Irish loughs such as Sheelin, brown trout of up to ten pounds will sometimes be found working a raft of olives or spent mayfly spinners in the wind lanes, and a few anglers have made a specialty of hunting these spectacular fish.

There is really no mystery to finding the areas that support the best populations of trout. If one narrows the search for what the Irish guides call shallows, you will soon be in a position to catch fish. Like the Inuit's hundred types of snow, the Irish lough fisher has a taxonomy of water and light conditions, including the characteristically Irish 'deep-shallow', the place to look for your better than average fish, for all the reasons specified for finding good fish in a river. Depending on water clarity, the deep-shallow is an area that provides security and food in abundance. On big waters like Corrib, these deep-shallows run for hundreds of yards, the bottom just perceptible in six to ten feet of green water. Once located, the angler sets the boat to cover the shallows in long parallel drifts. If there is a wave running, the drift will end in very shallow water near shore, since the trout can be expected to take advantage of the cover provided by the broken surface and are often taken in the 'smother' of the waves. The best drifts will run along the line where the shallow breaks into deeper water. This is a favourite haunt for the larger than normal trout, hunting along the drop-off with an eye on its escape route. A productive drift depends on judging the wind direction, staying a cast's length away from the drop-off so the boat doesn't spook the fish. A good man on the oars is the boat's most important asset.

On moorland lochs, the littoral zone is usually much narrower because of the poor light transmission in the peat-stained water. Many Scottish lochs sometimes have a littoral zone measured in mere feet, which necessitates a stealthy approach if fishing from shore.

The best highland lochs are shallow throughout, providing a littoral zone extending over the whole loch. These shallow lochs are usually well known for the quality of their trout. There may be plenty of decent trout lying in very shallow water, but striding along the shore, sky-lined with no background cover, waving your arms about in excessive false casting and lining the best holding areas is a sure way to send everyone packing for the security of deep water. This is possibly the reason most people think the Scottish lochs hold only small fish. Careful deep wading is far less disturbing and allows the angler to approach below the trout's angle of vision, fishing a short line to good effect. A well-handled boat is much more productive, of course, and permits the fly to be fished tight into the bank where often the largest trout are found. The North American enthusiasm for the float-tube hasn't caught to the same extent in Europe, but it has loads of potential for highland lochs.

One shouldn't underestimate the effect of lining the water with excessive casting. I put it right at the top of all the things you can do to spoil your own chances. Although there is something to be said for traditional methods, there is no point going to a trout loch with a traditional *attitude*. Everything depends upon conditions, and the most important of a trout hunter's skills is an open and enquiring mind.

2. Lessons from Corrib – the colours of Murt Folan

There has always been a special regard for the Corrib boatmen. Kingsmill-Moore's Jamsie was a prime example and these days, like their American counterpart, they prefer to be called professional trout guides, in keeping with that concept of rugged individualism. If you've never been sure just what a rugged individual actually looks like, spend a day with a Corrib trout guide. This was instantly made clear when we met up with Murt Folan.

Murt's approach is to size you up and fire a shot across your bow to see how you'll take it. If you laugh and shoot back in kind, you're in for a hilarious day on the water with a singular character, even by Corrib guide standards. If you go all red and stiff necked, it'll be, yes sir, sure that was a grand trout you frightened away with your line again there, sir, allow me to unhook your backside once more, sir. All day long. Within about three minutes of meeting him, Murt was referring to me as 'the big prick up in the bow'.

The first thing you realise when you set out with Murt is that immediately and in no uncertain terms he is letting you know that it is a waste of time to mess with anything other than his method or his flies. He's got Corrib *taped*. Even to the most cautious and sceptical of anglers, this has the effect of raising morale to a fever pitch. If you don't know Corrib, you should understand that you need confidence bordering on hubris to even tackle it. It's a vast thing, over forty thousand acres. Humility is just not an appropriate attitude. Anyway, crashing through a two-foot chop on the crossing to Greenfields that morning, the only thing missing in our boat was a loud speaker playing Wagner's *Ride of the Valkyries*.

As my friend Arthur Greenwood says, old Murt has forgotten more big trout than we'll ever see. If there's a trout to be caught in Corrib, well, Murt's your man. If you haven't heard this from someone else, don't worry, you'll hear it from Murt himself soon enough. He is definitely the man with the plan. He's got the experience – over forty years on Corrib – and he's got the flies. He's got the theory, and he's got the method. Confidence? That's not the word for it; Murt Folan has *certainty*.

I almost never fish anyone else's flies, but somehow when we arrived at our first drift of the morning I found myself with three of Murt's patterns on my leader. I also never fish three flies on a cast but I figured that, you know, when in Rome. Murt had me in his thrall. I had not the slightest reservation in throwing those flies out into the downwind wave…and what flies they were.

I was fascinated by Murt's running commentary as we began fishing. He did not miss a thing. A guide is supposed to influence the way things happen, but it is rare when you feel that he is fishing *through* you, that you are acting as a kind of medium for him. That is exactly what I felt that morning. Murt was inside my head, in touch with his flies almost to the same degree that I was, as if he was feeling the rod and line and the action of the flies himself. There was a constant feed of information and corrective advice from the stern. I'm sure a blind person could fish perfectly well with Murt as the guide.

Murt spotted the first trout to come to my fly before I did. It was a good one too, but it didn't close its mouth on the fly and didn't come again to a series of bracketing casts. Although we couldn't know it at the time, this was to be the pattern throughout that day, and the next. It is a testament to the force of Murt's personality and strength of conviction that we didn't collapse into a desperate fugue of fly changing from that point. The conventional wisdom has it that if a good fish refuses try him again, maybe with another fly. Murt just said to take it easy, the flies are good, it's the trout and the light that are variable. When they are going to take, he said, they would take these flies. I was interested in his first comments on the light. It soon became clear that light and colour were the bedrock of Murt's method.

Murt describes himself as a traditionalist. When I hear someone call himself that, it means I am about to be preached at, like when you meet those born-again folks in the street, the ones with the beatific smiles and the riot-control bullhorns. No one can be as evangelistic as a fly-fishing traditionalist. What's the big deal, anyway, do they need *disciples*? I don't know about Murt needing a congregation, but he's like no traditionalist fly-fisherman I've ever met. For one thing, his method is deeply mysterious and is rooted in the theories of colour and light, an oral tradition handed down through generations of Irish lough fishers.

Murt Folan with a nicely conditioned Irish lough brownie

Like Kingsmill-Moore, Murt believes in colour. He refers to them as *the* colours, so we know he's not talking about colour in general. The Irish tradition is an aesthetic one; they have the most artistic and colourful approach to fly tying in the world. Kingsmill-Moore's series of lough flies are good examples, although he was at pains to describe his rationale as a scientific one, with one hypothesis based on the effects of light beyond the visible spectrum. Like Murt, he believed in unexplained attractive powers in the colours themselves. Even the ubiquitous Golden Olive Bumble, one of the most popular lough patterns in western Ireland, shares no obvious resemblance with the natural fly in colour, form or movement. The Irish tradition is probably one of the best examples of how fly-fishing practice is influenced by the expression of a cultural character. In effect, the Irish lough tradition has been a great longitudinal empirical study on the responses of trout to colour and movement.

We've seen it before, the fantastic salmon fly arrangements of Kelson were regarded as deriving directly from the 'gaudy Ballyshannon' fly, to the dour consternation of Scrope and his contemporaries. It is hard to account for why the colourful fly won in the rivalry between the severe and drab Presbyterian dressings and the wild 'excesses' of the Irish style. With the return to simplified dressings on Scottish rivers in recent times, it is probable that the fancy fly was an expression of human aesthetics as much as it is a result of any real preference by the fish. The Victorian predilection for ornament clearly influenced fly making, and it is arguable that fly tying allowed an arm's-length expression and indulgence through colour that might have been otherwise frowned on among the black-coated Scottish gentry. What the old boys discovered was that colour can make a difference.

What I find interesting about Murt Folan's method is his approach to trout fly design. It is here, in design, that we see that he is indeed what he says he is – a traditionalist. Murt's flies are exquisite models of the Irish wet fly tradition, beautiful in their symmetry and attention to detail. His hackles are brilliant, a result of his critical selection of hackle necks with an eye for hue and translucency. His mallard shoulder hackles and golden pheasant crest tails are perfectly proportioned. Murt has an artist's eye for line.

The bob fly I fished for those two hard sunny days on Corrib was Murt's Father Ronan. All the fish I raised and caught came to that fly, fished fast on a long floating line. The Father Ronan is a beautiful, and without doubt the most colourful, trout fly I have ever tied on a leader. I've used the standard Scottish colour patterns such as the Dunkeld and the Blue Zulu, but Murt's fly seems to be powered by an electric current. The bright complimentary hues of the Father Ronan fairly radiate in the greenish limestone water of the Corrib.

Murt's method is to fish hard and fast, just under the surface. He fishes a very fast wet fly. I find it tiring and, frankly, a little monotonous to keep up the pace all day long. Not only that, it goes against my feeling that the bigger fish are too deliberate for the fast fly to be a reliable method in all circumstances. The idea behind the colourful flies is to give the fish only a glimpse of shape and a flash of colour. 'Make him chase it' said Murt repeatedly. This, it seems to me, is a kind of lough version of the river angler's induced-take technique. The fly is pulled quickly so that it travels just under the surface film, creating a slight bulge in the surface as it moves. It undoubtedly does a good deal of reflecting in the surface mirror as well, even on rough days. The whole thing is a matter of flash, movement, colour and fleeting impression, giving the trout no time to inspect the fly and just go for it. The impulse to chase is reinforced by the team of flies, according to my crackpot hypothesis for the response of trout to the bob fly.

Murt's choice of colour is a compromise, he says, the best choice to meet a wide range of light conditions. His certainty is in his fierce belief that his is in fact the best possible choice. As far as fly design goes, Murt is solidly classical, putting everything on red so to speak. He attributes great powers to 'the colours', as if part of a personal expressive aesthetic system. Murt, of course, has built his colour system empirically, by experience not theory, so although he has been urged repeatedly to write a book, he says he finds it difficult to find 'the words'. This is certainly not due to a deficiency in language skills; a day in his boat will demonstrate the extent of Murt's rhetorical range. The difficulty is in the illusive, mystical properties of the colours and the infinite range of light effects as conditions shift and change. You probably have to factor in an aspect of belief. As Datus Proper would say, this is art not science.

After two hard days of pulling flies, I had caught a couple of half-pounders and maybe a dozen more fish responding exclusively to the Father Ronan on the bob, but that was it. Murt was philosophical; the trout were just 'coming short' in that hard brassy light. We needed cloud and soft pearly light. Murt's certainty is built on having the time for conditions to become favourable to his method. I don't believe that trout play; if a trout shows to a fly he's on the verge of taking. He might have been put off the attack for some reason. Sometimes he'll miss the moving fly and spook himself. If he hasn't been spooked, it might need only a change of fly or size or some change in presentation to make the difference.

As an intriguing postscript to the Corrib lessons, we were left with a big question posed by a big trout. As we were winding up our operations on the last day the sun was, if possible, even harder and brassier. Bob Morton was feeling defeated. He hadn't enjoyed the constant hard graft of pulling wet flies for two days and was itching to experiment. I heard him remark that a Murraugh, the big red sedge, had just landed downwind of him, the first we had seen on that trip. It was last cast time, we were tired, the pub beckoned. I didn't even think really; I just hauled in, removed the Father Ronan, tied a hare's ear bodied Deer Hair Sedge onto the bob position and re-cast. The fly looked good out there in the light ripple – and it suddenly disappeared in a boil the size of a washbasin. After so much inaction, I struck too quickly and felt the hook prick the fish. There was a long moment's silence in the boat.

'Now, *that* was a grand fish there,' said Murt.

3. True colours

I was considering my fly boxes the other night, doing some serious tying, tooling up for the annual campaign in Sutherland. Unlike Murt Folan, I'm not really much of a colour person, and while I try to be objective in my conclusions regarding the ways of trout with a fly, I'm certainly no scientist. I remembered my first few Scottish seasons back in the eighties, trying to make some sense of the frankly bewildering range of trout patterns which, as recently as fifteen years ago, were regarded as the essential battery of the northern loch angler. In those days, a boxful of traditional trout flies resembled a Bavarian cavalry regiment turned out for the king's birthday.

My boxes still display a range of colours, but these days they look more like a camouflaged infantry unit – lots of dull olives, dun greys and earthy browns. This isn't an expression of my psychology, I actually love the look of those fancy ranks of blues, reds and gleaming silver, great old patterns that have been catching trout on the northern lochs for a hundred and fifty years or more. It's just that the flies that keep their position on the player's bench are the ones that catch the most fish for me, most of the time. Despite the many intriguing theories, over my half-century as a fly-fisherman I've found a rough imitation of some food form to be a more reliable approach than provoking the trout's curiosity or aggression. I say imitation, but I really mean impression – shooting for general characteristics and salient features rather than the specific details of natural insects.

The flies I actually use, as opposed to just tying and admiring, are invariably a rough impression of some natural insect. Many fly-fishing authorities have maintained that colour in a dry fly is relatively unimportant. They say that size, shape, and translucence are what makes a good surface fly. This makes sense to me, because a surface fly is usually seen by the trout against the light background of the sky, in silhouette.

Most of us just ignore all that common sense and try to capture something of the body and wing colour of the thing we are trying to imitate. Besides, there are enough instances where colour makes the difference that it should never be discounted completely. Gary Borger has marketed a highly organised colour system for fly tying materials, but I'm not convinced colour merits quite that degree of nuance. The impressionistic approach is widely accepted in principle, but, as in art, the logic of realism and exact imitation exerts a strong pull. Gary LaFontaine expressed some strong opinions regarding the effectiveness of certain colours in different light conditions and the possibilities of exaggerating them, echoing Murt Folan's empirical approach. With so many variables to consider, it seems to me that keeping the colours roughly imitative, but with an eye on colour as a possible trigger, isn't a bad way to go, and this brings us to the matter of dubbed bodies.

Dubbing, traditionally, is made from the fur of animals, but over the past decade or so synthetics have largely displaced natural fur from the list of tier's materials. Although some new synthetic fibres are very good, especially the finer dubbings for small flies, no synthetic matches the translucency of seal's fur or the bugginess of hare's mask. Mink is very good for finer work and makes an excellent binder and tonal mixer for a range of muted colours. Since mink coats and stoles went out of fashion there are hundreds of them showing up at auctions for next to nothing. Hare's mask is my favourite dubbing, it's dirt cheap and it's got the magic ingredient – trout appeal. A good hare's mask has an amazing range of textures, hues, and tones, the winter masks in particular. In fact, I usually replace a mask long before I use it all up. The best and buggiest material is found on the front of the face. Luckily for me, my friend Bruce Masson is involved with pest control on the South Island of New Zealand, and has an astronomical supply of European Brown Hares literally at his disposal.

Despite the prevalence of the new synthetics, especially in commercially tied flies, there is nothing like real seal's fur when it comes to texture and translucency, and as long as it is available I'll continue to use it. Seal comes in a wide range of colours, but I use far more claret, olive and black than any of the other hues available. Harder to dub than synthetics, natural seal retains volume better and produces a nice 'halo' effect caused by light through the stiffer fibres. This halo is observable in emerging insects and may be a strong stimulus to the trout, signalling an insect at its most vulnerable. For northern surface patterns I like the way a seal's fur body retains water, fishing hull-down in the surface. My sheet-anchor bob fly, the Deer Hair Sedge, is a prime example. Since it is essential that the DH Sedge fish properly, I wouldn't use anything but hare's mask or a mixture of hare and seal as a body material for that fly.

When it comes to my current go-to dry fly, the Deer Hair Emerger, colour does enter into my thinking simply because the fish get a good look at the fly's abdomen. Although size and shape are the most important considerations for this fly, it's reasonable to assume that the submerged abdomen makes colour a factor, especially during a hatch. For the northern lochs, a couple of shades of olive do the trick; from a dirty mustard colour, a mix of Golden Olive seal's fur and hare's mask under fur, to a dark, brownish-olive mix of the same materials. For ephemerids like the mayfly and lake olives, I'll use hare's fur mixed with some other type of dyed dubbing for a hint of colour, and for a more robust abdomen on caddis imitations, seal's fur mixed with the hare. What this amounts to is that my battery for the northern lochs displays a pretty narrow range of 'true' colours.

For June and July, although I don't really see what it represents, a good dark claret, a 70-30% proportion of black to claret seal's fur is by far the fishiest combination for northern brownies in conditions of cloud and low light. Obviously, the high contrast of that dark body is a big factor, but then again, the claret mix definitely works better than straight black. During a mayfly hatch, the dirty mustard DHE is a proven killer. Coincidentally, these two hues, claret and subdued golden-olive, are those used to such great effect on the Irish loughs.

When the lake olives or summer duns are on, a dark brownish olive to fiery brown mix of hare underfur and coloured seal's fur dubbing is good medicine, tied slim. It's hard to beat a robust and spiky hare's mask body for a sedge hatch. For fair weather, a 'Donegal' blue, and grass green seal's fur can be excellent, but they're the only true colours that I know that can be

Bob Morton works the shore of a northern Scottish loch

relied on to any extent. Sydney Spencer found the Donegal Blue to be a killer on what he called a 'blue day' on the Irish Loughs, but I have no idea why. It maybe has an explanation in Murt Folan's mysterious system of colour and light. It's not really a very common insect colour. LaFontaine said that the amount of green light in mid-day light makes green show much more intensely than other colours, but I don't know if that really explains why the fish react positively to such an unnatural colour. I say it's a fish thing, we just wouldn't understand.

4. Bob fly voodoo

The bob fly, the top dropper of a two or three fly rig, is a real mystery. Why is a fly in that position on the leader so attractive to trout and salmon? Most anglers have their favourite bob flies. Mine is the no-hackle Deer Hair Sedge. For others it may be a Greenwell, Muddler, Soldier Palmer, Claret Bumble, Butcher, Blue Zulu, or Kate McClaren – the litany of personal deadliest bob flies is a long one. The fact that the list seems endless is precisely what makes the idea of a specific pattern that is 'best' in the bob position slightly suspect. Everybody's got a personal special and deadly favourite, which suggests that the fly's position is at least as important as any particular pattern, probably more so.

One of the fascinating aspects of fly-fishing is that we can observe the fish's reactions, but we can never really know *why* it is reacting. We can't interview them and have only clues to the trout's behaviour, seen as if through a glass darkly, the reasons only dimly discerned. Dimly or not, I have discerned what seems to be at least a glimmer of why a trout will scoot past a perfectly good point fly and chomp down the bob fly. During periods of particularly heavy action on the northern trout lochs I have done some experimenting. The findings may be crude and subjective, even fanciful, but there is a pattern beginning to take shape out of the murky mysticism of fly-fishing tradition. And, let's face it; our traditional reasoning can be pretty murky. Much of what we do is because that's the way our daddies did it. You know; it works, it's always worked…shut up and fish.

Recently, I was interested to read in an American fly-fishing magazine an article by Dave Whitlock, in which he offers an explanation for the trout's reaction to the dropper fly remarkably close to my own intuitions on this matter. Whitlock is one of those anglers who approach the subject with a scholarly rigour and an artist's creative leaps of the imagination. His idea is simply that the use of more than one fly *excites* the fish. This idea is pretty similar to my own notion that the trout almost invariably goes for the bob fly because it is *competing* with the point fly, which looks like it is chasing the bob. Stay with me here. A trout is actually a pretty simple organism, after all, as far as mental horsepower is concerned. In fact, the term 'mental' implies a mind at work, which clearly isn't the case. Despite Lee Wulff's famous aphorism that in fly-fishing we fish to a salmon's mind, a trout or salmon is mostly a cluster of instinctive responses to changes in its environment and its prey, not really a thinker as such. Wulff was doing some head scratching himself there, pondering just why the hell a salmon would bother to rise for something as unnatural as a salmon fly when it doesn't need to eat.

As a boy, I noticed that if more than one trout went for a fly, a hook-up was pretty certain. One of the fish would always race ahead of the other fish to catch the fly. Back then, we often fished a team of two or three wet flies, down and across the current, the classic wet fly sweep. Many times, on those trout-filled creeks and rivers of my youth, I noticed that two trout would not only race for the fly but get into a dead heat for the dropper fly – passing right by the point fly. You'd think in a situation like that one of the fish would go for the point, it being the easiest to catch. There are enough flies to go around, why fight over them? When something like that is observed, we always attribute it to the special deadliness of a particular fly. To this day, I still impute special pulling powers to certain patterns because of these early experiences.

What I now believe, along with Dave Whitlock it turns out, is that excitement and competition are the prime movers here, not the pattern. I have proven this to my own satisfaction by putting the same pattern on both bob and point, and I've done it enough times that it seems conclusive to me. Keeping in mind the size and make-up of the trout's brain here, my idea is that, to the fish, one fly seems to be chasing the other. With respect to Mr Whitlock, and certainly without his consent, I would like to propose this as the Whitlock/Wyatt (dubbya-dubbya?) Theory of Bob Fly Seductivity. Like a cat, a trout has a built-in chase response to prey. It doesn't think about it, it just *reacts*. A trout has a far simpler brain than does a cat. When there are two or more prey items, the trout, with its simple reactions to a stimulus, gets excited (Whitlock) and into something like a race with the point fly (Wyatt). Okay, I know this all sounds more than a little loopy, but no more so than the idea that a trout prefers the *flavour* of one insect to another. Anyway, until someone finds a way to ask the trout what's going on, that's my story and I'm stickin' with it.

That might partly explain why a trout will seemingly select the bob position out of two identical wet flies. The semi-dry surface bob fly is another matter. The so-called 'dibbled' bob fly has traditionally been the loch styler's supreme tactic. The bob fly is designed primarily to create a surface disturbance. The powerful predatory stimulus of the struggling, vulnerable fly on the surface just overrides everything else. Pattern and colour are important only insofar as they help create an impression of something that the trout will decide to eat; beyond that, it's magic. All the fancy jay hackles, tags and ribs, etc, are just a kind of angling necromancy. That said, certain patterns are better bob flies than others. During June and early July, the simple, dark claret, no-hackle Deer Hair Sedge is the best bob fly I know for northern loch brownies in a good fishing wave. It has silhouette, contrast and vulnerability going for it. Put the DH Sedge in both the bob and point positions, which I have done plenty of times, and it is *still* the best bob fly. When presented with identical offerings, the trout will almost invariably ignore the point and surge toward the bob. If you've got a better explanation than the W/W bob fly theory for this behaviour, I'm all ears.

The deer hair wing, clipped head/thorax and soggy seal's fur body of the Deer Hair Sedge make a dynamite combination. It beats any other loch pattern, traditional or otherwise, that I know – barring my Deer Hair Emerger, which will out-fish it in calm conditions or during a hatch. Why does the no-hackle Deer Hair Sedge make a better bob fly than most others for northern Scottish loch trout in June and July? Why does it appear to be specific for the northern loch trout at that time of year, and less effective the further south you go? I don't know the answer to these questions, but intend to keep working on it. I think of it as my own longitudinal empirical study, if you will, and if I'm lucky I might have some answers before I'm pushing up daisies.

The traditional Irish 'Bumble' design of lough flies is certainly worth analysing. There is no arguing with the fact that they work. Thousands of British and continental anglers rig their cast with two or three of them as soon as they cross the Irish Sea, although they wouldn't dream of using a rig like that on their home waters. In itself, this makes me think there is more orthodoxy here than meets the eye. Top guides like Basil Shields at Oughterard have brought some fresh thinking into the lough tradition, but no one would suggest that the Irish wet fly is obsolete.

The basic Bumble design is an excellent one, essentially a seductive mix of light effects, colour and 'significant form'. The Bumble is fished in the surface film, barely submerged so that it causes a bulge in the meniscus as it is moved. All predatory fish in salt or fresh water are susceptible to this stimulus. The Dabbler evolved from the old Irish wet fly as a sub-surface pulling fly. Compared to the Bumble, the Dabbler's design is a relatively crude one, the main feature being its solidity and presence. The hackles of the Bumble are resistant to the water as it is moved in the surface, like an insect struggling and vulnerable. Everything from mosquitoes to field mice are eaten by trout as they try to swim across the surface. Pike and even large trout are commonly seen to prey on ducklings. Fish soon learn that the best meal they are likely to get is associated with a surface wake. The only problem with this explanation is that the Irish wet flies are sometimes very effective when pulled fast under water, like no bug under the sun.

The true lough-style wake patterns are the sedges. Usually, the Irish flies have a palmered hackle for maximum effect. Recently, many top Irish anglers have lashed deer hair wings onto semi-dry sedge patterns like the Green Peter. For moving top-water flies, this makes a lot of sense, but for more static presentations, I think the no-hackle style is better. Old wild trout hands Malcolm Greenhalgh and Mike Weaver have found the no-hackle elk or deer hair sedge to be a better fly than Al Troth's palmered version; Greenhalgh considers it one of his best all-round dry flies. That has certainly been the case everywhere I've used it, and I believe that the clear outline of the sodden body of the no-hackle fly gives a stronger signal of a sure thing to the trout.

5. The static dry fly

Upon my arrival in Scotland twenty years ago, I made a determined effort to get to grips with the loch style approach. Everyone I met fished this way so I re-equipped myself with longer rods than I was used to in Canada, eventually working my way up to an eleven-footer before I

A good stillwater brown goes back where he came from

decided that I was making a lot of unnecessary work for myself. I learned the classic bob fly technique from good anglers who had done it all their lives, and who had learned it from anglers before them. We caught bags of fish and could have fished happily on forever, but didn't. The old loch style works as well as it ever did, at least on lightly fished waters, it's just that the range of tactics has expanded. For me, the traditional loch style wet fly method is a relatively minor tactic.in a repertoire of stillwater techniques,

There is no doubt that competition has revolutionised the strategies of stillwater trout anglers, whether one agrees with the idea of fishing competitions or not. On hard-fished waters, in situations where the number of trout caught is the only measure of success or failure, new tactics evolved that caught fish when conventional methods blanked. In his definitive book, *The Pursuit of Stillwater Trout*, Brian Clarke outlines the imitative approach to contemporary loch style angling, particularly the dry fly and nymph, and it has certainly influenced my own ideas on how to catch wild trout in stillwaters anywhere.

On the big English reservoirs today, the use of the static dry fly is a standard tactic. Even stocked trout quickly become boat and line shy when teams of anglers comb the water continuously. On many lakes the angling is literally continuous from dawn to dark. To get the edge in tough conditions some resourceful anglers found that by fishing fine and far off with dry flies and damp/dry emerger patterns a few extra fish could be picked up, making the difference and often winning the contest. In a short time, the stationary dry fly has become a major tactic for summer reservoirs and is considered an important part of what is referred to as the loch-style. By the end of the twentieth century, the flexible eleven-foot rod had given way to shorter, faster rods made for covering the water with a longer line and quicker pick-ups. Experienced loch-stylers use fewer casts to reduce disturbance on hard-fished waters, targeting fish that have become inured to both the old short-line dibbled fly and the stripped wet fly. These methods still get plenty of fish and the trout occasionally like to chase a fly, but there are times when pulled flies will catch nothing at all.

The traditional loch style wet fly still holds sway in Scotland and Ireland, but things are changing there too. On reservoirs the conventional tactic is the stripped sunk lure, but on wild trout lochs the team of traditional wets is still the choice of most anglers. On the big Irish loughs, since the introduction of the Dabbler style wet fly, lure stripping rapidly became a standard technique. It catches fish too, particularly when the fish are feeding aggressively, but on those bluebird days, with no wave to obscure the boat and line, the pulled sub-surface wet fly is next to useless. It's not that the trout have become wise to the flies in use, but wary of the commotion caused by the stripped fly methods. Not only that, but when you slow traditional wet flies down they don't make a very convincing impression of natural food forms.

Several prominent guides on the Irish loughs make the static dry fly a standard tactic, turning to it when conditions don't suit the pulled fly or when targeting difficult fish. Some radicals among them have taken to fishing the static dry and sub-surface nymph all season through and regard it as a selective tactic for the larger fish. Like the reservoirs of England and Scotland, the fish on the popular loughs see a lot of boats, lines and flies. Rutland and Corrib, for instance, accommodate thousands of anglers over a season. When things go quiet many anglers will accept that the fish are just not on, and don't do much other than change flies or the speed of the retrieve in an effort to coax up a fish or two.

If you've done much stillwater fishing on calm days you will have been frustrated by the way the trout seem to rise just beyond casting range of the boat. You might put this down to the natural wariness of wild trout, but are surprised to find that even recent stockies will exhibit this annoying behaviour. It's true that freshly stocked trout, conditioned by fish farm routines, are sometimes even attracted to a boat, but with sustained pressure even farm fish soon start to avoid the commotion produced by fly lines. Wild trout, on the other hand, are naturally wary of danger from above or from the shore even if they don't know what is causing the disturbance.

On the northern Scottish lochs the trout are not always as daft as they are reputed to be. It is certainly the case that the small desperate brownies of the overpopulated lochs can seem positively suicidal, but the better fish are usually as canny as brown trout everywhere. What many anglers don't realise is that by refining their technique and fishing as they would on a heavily fished reservoir, they will catch fish of a quality that will surprise them. A team of big traditional attractor flies and coarse leaders will still get them a bag of three to the pound fish, and this is what many northern anglers are content with. They leave the loch believing that it is full of 'wee broonies' and have plenty of reason to be content, but they have missed an opportunity.

I recently watched a boat of visitors to a well-known loch work down a shoreline, guided by an estate gillie. Two anglers fished a half-mile of water, casting and pulling wet flies in the traditional manner. They caught three or four small trout in two hours and retired to the lodge. The sports undoubtedly reckoned the loch was 'off', or there were no worthwhile fish in it, or the gillie wasn't trying hard enough. The gillie probably reckoned that his sports just couldn't fish for shite. Conditions weren't ideal, but my partner and I had been doing pretty well. Between us, we had about a dozen trout from a pound to a pound-and-a-half, and had returned over thirty more from ten to twelve inches. We even got a nice two-pound sea-trout to cap things off. All the fish had come to the Deer Hair Sedge or Deer Hair Emerger, fished static on a long leader. Not a great day for that loch, but good fishing anywhere.

Over time, results like that tend to change the way you fish. I don't pull wet flies much anymore. I've found that fishing a damp/dry sedge or emerger, near static or dead in the water, will outfish any other method in June and July on the Scottish lochs, in terms of both numbers and size of fish. I'm so convinced of this that I'll go even further; the static dry fly is a selective technique for the larger fish. You'll get as many smaller ones at times, but your average weight will jump. The bigger trout that *might* take a pulled wet fly will almost certainly take the static dry, although the converse is not true. It's simply a matter of the bigger fish going for the sure thing. If there is a good wave, I'll work the bob fly a little, but only enough to cause a subtle disturbance, no more. Even in a fairly rough wave, I'll do little more than keep up with the slack line as the boat drifts downwind. While the waking bob fly has an important place in my repertoire of tricks, the stripped wet fly has been relegated to my desperate measures file. If conditions demand a sunk fly, I usually go directly to nymphs or baitfish flies.

During a surface rise to a hatch, the static damp/dry fly is the deadliest technique I know for loch trout. If the trout are showing themselves, it always pays to take a moment to figure out what a particular fish is doing before going into action. Broadcasting all around the boat is always less effective than targeting a specific fish. A fish that is feeding will stay up on top until the food is gone or it is spooked, so again, presentation is the thing. Judging the path a trout is taking on its feeding cruise will allow you to have your flies in its way when it arrives within range. Having someone on the oars who is friendly to your desires is undoubtedly the best situation, but not everyone is content to row while the other fishes. A fishing buddy who will take turns on the oars is worth his weight in Gold Ribbed Hare's Ears.

More suggestive fly designs have replaced my old standards almost completely, except for the good old Grey Duster and the Blue Upright, excellent hackle patterns that will match any dun or spinner on the water. A few hackle spiders and sparse emergers for chironomid hatches are essential, and for terrestrials I'll always have a range of peacock-bodied flies like the Red Tag and the Grey Hackle, palmered or otherwise. Others rely on impressionistic emerger designs like those of England's Dave Shipman. When the trout are feeding on ephemerids and terrestrials, the static dry fly can be the best tactic, by far. There are several reasons for this, but the most important is the attractive appearance of the fly in the surface film. The dry fly is obscured by the distortions of the meniscus, and that's a good thing. A wet fly is in full view and must rely on other factors for its pulling power. The dry fly only has to present a couple of primary aspects of resemblance, size, basic shape, maybe some colour, to do its job. The rest is down to the angler's skills of observation, stalking and accurate casting.

The biggest obstacle to catching fish on busy waters is the disturbance caused by boats and fly lines. Trout in a heavily fished lake are just as spooky as a fish in a New Zealand river or a Hampshire chalkstream, it is just that we can't see them react to us in the same way. The trout may only be conspicuous by their absence. What we make of that absence will decide whether we have a good day or a blank. Equally important is to not *expect* a blank because of what might appear to be adverse conditions

6. Fishin' Impossible – lessons from Tasmania

The sun flashed like an arc welder as it rose through the branches of the gum trees. The great expanse of Arthur's Lake was as placid as a bird bath.

'Looks good,' said Brett Wolf, who had come up beside me at the big picture window.

I'm thinking, what are you, *nuts?*

'Looks pretty flat and bright to me, Brett,' I said. He was clearly doing that 'guide talk' thing, wherein the guide tries to pump the client's will up to a level that it becomes at least bearable for the rest of the day, like a WW I trench sergeant trying to get his grim faced men over the top.

'Yup,' said Brett, 'just needs some bugs on the water as it warms up.'

He walked over to the gallon pump container of thirty-weight sunscreen that sat on the end of the bar and squirted about a cupful into his hand, applying a thick white coat of the stuff over his face and neck. His grinning death mask visage seemed appropriate to the morning's prospects.

Great, I sighed, just my luck. Travel to the best trout lake in the southern hemisphere for a sunburn. My heart sank as I looked out of the big picture window of the Blue Lake Lodge's dining room. Not that it wasn't a beautiful scene; it's just that I'd seen fishing days begin like that many times and it always spelled disaster. I was recently skunked on two consecutive trips to Ireland for precisely these reasons.

The memory of similar mornings on Corrib was still raw. It was going to be another one of those days, cloudless, gorgeous and fishless. We all know this, right? Brown trout lochs and bright weather just don't mix. We have pet theories for why this is so. Trout don't have eyelids, we say; brown trout hate the light; it hurts their eyes, and so on. These explanations seem to jibe with experience. When we see that harsh brassy light that accompanies a big northern high-pressure system we feel hopeless. We go through the motions and expect the worst.

I had come to Tasmania to hook up with Brett and Rob Sloane, publishing editor of *FlyLife*, the smart Australian fly-fishing magazine. It was a great opportunity, to fish with two of the hottest rods in Australia, on one of the world's best trout lakes. Arthur's Lake is famous for its sight fishing, hunting big, cruising and tailing brown trout in shallow water. Rob and Brett are

In Scotland, conditions like these are considered impossible for traditional wet fly tactics

both from fishery biology backgrounds, Rob being District Manager for the Tasmania Inland Fishery for many years before starting *FlyLife*, which he runs with his attractive wife Libby. Brett and his attractive wife Simone run the superb Blue lake Lodge. It seems to me that these guys have got it, you know, sorted.

Rob had told me that Brett was a great guide, the best, and I had been getting progressively more excited as this trip drew closer – it was looking more and more like a sure thing. Until, that is, I looked out onto that lake. Now, I know better than to trust my own excitement. I know that the chances of success are in inverse proportion to my sense of an impending sure thing. A finely tuned sense of irony, developed over a lifetime of fishing disasters, allows me to combine a rising feeling of excitement with the acceptance of certain doom. Like a dog stealing a steak from the table, simultaneously drooling at the prospect of all that pleasure and whimpering at the inevitable beating.

In minutes we were sliding across that mirror surface in Brett's roomy and very serious boat. Oddly, Rob and Brett seemed unconcerned by the conditions. All they wanted to find was some food on the water. There wasn't any. I reckoned we were going for a boat ride. I decided to relax and adopt the tourist attitude. This is the fallback position for anglers, in the knowledge that millions of people happily regard something like a sightseeing boat ride as value for money. If the fishing is crap you just go tourist, lie back and enjoy it. Liquor helps. Margaret, my ex-wife fishing buddy, conducts these trips on that basis. The fishing has to be pretty damn good for her to get out of her beach chair and pick up a fly rod. With a veteran's eye for the main chance, Margaret decided to stay at the lodge and work on her tan. To her, a sure thing is sunshine, a whisky soda, and a good book.

Don't get me wrong. It was still a fishing day, and even a bad fishing day is worth a month of the other kind. Arthur's Lake is a big natural lake that had its level raised in the sixties. In those days, I guess, gum trees weren't worth anything, so they just left the surrounding shore fully treed. Now, forty years later, the skeletons of these great trees stand all around the shore in a few feet of water. The scenery was strange and beautiful, a bit weird actually, but like all good fishing places you grow fond of it quickly enough.

Brett took the boat into a broad shallow bay, where the weedy bottom was visible for fifty yards in all directions. Nothing stirred. He manoeuvred the boat by operating a silent bow-mounted electric motor, and we prowled off shore looking for life. Since it was so late in the year the boys didn't expect to see much this early in the day. Nevertheless, we probed among the gum trees, pot-shotting any likely looking holes in the weeds. For these guys, sight fishing means dry fly fishing. Brett had set me up with a two fly rig; a Red Tag on the point and a mahogany coloured parachute 'dun' on the bob. There were no mayflies on the water, and Rob reckoned that if anything were on the water it would be beetles. The Red Tag, a simple Brown Hackle Peacock with a red wool tag, looked pretty beetle-like to me, so when Brett wasn't looking I cunningly replaced the parachute dun with another Red Tag.

The flies apparently looked good enough to a fish as well, because when they dropped into a little hole among the weeds and tree trunks one was immediately taken in a large boil. This fish came out of the water three times and we saw it was a real cracker. It weeded up immediately, which quietened it down some and Brett got hold of it, as beautiful a three-plus pounder as you'd dream of on Corrib. Okay, I'm thinking, *that* was encouraging. It wasn't ten minutes before I had another one of the same size to the Red Tag. By now, the sun was even more dazzling, and the water, if anything, even flatter – so Brett decided we should head for open water.

Brett Wolf hefts a typical Arthur's lake brown that fell for the good old dry Red Tag

Right, I'm thinking, he *is* nuts. Why leave the shaded pockets among the trees, and known trout, for the desolation of open water? The reason, it turned out, was that Brett wanted to find some scum lines. Scum lines are created by wind lanes; the other thing that Brett wanted to find. Of course there was no wind, so he figured that we'd maybe find some fish picking the leftovers of an old wind lane. I've known plenty of guys like Brett. Enthusiasts. Optimists. The glass is always half full. Sixteen years of fishing with a gang of Scots has knocked that sort of gee-whiz Pollyanna attitude out of me. I know a grim proposition when I see one. But, damned if Brett didn't find a fish. Way out on that featureless blue expanse, he spotted a trout rising. I didn't believe him, because I couldn't see zip. Finally, after creeping along for a hundred yards with the electric motor, he pointed out the tiniest, insignificant blip on the surface, still seventy yards away.

'Wo!' said Brett, 'He's a good one! Look at that nose! He's coming this way! Get ready!'

I'm going...*eh*?

First of all, I thought, how could he even tell if that was a trout out there, let alone a good one? Second, if it was a trout, how in the hell were we supposed to catch it in these conditions? A rifle,perhaps? But no, I was clearly expected to make a cast at this fish, and Brett urged me to stay low as we crept toward it. Finally, Brett stopped the boat and we waited. I had thirty feet of fly line trailing alongside the boat for an instant water-haul, and another twenty coiled at my feet, bonefish skiff style. The lake was literally like a mirror. Then, almost imperceptibly, the nose poked out of the glassy surface, fifty feet away.

'Watch him', said Brett, 'there, moving right! A cast and a half, go, go!'

Somehow, I managed to keep my feet out of the line and make a good forty-foot throw, putting the flies about six feet ahead of the last tiny blip. We waited. A new minnow-like blip appeared where one of the flies was, I lifted and he was on. I couldn't believe it. It was not a wee minnow at all but a chunky two-pound brown trout, and he was all over the place. We brought him to hand after a spirited tussle and let him go. Okay, I'm thinking, what's going on here? There was no wave. There was no hatch. Trout don't have eyelids. This was not supposed to be happening. By now there was an occasional zephyr ruffling the surface as the afternoon

Rob Sloane nets another nice Tasmanian brownie in what Scottish anglers would consider impossible conditions

convection built over the lake. These died away almost immediately, but they created something that, with some imagination, you could call a wind lane. When one appeared, say a mile or so off, Brett would fire up the big 150 and we'd fly toward it. When we got near it we shut down and watched. Every time, somewhere out there, Brett or Rob would spot a fish. Now, I like to think I'm pretty good at spotting fish, but for the first couple of hours I saw nothing. It always took one of them to act as rangefinder and call out co-ordinates. Eventually I got so I could spot one without their eyes, but it brought the cold realisation that I've been ignoring catchable fish all my life.

The wind lanes did not have to be well defined to attract trout. The slightest breeze would form a swathe of debris and terrestrial bug life, no matter how sparse. These fish took advantage of very little food on the surface, the reward for loafing along, sipping the occasional beetle or other vulnerable bug trapped in the surface film, was greater than that of hunting and chasing minnows, etc. The important thing was not to spook the fish and I spooked several, good ones, just by false casting, fish I didn't even know were there until Brett pointed them out.

One might expect the trout in conditions like these to be pretty picky about what you threw at them. Maybe on other lakes they might be, but I'm not so sure. A fly in the surface film is a fairly indistinct thing, after all. It's really a matter of getting the size right. These fish were expecting beetles, and the Red Tag with its peacock herl body was near enough. In that region there are gum beetles with a spot of bright red on their underside, so it's possible that the red wool tag did the business as a confirming trigger. It made me think of the red-legged Heather Beetle, or Bibio, on Scottish lochs, usually associated with bright sunny weather in late August. I remembered flat calms in conditions almost identical to our day in Tasmania, and the hopeless feeling in our boat, even as trout were obviously rising here and there. That day on Arthur's Lake was a reminder that, too often, the greatest obstacle to success is your own state of mind.

* * * * *

6. Stillwaters II: The Northern Scottish Lochs

There are times when I have stood still for the joy of it all, on my way through the wild freedom of a highland moor, and felt the wind, and looked upon the mountains and water and light and sky, till I felt conscious only of the strength of a mighty current of life, which swept away all consciousness of self, and made me part of all I beheld.

Viscount Grey of Fallodon
Fly Fishing

Suilven, Assynt, Scotland

1. Adventures in the holy land

You don't really choose your home waters; they choose you. I grew up in southern Alberta, learned to fish on the Sheep, Highwood, Crowsnest and Oldman rivers, graduating to the mighty Bow in my teens, all serious fly-fishing waters that became international destination rivers over the short two decades that I fished them. The Skeena country in northern British Columbia chose me for a few years, an example of how fly-fishing can exert a truly irresistible influence on a young man's life. I fell in love with the Morice and Kispiox rivers, and especially the Stellako, on which I was lucky enough to live for a few years. Then, as fickle as a schoolgirl, I had a lengthy crush on the steelhead rivers and tidal estuaries of Vancouver Island; but it wasn't to last. For the last decade and a half, although I've got a steamy affair going with the crystalline rivers of New Zealand's South Island, I've been chosen by the dark, whisky-tinted waters of Scotland. I sense now is that it is all one place, and it's inside me. Home waters are where the heart is.

On the maps the region is called Sutherland, but the old Gaelic name for the part we haunt is Assynt. My fishing pals and I refer to it as the Holy Land. Space being the world's last great luxury, this is a place where you can indulge yourself. It is glacier country, or was, and it has that sculptured quality to the landscape. It is open grassland, visually much like the prairie I grew up in and I feel at home there because you can see so much nothing, but this region is wet, or should be. The wetness and the calciate up-thrust known to geologists as the Durness Limestone make it good trout country. The terrain is mostly rock and bog, so until they develop better ways to sell bog the only commercial use of it involves deer, sheep, tourists and the dirty little business of salmon farming. Despite a shameful level of tax-shelter conifer monoculture, there is still a vast area of open land, and the legal freedom to roam and feel alone.

Those who fish the hill lochs are kin to the mountain climber and the solitary hill walker. The objectives may be different, but the engagement with that landscape certainly stems from the same source. To fish the northern Highlands is to have accomplished a thing of a different order, a level of competence in a range of outdoors skills and techniques, and to have demonstrated, to oneself at least, an understanding of something profound and, well, serious.

The emptiness is palpable and somewhat forbidding, seeping into your consciousness and giving proceedings a certain edge, as J.C. Mottram described in 1921, in *Fly Fishing: Some new Arts and Mysteries*. 'Can one forget the lonely, barren, brown tarn up among the mountains? A few stunted rushes grow at the shallow end; islands of grey granite dot its surface; little foamy waves beat its rocky shores; the grey solemn face of a mountain bends over it, looking always steadfastly into its sepia depths, watching, watching day and night, year in year out, spellbound. At first you see nothing of this, but as the day passes you begin to see and feel that there is some subtle force keeping these two, the mountain and the tarn, thus mesmerised. The day's fishing is done, you pack your rod; there they are, the big mountain and the little tarn, unmoved; you shout, you halloa, hoping to break the spell, but they only return your words; fear seizes you, a great longing to fly from this unknown comes upon you; heedless of the uneven ground, you hurry down the mountain side; what joy to reach the King's Highway, to see the cottage light's bright ray; such is the mystery of water.'

It is not a landscape that invites the tourist approach to things, but one that must be engaged with at some deeper level. This is its appeal to the thousands of hill walkers and climbers who head north every year, some of whom, it must be said, do not return to their urban lives again, usually through some underestimation of the very real dangers in this brooding landscape. It looks like what it is. After a period alone in a wild landscape you tend to renew your appreciation of other people. A week of this solitude, and the whisky, will turn the sourest misanthrope into a regular Sammy Davis Jr.

To anyone familiar with the huge expanses of the North American west, Scotland may seem pretty tiny. I suppose it is, but the thing about Scotland is, it's dense. By that, I mean that you

Working the upstream wet fly on a highland spate river

get a tremendous variety of terrain and micro-cultures packed into an area the size of, say, a good sized Californian shopping mall. It takes me less than five hours to drive from my home in Glasgow to Lochinver, in Sutherland. In that time, you travel through what seems like at least three distinct geographical and cultural zones. Between the sprawling sectarian raffishness of Glasgow and the industrial central belt, to the scrubbed grey Puritanism of Aberdeen on the east coast, only a two-hour drive, there are linguistic gates to daily life to which only a local birth certificate will permit access.

The nearest village to our favourite waters is Lochinver, about as close as we get over here to a fishing town like West Yellowstone in the States. There are, however, big differences. Lined out primly along the top of the Inver estuary, Lochinver is just a place where you can buy some supplies and liquor, eat a cheap breakfast at the Fisherman's Mission, or sink a pint at the Culag bar. In fact, it is closer in some respects to what existed in America before the big leisure and fly fishing boom of the seventies and eighties, like the old coal mining towns of Alberta's Crowsnest Pass, without the slag heaps. For instance, there are no specialist fly shops, guiding services, float trips, fishing contests or international professional fly-tying conventions. There are several reasons for this, some of which are specifically cultural, but it's mostly because most folks over here just haven't twigged to the concept of trout fishing as a business. I think of this as a sort of golden age, which, because things inevitably get worse, will certainly be regarded by the boys and me as the Good Old Days.

Good fishing, to anyone who has been doing it for any length of time, means you come close to reconciling your desire with the potential of the water. In Alaska or New Zealand we know that a big fish means bigger than anywhere else. However, in most of North America and Europe, the natural range of the wild trout, a foot-long brownie is a good fish. Big starts at about fifteen inches and weighs maybe a pound and a half. By these criteria the fishing in Sutherland is much better than fly-fishing for wild brown trout ordinarily gets.

During June and early July there is usually a hatch of Mayfly on most of the lochs. This isn't the ordinary large Lake Olive or Summer Dun, although those flies are also common. These northern lochs have an honest to goodness hatch of *Ephemera Danica*, the legendary Green Drake. These critters are big, with bodies at least an inch long, and I've seen nymphs over an inch and a half. In July, you will also see the Murragh, or the Great Red Sedge, some of which are grey-blue. In flight, these things look more like small birds than flies and when one has you in its flight path it's hard not to panic. These animals may explain the northern trout's penchant for huge flies dragged over the surface.

The first day or two, you might indulge the base desire to catch a ridiculous number of trout. Those of low character might even keep score. By the third day you will probably be thinking about how to find those big fish and begin scrutinising the topo maps. There are hundreds of trout lochs here, and many hundreds more across the north of Scotland. All have trout in them. The lochs with the best average weight of fish often lie on rock with some limestone in it. Some have only a few big old lunkers sharing a good food supply – these lochs will really test your mettle. Boggy lochs are normally too acidic for quality trout, but there are exceptions. Look for weed-beds, not reeds. A mud or silt bottom produces the Mayfly hatches. Lochs with good spawning usually have huge populations of small, if perfectly formed, trout. In these waters, you will have to sort out the bigger fish from the hundreds of half-pounders – not unpleasant work in itself. This kind of fishing sets you up for the inevitable tackle-buster that will come sooner or later. You can become pretty cavalier after a run of half-pound fish and will pop a leader on a two-pounder before you know what hit you.

2. The limestone lochs of Cape Wrath

Things got off to a great start. I've lived in Scotland long enough to realise that it was probably a bad sign. However, the loch was alive with rising fish and on the second drift Al Pyke covered a portentous boil and felt the weight of a solid twenty-incher. The fish spent most of the next minute or two in the air and then fought it out right to the boat. It took a size eighteen wet spider and was certainly the prettiest trout we had seen over the previous eight days on the Sutherland trout lochs.

The trouble with great starts is that they lead to high spirits and hubris. In their hearts, Scottish anglers know that high spirits are wrong and will end in certain and well deserved humiliation. The rise boiled away for over two hours and we had only one more trout to the net, a cracking pounder that would have inspired effusions of admiration only days before, but which now received summary treatment at the boat side and sent home to grow up. We were after bigger stuff. Those big trout chugging away out there completely ignored our increasingly anxious efforts. We understood our penance was at hand.

Charging back to the hotel to scoff down some dinner, we were back on the water by nine. It was blowing and raining harder than ever – they don't call it Cape Wrath for nothing. At half-past eleven, Al stuck another trout, an even bigger one this time, and played it out in the blustery twilight. This fish, a superb three-pounder, took a dark claret, no-hackle Deer Hair Sedge dragged through the waves in the rain and gloom. Given our level of discomfort, we

Al Pyke bags a good Caladail 'buzzer' feeder on a small wet spider

reckoned we had probably got what we deserved and had squared things up with the fish gods. We squidged our way back to the darkened hotel and collapsed into our beds.

Al and I had decided to cap off our week in Assynt with a couple of days at the Cape Wrath Hotel. I had never fished the famous limestone lochs and we thought it would be a way to decompress after our annual total-emersion trout camp experience, not to mention chance to reconfigure our blood chemistry. Also, a day or two in the company of polite folks couldn't hurt before we returned to the world. Nobody is more polite than Jack Watson, erstwhile proprietor of the hotel after almost twenty years of keeping large groups of anglers happy. I looked up from my breakfast to the smiling face of Jack doing the rounds of the tables and co-ordinating the day's fishing. At his side was the new owner, Michelle Robinson, observing Jack's performance with pleasant anxiety.

It is, after all, her first venture into the hotel business – and a famous old fishing hotel at that. Her smile was fixed like a first-time father scrutinising a new baby for familiar body parts. It was clear that she was trying to make sense of the codified language of fly-fishing as he expertly counselled each party on the choices and opportunities for the day. Judging by the look on Michelle's face we may as well have been speaking Chinese, although it was obvious that she intends to learn as much as possible about this fishing thing while she has Jack around as advisor. Somehow, we pulled the straw for another day on Caladail, the Eiger of Scottish wild trout lochs. This suited me, since I was now in the serious big fish groove. After a week of fifty trout days, I was in the mood for something more astringent. I dunked my toast in my egg and thought to myself, all right Cape Wrath, bring it on.

Of the several lochs fished from the hotel, Caladail is the premium water, but not because it produces most fish. Borralie is better in terms of numbers – it gives up good catches of wild trout averaging a pound or so, with a sprinkling of two-pounders to keep one focused. This is excellent trout fishing by any standard, and has the added opportunity of being fishable from the bank. If you tire of sitting in a boat all day, as I do, the chance to fish on your legs is inviting. Deeper than Caladail, it provides a more definite drop-off that can be fished well by careful wading. You won't find a better class of trout anywhere. The fish are superb in colour and condition, glowing with health and vitality. When hooked they 'light up' like mahi-mahi and throw themselves all over the shop, resisting vigorously right to the boat. There are some seriously big trout in Caladail, up to five pounds and more. Little Loch Lanish has even bigger ones, sometimes caught in the wee hours by fanatics.

Pyko's big golden fish spent almost as much time out of the water as they did in it. Al wore a kind of stunned expression throughout the next day and had trouble coming to terms with the fact that he had caught two such specimens in one day. It's just as well, because over the next day he had only about three rises to his flies. We skipped dinner to stay on the water, and Al was so worn out by his day's frustration that he balanced himself on the gunnels and went to sleep for almost an hour. At the other end of the boat, I had a reasonable day's fishing, with five beautiful pound fish brought to hand and released, and maybe a dozen hooked out of twenty rises or so. Almost all of the trout were in the pound class, with only two bigger ones hooked and lost. Tough maybe, but good fishing all the same. I possibly pricked a couple of larger ones, but it's hard to say. Harder still to figure why I should have got all the action, but I've got a few ideas.

Reflecting on the first afternoon of watching those big trout plunging for three hours and making probably a thousand futile casts, we talked it over with other anglers in the de-briefing room, (AKA the bar). Neil Toft and his pal Dave (speaking of fanatics) had fished the other boat

Pyko with a cracking Caladail fish taken at dark on a big Deer Hair Sedge in foul conditions

and had about the same result. They'd had some smaller fish before lunch, but once the fish started working the surface the responses fell to almost zero.

Dave reckoned it was the flies. Like us, they saw the big flock of black-headed gulls and terns wheeling for the olive duns and reasoned that the trout were on them too. We all noticed a lot of big dark buzzer (chironomid) shucks in the water as well, and thought that maybe the olive hatch was masking the reality of the situation. Dave, who has clearly pondered this type of thing too often, feared there might have been even another level of masking going on, with an inscrutable third player in the form of 'wee small black things' on the water. Fighting back that kind of fly-fisher's paranoia, a slippery slope, I decided that the trout were zeroed on the buzzers, which at least accorded with the irreducible fact of Al's beauty on the spider.

On the second day we had better conditions, less wind for one thing, and no real rain by the previous week's standard. The fishing was slow until after lunch when the birds started searching the middle of the loch again. A few olives appeared and a few trout followed them up, but there was no big buzzer activity as on the first afternoon. By three there were enough trout rising to make it interesting, and I made sure to pay strict attention to what was happening this time. I got almost all of the action, although only a couple of the larger fish rose to my fly. I had switched to a single dry fly, a size eighteen Compara-Dun with no tails (since I didn't have an eighteen DHE). At the time, I didn't feel confident that the flies were exactly right, but I now believe that it wasn't the flies at all. They were good enough. I'm convinced it was technique and presentation that let us down. Only with hindsight did I see what was going on.

Caladail is a goldfish bowl, but it's the anglers that are under scrutiny, not the fish. You never see the trout, although the pale marl bottom is clearly visible over the whole loch. The water is literally gin clear, and you might expect to see an occasional fish dart from beneath the boat once in a while. You never do, because they casually swim out of your way by the time you reach them. Time after time, we drifted down to a pod of rising fish only to have the area go quiet when the boat reached it. It was as if a lifeguard had blown a whistle, everyone out of the pool. It's no surprise, really.

Caladail gets fished constantly throughout the season. It's not much more than twelve feet deep anywhere. There are three boats on it, all rowing up wind and drifting back down the wind, rods waving and lines thrashing the water like a team of combine harvesters working a big wheat field. Many loch anglers don't realise that trout can be made line-shy by repeated casting and line flash. Observing the fishless zone around the edge of most of our heavily fished reservoirs, where the trout cruise just beyond normal casting distance, is instructive. Although it is deep wading that is usually blamed for this effect on the trout, in the trout-spooking sweepstakes I'd put casting, especially false casting, well ahead of wading. This is certainly not a new idea. Almost a century ago, Mottram wrote that he considered the rod and line to be the greatest factor in spooking trout, much greater than the angler himself, who is usually positioned well below the angle of the trout's perceptual window. Trout react instantly to objects overhead, whether they understand them or not; the shadow or flash of a line may trigger a genetic memory of predators from above. The traditional high rod tip of the loch-style angler can defeat its intended purpose.

I got some action for these reasons: I was throwing maybe forty to fifty feet of line with an eighteen to twenty foot leader and a single fly; I was casting less often than Al, who threw about two casts to my one; I was fishing my flies dead in the water, while Al was pulling his team of wets. I was also stopping my cast well above the surface so the long leader would straighten out before the line touched the water, trying to avoid line splash and as much as possible; and I kept my rod tip low. There might have been other small differences; maybe my three-pound co-polymer tippet didn't make as much disturbance, and maybe my flies were sitting in the surface differently. Whatever, it wasn't magic.

These are all small details of presentation, but they added up to more responses from the fish. Something has to account for the difference in action at two ends of the boat. It also accounts for why we didn't get any big fish. With little wind to give us cover, they just stopped rising as the boat neared and swam around the area disturbed by the lines. It seems the fish are not so much put off by the boat itself so much as by being 'lined'. The younger fish, about a pound in weight and not yet shy of the line effect, were still susceptible to the fine and far-off dry fly technique. Normal high-rod, short-line, loch-style techniques are futile, as is belting out endless twenty-yard casts. I think the drifting boat is a handicap, and next time will maybe try to anchor discreetly near one of the weed beds and wait for things to begin. Returning to the head of the loch for each drift should be done up the shoreline in shallow water, not by ploughing through the prime fishing areas. Quietly stalking the shoreline on foot, Tasmanian style, is another possibility, as is a float-tube. In other words, the customary 'fish the water' approach, beating a swathe down the loch, is a no-hoper. We didn't get a chance to try it again with these considerations in mind, but I will approach that water differently next time. Fishing at night holds the greatest potential, but you'd need to prepare yourself before arriving by staying awake for a few nights. Tacking an overnighter onto a full day's fishing would be pretty gruelling. A cozy bed is a hard thing to pass up after a long day in the boat.

* * * * *

FLIES
a trout hunter's go-to selection

Fly portraits by
Hans Weilenmann

Deer Hair Emerger

DHE Tying Seqence

1. Tie in a bunch of deer hair, tips forward, leaving enough space to dub the thorax. Wrap down the butts of the hair and take the thread well around the hook bend. Leave a long tag end of the tying thread or use as a rib.

2. Dub the abdomen to the wing base. Wind the tag end up the abdomen as a rib, counter-wise to the dubbing. Tie off ahead of the wing base. Take the tying thread to the hook eye.

3. Dub the tying thread with spiky fur from a hare's mask. Wind the dubbing back to the wing base, forcing the wing into a vertical posture. Take the tying thread forward again through the dubbing and whip finish. Pick out the guard hairs of the thorax.

Deer Hair Sedge

Jerry's Bucktail

Deer Hair Emerger: fishing posture

Deer Hair Sedge: fishing posture

CDC & Elk: fishing posture

Dirty Duster: fishing posture

Emergers

Klinkhåmer Special (HvK)

Snowshoe Hare

DHE Rough Olive

DHE Stripped Quill

Wee Hare Emerger

Partridge and Olive Emerger (HW)

Hans Weilenmann's CDC & Elk series

CDC & Elk

CDC & Elk Cripple (B Salzberg)

CDC & Elk Spent

CDC & Elk Diving

Hans Weilenmann's Emergers

Itty Bitty Emerger

Partridge Caddis Emerger

Clipped Hackle Dries

Badger and Black

Grizzly Palmer

Red Quill

Blue Upright

Dirty Duster

Grey Duster

Nymphs and Buzzers

Dark Hare's Ear (bead head)

McPhee's Pheasant Tail

Simple Damsel

Simple Sedge Pupa

Grey Boy Buzzer

Teeny Nymph

Irish Style Wet Flies

Claret Dabbler

Green Octopus (variant)

mithy

Veyatie Black

Wet Spiders

Woodcock and Hair Lug

Woodcock and Yellow

Baitfish Imitations

Matuka Muddler

Desolation Baitfish

Bullet Head Bugger

Sloane's Fur Fly (variant)

Terrestrials

McPhee's Wee Muddler (Cicada)

Red Tag

7. Fly Design

There is a difference between the perfect imitation and the perfect fly (the former not desirable and the latter unattainable).

Gary LaFontaine,
The Dry Fly – New Angles

A beautiful Kootenay cutthroat to the DHE

1. Never-fails

Fly-fishing is a weird, subjective and variable experience, and there are more than a few persistent puzzles for a beginner. One source of bewilderment is the vast number of fly patterns. This is actually a problem, at least until you have come away skunked a few times and begin to suspect the reason might be the wrong flies – and not the weather, the water temperature, the time of year or time of day, your wading, your casting, your leader, your concentration, whether you have spooked the fish, whether someone else may have spooked them or caught them already, or if the water you are fishing has now, or ever has had, any fish in it.

The 'which fly' problem, the armature for many a pot-boiler in the hook and bullet press, is customarily framed thus; 'If I was limited to only one fly…'. The idea has been taken to extremes in Jack Dennis' famous One-Fly fishing competition, held at Jackson Hole, Wyoming, in which contestants actually fish all day with one fly only, no changing whatsoever, as if fly-fishing isn't hard enough. Predictably, contestants have cunningly developed the Swiss Army Knife of trout flies, with extra wings, tails, hackles, rubber legs, etc, any of which can be clipped, snipped and shaped to the basic characteristics of any emerger, dun, spinner, nymph, fish or terrestrial bug known to Ernest Schweibert.

The one-fly contest only serves to illustrate the depth of our looniness, rooted in the basic mystery of angling. Ortega explains it in terms of the primitive hunter's anxiety toward the scarcity of the game. It is the prey's absence that gives the hunt its essential character. Put simply, the fact that game is scarce is why we have to hunt it in the first place. If game had been plentiful and easy to catch, socio-biologists claim that we would not be the kind of being we are today. Early hunters were plainly mystified about how, when, why, or if the game would show up. Clearly a magical appearance for the benefit of humans, it gave rise to what anthropologists refer to as *homocentrism*, the humanistic 'central position' view of the world – and, by the way, society, religion and art. So, the next time someone asks why you fish, you can assert with confidence that civilisation as we know it depends on it.

In other words, as we anxiously finger those Klinkhåmer Specials and Gold Ribbed Hare's Ears, we are enacting something similar to the ritual performed in the caves of Lasceaux 40,000 years ago, evoking the absent prey, 'making it real' in our imagination so we can begin our hunt with at least a degree of confidence – or failing that, hope. Hope is one thing, but nobody likes to believe it's all down to dumb luck. This is where voodoo comes into it. A lot of flies imitate fish food and some are just plain attractors, but a few, at least in our expert hands, are special. They seem to possess special powers. So, we weave our personal fabric of magic, art, science and simple bloody-mindedness, and damned if it doesn't work!

But, let's face it, flies don't take up much space and they weigh next to nothing, so what's the harm in an over-stuffed fly box? None, whatsoever. The thing is, you want to have that little group of never-fails, what our state-side friends call your go-to flies, to fall back on. With these at the ready, if there is no hatch or things are just slow, you don't get trapped in one of those desperate three-hour fly changing episodes. With an overstocked fly box, these situations offer a glimpse of the true arbitrariness of the universe and can send you home in an existential funk. When things are like that, I just fish with the flies I know would catch fish if conditions were perfect. That may not sound like much of a strategy, I know, but it's surprising how often it works.

My personal line-up of go-to flies is fleshed out with plenty of other patterns for specific situations, and usually one of these will fill the bill for a singular circumstance. These at once increase and limit the possibilities open to me, and reduce the feeling of a crap-shoot. I've lately included a particularly hot design by my friend Hans Weilenmann, the CDC & Elk. It's easy to tie and I know it works. If I didn't have my own pet never-fail, my Deer Hair Emerger, it would be right up there on my front bench. Hans and I have something of an inter-continental rivalry thing going – whose fly is the best go-to in any and all circumstances – as if we really did only have one fly. It's a no-win contest, of course, but a lot of fun, and it leads us nicely to the idea of originality in fly design.

2. Originality

Like the rivers and lakes where they have evolved, the fly-fishing tradition is fluid and constantly

A fine back-country fish goes back

photo: Bruce Masson

changing. Tradition is an older word for the cultural studies boffins call an historical context, and things only make sense when seen in a context. All the recent and spectacular developments in technique and equipment have taken place against and within a framework of tradition. A fly rod, no matter how fancy or high tech, tends to look pretty much like a fly rod always has, a graceful blend of elegance and function. That's tradition at work. It must be said, however, the modern fly rod is to nineteenth century examples what the F-16 fighter is to the Sopwith Camel. Just because their rods still look more or less like fly rods always have, nobody would say that the pioneering graphite work of Gary Loomis, Don Green or Jerry Siem isn't original. It's just that the improvements they brought to the tools are important only within a functional and aesthetic tradition. So it is with fly-tying, but since rod design is considered to be technology and fly tying is thought of as something akin to an expressive art form, on the originality issue some fly-tiers can be as touchy as opera singers.

Take my friend Hans. He's got a good fly and he's pretty enthusiastic about it. So much so that he uses it for just about every situation encountered on a trout stream. Says it's his best dry, emerger, nymph, wet fly and streamer, certainly a broad remit and what we call an all-rounder. Hans calls his fly the CDC & Elk and says modestly that it's based on Al Troth's classic Elk Hair Caddis, but there are some significant differences. Instead of the hare's ear body and the palmered hackle, Hans' fly has a CDC feather wound as a body. As it is wound, the fibres that stick out from the CDC serve as a kind of soft, mobile hackle. The wing isn't actually elk hair but medium deer hair, the butts clipped to form a nice semi-muddler thorax or head. There are some fine points to its tying, but even by this description you can see that it's got all the ingredients of a good fly, most importantly the aspect of life. By the traditional criteria for fly design the CDC & Elk is highly original. While not shy about extolling his fly's virtues, Hans is always the first to point out its bloodlines, despite the fact that the only similarity to Troth's fly is in the wing, and even that has some obvious differences. Hans' fly is not simply a pattern, it's an original design.

That's an important distinction. Most fly patterns are conventional variations in colour and minor details of construction on a basic design. Halford's dry fly series were extreme examples of this narrowly codified form. Salmon flies are another classic example. In a black and white photograph only a few salmon flies would stand out in terms of unconventional form and design. Ally's Shrimp, the Francis Fly, the Temple Dog, and the dry Bombers are good examples of unconventional design. Like Hans' CDC & Elk, these flies represent significant originality in the thinking behind them. Other innovative trout fly designs are the Wulff's, the Pheasant Tail Nymph, the Compara-Dun (Haystack), the Muddler Minnow, the Woolly Bugger and the Humpy. There are plenty of others, but you get the idea.

Most fly-fishers have viewed the culture as a free exchange of ideas. The literature has always spoken in terms of a brotherhood of anglers, which by now includes more than a few sisters. When one of the brothers comes up with a good fly, most of us like to hear about it and try it out. It's also a real charge when you hear that somebody has done well with a fly you made up. The Internet has turned this into an explosion of information and shared experience. As Hans says, the effect of this explosion is that there are no more 'local' patterns.

There is another angle, from the folks I think of as the originality police, tirelessly on guard against unseemly displays of enthusiasm for one's own achievements. Their missionary zeal has spread to all corners of the fly tying world, producing variations epitomised by the Nova Scotian metaphor of the lobster barrel, based on the understanding that you don't have to put a lid on a barrel of lobsters. Every time one tries to climb out the other lobsters pull it back in.

I've got a fly that I commend to the brothers and sisters, not out of a pathetic aspiration to immortality, but just to share it around among the bubs, you know, like a bottle of whisky. I admit I'm pretty enthusiastic about this fly. My fishing pals are sick of hearing about it. They go, 'Pu-*leez*, Wyatt, don't start!' I was doing a couple of magazine pieces on this fly, so, just to make sure I wasn't treading on anyone's creative toes, I reckoned I should do as much research as possible, to see if it was already in circulation before I began blowing off about what a genius I am. I got plenty of positive and helpful advice from anglers and fly-tiers all over the globe, some reports of success with my fly on difficult fish, and a few lobster-barrel responses, apparently intended to keep my ego in check. My fly was described as being identical to Fran Betters' Haystack, to Al Caucci's Compara-Emerger, and a host of identical flies that had been on the scene for donkey's years. I heard of a New Zealand fly called the First Choice that turned out to be a fairly straight-up cover version of the Klinkhåmer Special. I heard about guides with fly boxes stuffed full of 'my' fly from Oregon and Norway. At first, my enthusiasm was somewhat deflated, but as I tracked them down, I found that these creations were either imaginary, entirely different, or shared only partial resemblance to mine, but all had the same thing in common. None, apart from the Klinker, the Compara-Dun and the Haystack, had so far been published in any magazine, book, fly catalogue or website.

Al Troth told me recently, 'Flies make themselves famous'. If these nearly identical flies have been around for years, I wondered, why haven't we heard about them? If my fly was out there somewhere, it was successfully being kept a secret from the rest of us. What this search confirmed was that no particular fly, at least none circulating in the public domain, incorporated *all* of the features of my fly. I began to think I might actually be on to something – a 'new' trout fly. Now, I really *was* excited, tempered by the realisation that, for me, somewhere along the line, what qualifies as exciting had changed significantly.

If you've been around the track long enough you know that a new fly, no matter how good you think it is, is no magic bullet. With few exceptions like the Elk Hair Caddis, the Royal Wulff, the Grey Duster, Adams or the Gold Ribbed Hare's Ear, most great new flies eventually join the ranks of just 'good flies'. Why this is I can't say, except that it's probably got something to do with the fact that the fly on the leader when the fish start to rise is often the 'only fly they'd take'. For instance, on Scottish salmon rivers these days, eight anglers out of ten will be using a variation of Ally's Shrimp. Ergo, it continues to hold pre-eminence as the hot fly. Trout flies are different, of course. Arguably, imitating the food of an actively feeding trout is a different matter than stimulating a vestigial predatory or aggressive territorial response from a salmon or steelhead.

The point of this epistle, I guess, is just to say that there really is no such thing as true originality – the apple never falls far from the tree. Nothing is created, god-like, from a vacuum. Claims of originality in fly design are no different from originality in art, including *avant-garde* art. Innovation, even among Turner Prize wanna-bes, is dependent upon well-established traditions of form. The very idea of something new is consequent on something that precedes it, something old. More than ever, in the new world of the Internet and the information culture, we understand that information is pointless unless shared in a context. Otherwise it's just noise. As we enter the age of what might be thought of as collective originality, the main thing to remember is the point of it all, to share one of the finest experiences in the world, simply trying to catch a wild fish in natural surroundings with a fly of your own making.

3.The prey-image: fresh angles on selective trout

When we try to figure out why a trout behaves the way it does, we are creating a theory. The

Dumb blondes? Wyatt admires a typical Kootenay cutt

premise for mine goes something like this; in its way, a trout is no less a predator than a lion. We have all seen enough TV nature programmes to know that the king of beasts does not normally waste much time or energy chasing things it can't catch. In fact, big male lions don't waste time chasing anything. They let the women do it. Lion cubs, on the other hand, are always trying to pounce on birds, grasshoppers and flies. It's how they learn to hunt and pounce. They are learning what they can catch and, just as importantly, what they can't. By the time you are a full-grown lion you know that the best bet is the prey that shows signs of slowness, weakness, or just lack of awareness. Basically, if it looks like dinner can outrun you, forget about it. As a corollary, all defensive decoy behaviour among animals, such as a hen-bird's dragging of a wing to lure a predator from her nest, is based on the predator's hard-wired impulse to attack a defenceless target, the sitting duck.

In their quiet and slimy way, trout are no different. A single *Baetis* dun does not contain that much nutrition, so a trout needs to eat a lot of insects to make up for the expenditure of energy to catch them. The big difference between lions and trout is in the way they get their food. Lions and pelagic fish like tuna are chasers, while stream trout are efficient interceptors. Gary Borger says that trout don't miss, that what we interpret as misses are refusals at the last moment, caused by something wrong in the appearance or behaviour of our fly. While I agree that drag is usually the culprit in refusals, his assertion that trout don't miss is off the mark itself, especially with regard to moving flies. Loch anglers frequently see trout miss the bob fly, or a dapped fly, and then search around for it, sometimes taking it or the tail fly in a second attempt. The fact that they go for it again convinces me that they weren't put off by the way it looked or behaved; they just missed. Young trout often encounter a dun that flies or is blown away by the wind just as it is about to be eaten, a waste of energy. It wouldn't take that many misses to modify the trout's behaviour to the extent that the dun is often completely ignored. Large fish have usually found an easier, more reliable, and energy efficient way to obtain food.

Manipulating the food supply can modify the behaviour of laboratory pigeons and chickens, so it's likely that a trout is capable of learning to some extent. It's possible that they learn to ignore the insects that look ready to fly. That's maybe one reason why it's rather a waste of time to strive for the impossible, to make perfect representations of adult mayflies and caddis. Even if it wasn't practically impossible, which any comparison between the most realistic of close-copy imitations and the natural will demonstrate, it's rather like trying to imitate a perfect healthy zebra if you were trying to catch a lion. All predators, including us, have one thing in common; they are suckers for a sure thing. People involved in predator control know that if you want to lure a fox, make a noise like a wounded rabbit – what we might call an audible trigger. Trout are sight feeders, so what we want in a trout fly is a convincing prey-image that incorporates one or more visual triggers. This narrows the field to representations of hatching nymphs, emergers, cripples and spent spinners as the main phases of the hatch to study, the sitting ducks. If you've got everything right but the correct phase of the hatch that the trout are keyed to, your fly is out of context in terms of the trout's current food supply. It's not so much a sitting duck as, say, a rubber duck.

In 1966, W. H. Lawrie wrote in *Scottish Trout Flies*, ' …on particular occasions, trout will ignore both the dry fly floating cocked high on the water surface and the sunk wet fly or nymph – a circumstance which has baffled many a fly-fisherman… This is far from being over-refined theory, trout have demonstrated time and time again without number that they can and do distinguish between flies floating on, in or under the film that constitutes the surface of the water'.

For most of my adult fishing career I've been quietly embarrassed about not getting more involved with insect identification and serious, scientific hatch matching. Although I've never felt disadvantaged by this ignorance, in terms of my success rate, I've secretly feared that one day on some high profile trout stream I'd get what I deserved for being so lazy, thoroughly skunked and humiliated, surrounded by sneering experts wearing those little half-moon spectacles. I've made it through almost fifty years as a fly fisherman without this happening, and if I stay away from the Henry's Fork of the Snake during the Trico hatch, I reckon it won't. I feel like I get my share of trout and just accept that, out there in selective trout country, the real hatch-matchers must be catching one hell of a lot of fish. This is really just a rationalisation for behaviour that I have no intention of changing, but now that I can count my remaining good trout seasons on my fingers and toes I've begun to do some thinking about necessity.

That old misanthrope Shopenhauer stated that 'freedom is the recognition of necessity', and I've neatly rolled that idea into my theory of trout behaviour and fly design. I feel that a great burden has been lifted from my shoulders. For one thing, I no longer have to be embarrassed at not knowing the Latin names for mayfly subspecies. I just go, 'Okay, emerger, dark, size sixteen'. What gives me the confidence to be so cavalier about it is the knowledge that some really great trout anglers use only a few favourite flies in almost every situation, and most of their go-to flies look pretty much like mine.

The premise for my theory of fly design, if I may call it that, is that any selectivity going on in a trout's brain is with regard to its recognising it as prey and locking on to it. This hard-wired behaviour is necessary and adaptive – it gives the trout its best chance of success. It also gives us a reasonable chance of tricking it into eating our fake bug. Like the wounded or infirm caribou, the natural fly that presents an aspect of vulnerability is doomed to stand out from the herd. This leads to the conclusion that our artificial flies should in fact stand out to some extent from the prevailing food form, but not look different enough to put the fly out of context. LaFontaine makes a similar argument for exaggerated features to get the trout's attention. It's the likeliest explanation for why a trout will often choose our relatively crude impressions from hundreds of perfectly good naturals – they get noticed. If we pursue the logic of the African predator analogy a bit further, let's consider a zebra that had no stripes, or was a bit bigger than the other zebras. A strict interpretation of the selective behaviour theory would suggest that a lion might reject such an odd animal as prey. In reality, such an unusual zebra would be lucky to see its first birthday. Among prey animals, individuality is not an adaptive characteristic.

When you compare a conventional dry fly to the natural *subimago*, it's clear that among a raft of natural duns the artificial fly stands out like a goose in a hen house. This idea happens to fit both LaFontaine's thinking on the reasons a trout will select an artificial from among a hatch of naturals, and biological concept of the predatory search-image. After all, it can't be the case that the trout are eating your nice parachute Adams because it looks *more* lifelike than the naturals. It must be that, within certain parameters, the trout will accept a variety of things that look roughly like familiar prey, but which stand out from the rest enough to attract attention. It is a matter of primary and secondary stimuli, or what we fly-fishers refer to as triggers. The prey-image hypothesis is not a new idea for behavioural ecologists, but accounts for feeding behaviour that anglers have traditionally treated as mysteries, or attributed to very un-troutlike capabilities such as suspicion, reason, even taste.

This approach to fly design is just approaching the problem with a different emphasis than Brian Clarke and John Goddard in *The Trout and the Fly*, or John Roberts in *To Rise a Trout*, expert and innovative anglers who, like most authorities on the dry fly, emphasise the imitation of the fully emerged dun. In these books the authors suggest that Swisher and Richards' no-hackle designs don't really work that well, at least on the trout in their waters. The implication of this difference in experience is that maybe the English chalk-stream brown trout are more interested in the perfect subimago than other (American) trout. Putting far too fine a point on it, that's like saying English foxes are less interested in garbage cans than their American counterparts (Roberts does display what appears to be mild pro-English chauvinism in his preference – you don't want to get him started on baseball caps). Although Roberts acknowledges the trout's predilection for the emerger and spinner throughout the book, the

The wild trout is essentially an oportunistic predator, with periods of 'tunnel vision'

premise of *To Rise a Trout* is conflicted, to borrow a term from pop psychology, by its emphasis on the challenge of imitating the dun. Anglers are increasingly aware that it is the hatching nymph and emerger that are central to dry fly fishing, not the dun.

Anglers have always known that trout feed upon hatching insects, but Frederick Halford launched the modern tradition of 'exact imitation' of the dun. Ernest Schweibert popularised the taxonomic approach with *Matching the Hatch*, and introduced that phrase into the fly-fisher's lexicon, but Doug Swisher and Carl Richards framed the contemporary concept of discriminating trout in their seminal book, *Selective Trout*. Since its publication in 1971, with sales of over 150,000 copies, *Selective Trout* has firmly imbedded the idea of the suspicious trout in anglers' minds. In its opening chapters, Swisher and Richards lay down the premise for their approach, stating emphatically that the most important factor in an angler's success is in the fly's capacity to convince a trout that it is a real insect. You can't argue with that, but they go further, stating that realistic imitation far outweighs the role of presentation, which they lump into a handful of 'excuses' for not catching fish. They claim that trout are getting more selective as they are increasingly being fished for, caught, and released, and that the only antidote for this is even more realistic imitation.

Despite the tremendous quantity of sound information that *Selective Trout* contains, especially its emphasis on essential triggers in a successful fly's design, I think there is something fishy about the theory that underpins it. The idea that angling pressure and spookiness produces heightened discrimination in trout is common currency in fly-fishing discourse, and to question it is to challenge some of the greatest contemporary authorities. My temerity is bolstered by the knowledge that some of the great anglers of a century ago challenged the primacy of exact imitation over impressionistic suggestion and presentation, in some cases on rivers where angling pressure was greater that it is even now. There are some lacunae, or unexplained gaps in the selective trout concept, and the theory contains what might be called 'work-arounds'. The fly-fishing discourse is a kind of long-running debate, spirited but friendly, so in keeping with that spirit maybe it's time we unpacked the selective trout theory.

Where the food supply is restricted to a single type, or for short periods during one phase of a sustained hatch, trout may develop narrowly constrained feeding habits, but the exclusively selective trout is a rare beast at the extreme end of the spectrum of fly-fishing problems. It's a mistake to think of all trout as picky eaters. Unless you specifically target selective feeders, and restrict your efforts to spring creeks or chalkstreams during major hatches, what you are far more likely to encounter these days are disturbed and spooky trout, which is not the same thing as suspicious and selective trout.

Swisher and Richards are at pains to link trout selectivity to spookiness. They don't separate these behaviours, making it difficult to say just which is the primary response, and claim that selective behaviour is increasing on hard-fished streams. Their theory puts the trout's capacity to learn above deeply ingrained, probably genetic, behavioural traits. Spookiness may be increasing with increased angling pressure, but it does not follow that selectivity is increasing because of it. If that were the case, after two hundred years of unrelenting pressure, the trout on some public British rivers would be more or less uncatchable. They aren't; the flies used a hundred years ago are still catching trout, in the same old ways and in the same old places.

Behavioural ecology treats spookiness and selectivity as distinct behaviours. To my knowledge, no causal link between the two has been established. In fact, contrary to Swisher and Richards' claim for such a link, biologists have established that when animals like trout are in a predatory search mode their search-image leaves little room for anything else in their brains, including their own safety. Even large brained predators are at their most vulnerable when engaged in hunting, including us. Limited attention is a feature of all predatory behaviour. This suggests that not only is selectivity not caused by spookiness but trout in a *non-selective* feeding mode are probably at their spookiest, a fact born out on New Zealand backcountry streams. Closer imitation will not overcome a disturbed trout's spookiness – only careful presentation can do that. Further, a strong predatory stimulus such as the impression of vulnerability is much more important in a trout fly than the minor details of its physiognomy. Unless one purposely limits his efforts to them, truly selective trout, especially those feeding exclusively on the subimago phase of a specific hatch, amount to only a fraction of the trout one will encounter over a lifetime of fishing.

The window for what we interpret as selective behaviour is actually quite narrow, observed only when the trout's prey is super-abundant, or on waters where a single type of food is predominant. Keyed to a specific food-form, the trout simply ignores anything that does not fit its established search-image and which lacks the stimuli to trigger a predatory attack, what biologists call its functional response. Together with important aspects like size and general shape, these stimuli, or triggers, constitute a fly's prey-image. Over a sustained period these triggers might be reduced to one or two salient features. Build something like these into your fly and you've cracked it. A good example is the crayfish-feeding trout of certain Chilean rivers. These trout just don't eat anything else. Any big, dark, deeply sunk fly that has the size, the necessary bulk, and maybe some feature that gives the vague impression of claws, works fine on those big trout, but not much else will. This idea accords with recent findings that the human brain is hard-wired, so to speak, to respond to certain prime visual stimuli called representational primitives. Trout have a far smaller and simpler brain than we do, with some important structural differences, but the principle probably holds for them as well. As far as the discriminatory powers of trout are concerned, what we are observing is not suspicion and selectivity but the occasional preoccupation of a very simple predatory brain.

In situations where a single food-form is present in large numbers it does not pay for the predator to hold more than one search-image in its brain at one time. When such prey is abundant for an extended period of time, the trout can afford a narrowly defined search-image, ignoring anything that does not conform, to the extent that it displays what we call extreme selective behaviour. In normal circumstances, however, when food is scarce and varied, the trout has to be able to take advantage of changing circumstances and respond to different food-forms. Several prey species may be present during a hatch and trout often respond to several kinds of prey at once, a fact acknowledged by Swisher and Richards. They attribute this to 'periods of reduced selectivity', as if the trout's powers of discrimination had a dimmer switch. That's close, and in fact, biologists studying predatory behaviour have observed something that explains why trout respond to our vague and inaccurate impressions in the first place. What we anglers have going for us is that when predators have to respond to several different food types they have trouble remembering and detecting them. A search-image that is not too narrowly defined permits the fish to recognise other opportunities to eat. Even during a hatch, a single insect presents to the trout a wide range of shapes and postures, all of which contain triggers to a predatory response. If this weren't the case our impressionistic flies wouldn't work during a hatch at all, ever.

Experienced anglers, including Swisher and Richards, have always acknowledged that even selective trout will usually select an artificial emerger or surface nymph when the water is covered with natural duns – confirmation that an outstanding primary stimulus such as the fly's posture can over-ride a well established search-image. Al Caucci says what makes his Compara-Dun and Compara-Emerger so effective is simply the lack of a hackle. He says this alone contributes the essential aspect of vulnerability. This is not a new idea in itself. Ogden's old Gold Ribbed Hare's Ear is the prototype of the modern no-hackle dry fly, and very early European trout flies commonly had no hackle. In several contemporary versions, the GRHE is still among the great takers of trout. Swisher and Richards based their groundbreaking efforts in fly design on the same essential aspect that Fran Betters exploited in his Haystack and Usual. Caucci derived his Compara-Dun on Betters' Haystack, which has been fooling the Au Sable trout for decades, a perfect example of the fly-fishing tradition at work. Swisher and Richards' Hair-wing No-hackle Paradun is for practical purposes identical to the Compara-Dun. All these flies are out of the same kennel. Simple and rugged, I'd fish them anywhere.

In To Rise a Trout, John Roberts is dismissive of the Compara-Dun because it does not give an adequate impression of a floating dun's body, and none of the leg signature, its 'footprint', on the surface. He's right about that. Roberts admits it catches trout but, he says, so would a cigarette butt. A tad harsh you might think, since the cigarette butt objection can really be applied to any design. Anyway, that's rather like criticising a butcher's shop for not selling cream cakes. Caucci and Nastasi do not intend the Compara-Dun to do what Roberts asks of it, that is, imitate the fully emerged or perfect subimago. In fact, the Compara-Dun does not really imitate anything in particular, but presents several essential triggers to predatory behaviour. LaFontaine considered it an absurd imitation but one of his favourite flies. Besides, the cigarette butt remark probably says more about the fish farm origins of the trout in some venerable English chalkstreams than it does of the effectiveness of the Compara-Dun.

In *The Trout and the Fly*, Clarke and Goddard support Vincent Marinaro's thesis that the body of the subimago is unimportant, and except for the tips of the upright wing and the impression of its legs in the surface film, the trout does not see much of a natural dun as it enters the perceptual window. Central to their new approach was their design for the Up Side Down Paradun, tied so the hook and body do not penetrate the surface, effectively destroying what they call the footprint of the perfect dun. The tail and hackle of their fly keep the upside down hook and body clear of the water. There is no doubt that a fly's posture and its visual effects in the surface are powerful triggers. Clarke and Goddard's footprint theory centres on presenting a strong stimulus to the trout's predatory response. The footprint thesis has a lot going for it. It's logical, and the USD Paradun undoubtedly catches lots of fish, but some of their conclusions are open to question.

I'm just not convinced that the hook is much of a problem. Even if the exposed hook might act as deterrent, which in my experience is very seldom, it can be over-ridden by the primary triggers in our fly's design. A trout cannot possibly understand what a hook is. If it could, the north English and Scottish tradition of fly tying, if not all artificial flies, would not exist. The River Clyde and Tummel style wet flies are essentially a bare hook, a wisp of silk or dubbing and a single turn of hackle. These minimalist wet flies were designed for maximum effectiveness, by professional anglers on hard-fished public rivers, for small but mature trout that are notoriously hard to fool. It is well to be reminded of that cranky old market fisherman, W.C. Stewart, who regarded twelve pounds of trout a 'required' bag, every day. At three to the pound, that's a lot of trout from streams that received far more pressure than they do today.

The River Tummel style wet spider is all hook. With no surface distortion to mask it, the trout have a clear view of a wet fly's make-up. It begs the question as to why trout on one river should react to a rather distorted sight of the hook on a dry fly, while trout on another river,

Sometimes things go really well. Hooked up on the Mataura   *photo: Margaret Mitchell*

presumably just as wary, will take a wet fly with a clearly visible hook. In *Emergers*, Swisher and Richards describe the opportunism of trout during the massive behavioural drift of caddis pupae and other invertebrates, occasions when you might expect the fish to be at their *most* selective. They say, 'Although fish may feed extensively on the drift, they are at the same time opportunistic, feeding on other available insects that may be present in great numbers – insects not found in the drift'. This is demonstrably true, but is in direct conflict with the basic premise of the selective trout theory. Are we to accept that selective behaviour is restricted exclusively to dry flies?

Scottish Trout Flies, published in 1966, is a remarkable little book, one of the few that analyse the Scottish traditions of fly design. Lawrie made some telling observations regarding fly design that are universal in application. Discussing the extreme austerity of the River Tummel style wet fly, he encapsulates a theory of trout behaviour that seems right on target today. He writes, 'The Tummel fly, in fact, seems to lend support to a theory that provided a fly is lightly dressed and correct in form and general colouration, and is fished at the proper water level so that it is noticed, *trout will see what they wish to see and accept such a fly on that basis*' (italics mine). On the face of it this may not seem especially profound, but it is possibly the most important thing we can understand about trout behaviour and fly design. I don't think trout 'wish' anything, and would maybe substitute the word 'anticipate', but if you put Lawrie's theory against the behavioural ecologist's prey/search-image concept there is not a hair's width of difference between them. In fact, Lawrie's idea was contemporaneous with Nikolaas Tinbergen's groundbreaking theory of the search-image. It accounts for several hundred years of fly-fishing success and still holds water, even after trout got smart.

The almost incredible success on very technical rivers of the San Juan River style bloodworm patterns, simply thread wrapped up a hook shank, is another example of trout seeing what they expect to see. The no-hackle epoxy and 'anorexic' buzzer designs recently developed for British stillwaters are just as extreme. With close-up underwater scrutiny the fish could easily compare these flies to the natural, if they had the cognitive capability to make such a comparison. It's clear that the very visible hook is over-ridden by some essential feature of this simple design, and that the fly accords roughly with the trout's generalised and inclusive search-image. Incidentally, employing the induced-take technique, Oliver Kite famously demonstrated that trout readily accepted a bare hook, a response triggered solely by its movement. It is worth noting the similarity between a bare hook and the curved posture of the natural chironomid pupa.

If the only aspects of a dry fly clearly visible to a trout are its wing-tips and whatever parts penetrate the surface, first observed by Ward and Mottram, among others, early in the twentieth century, and backed up by the observations of Marinaro, Clarke and Goddard, it seems to me that more thought should be given to exploiting these two primary features rather than fighting the hook's tendency to penetrate the surface. John Roberts admits that the tail of the standard dry fly bears no resemblance to the tails of the natural dun, which is probably not even seen by the trout. Despite the fact that no healthy dun rides the surface with its tail in the water, Roberts defends the use of the hackle fibre tail in the construction of dun-imitating dry flies, including the USD Paradun, on the pragmatic grounds that it is necessary to support the body of the fly above the surface. Right about here, in the effort to make reality fit the theory, the old exact imitation dry fly concept goes pear-shaped.

Clarke and Goddard correctly point out that, in actual fishing situations, your orthodox dry fly is often fishing awash, the hook and body penetrating the surface. Like a little life preserver, the nice expensive genetic hackle supports the body, suspended hook-down in the meniscus. Even when treated with floatant, the hook and hackle tips usually penetrate the meniscus. In practice, even the USD Paradun will often float with its body in the surface film, but it still works, like many of our impressionistic flies. This is only a problem if, like Halford, we believe it to be a bad thing. Even when badly cocked, not floating as it was designed, the USD Paradun falls roughly within the range of shapes and sizes that the trout recognises as prey. It conforms to the trout's search-image, more or less.

The posture of all parachute and no-hackle duns is not really that of a dun at all, but either an emerger at the moment of ecdysis, a 'stillborn' dun, or a cripple. John Roberts recognises this in *To Rise A Trout*, but discusses it in terms of the importance of representing the legs of the perfect dun. Although he does not state it so baldly, it could be inferred that trout select the perfect subimago in preference to emergers, stillborns and cripples. This just does not seem reasonable and is something I've never witnessed. Too often, I've watched rafts of available duns being completely ignored by trout for that to make sense. If the duns were a preferred prey, trout would certainly take advantage of such a plentiful food source as long as it was available. They often don't, giving rise to the idea that the trout have become sated. A trout packed to the gills with mice or stickleback fry is one thing, but I've never seen a trout so stuffed with duns that it quit eating. Usually, they keep rising until the hatch is finished.

I have the utmost respect for Roberts, Clarke and Goddard, so I hope my remarks are taken in a friendly spirit of debate, but to my mind the approach in *The Trout and the Fly* was conflicted by its preoccupation with the dun. Although I am sure it works, I think the rationale behind their USD Paradun was barking up the wrong tree. It's the same tree that Swisher and Richards surrounded back in 1971, in *Selective Trout*. Swisher and Richards base what they refer to as a scientific approach on a single premise: that close imitation is the most important factor in getting a successful response from a trout. They put close-copy imitation well ahead of what they call anglers' excuses regarding presentation. As a hard-core presentationist and impressionist, I'd argue that surface penetration and a clearly presented body outline in the meniscus, historically regarded as bad form by Halfordian dry fly men, is why most conventional dry flies work at all - not because they make even a passable imitation of a fully emerged dun.

Roberts says that Swisher and Richards are attempting to do the impossible, catch 100% of the trout. He not only accepts that some trout become preoccupied with duns but takes the uncharacteristically defeatist position that a percentage of such selective trout are simply uncatchable. To me, this seems to be at cross-purposes with his support for Clarke and Goddard's USD Paradun, a design specifically aimed at the *most* difficult of selective trout. To be fair, I suspect that John Roberts is actually a closet presentationist, well aware that some trout are so spooky as to be practically uncatchable, and with trout like that better imitation just doesn't cut it. His uncatchable trout are just too spooky to approach in daylight with a fly rod.

Science often has 'strong' and 'weak' versions of theories, a strong theory being one that has the most counter-intuitive and far reaching implications. On regularly fished English chalk streams and American limestone creeks where the selective-trout concept was developed, trout have been observed to rise, inspect and reject dry flies that fail to meet their critical scrutiny. Although it is always closely linked to trout wariness and fishing pressure, this behaviour has been popularly interpreted as a display of suspicion toward our fly, that it is not a genuine insect. Moreover, the so-called educated trout is understood to be *choosing* between types of insect for some reason. Not only does our artificial have to look lifelike, it must look like it belongs to a specific species in detail – we must accurately 'match the hatch'. If that isn't enough, these fastidious and suspicious fish choose to eat only those insects that present the footprint of the perfectly formed, adult subimago, or dun. Since it asks us to accept such a high degree of awareness, rationality and preference in the trout, we might call this the strong version of selective trout theory.

To some extent, since the observers have been anglers of the highest calibre, I must bow to their expertise, but the sheer number of different designs and patterns proven to be successful on wary and selective trout augers heavily against the strong version of the selective trout theory. In 1921, G.E.M. Skues made a point of illustrating *The Way Of A Trout With A Fly* with a photograph depicting ten very different regional fly designs, all intended as imitations of the same natural dun, hatching at the same time on rivers around the country. This is not surprising in a country where differences in the local spoken dialect are noticeable between river valleys, but thinking such local differences extend to the trout in those rivers is maybe stretching things too far. When you note the considerable variation in modern flies designed to represent identical insects, very successful flies at that, the selective trout concept gets even more interesting.

It's undeniable that trout key their feeding response to particular prey and sometimes reject our flies, especially in strong hatch situations, but there are better explanations for a trout's refusal than its suspicion that the fly is a fake. One likely explanation is that our fly lacks the essential confirming triggers, including the most important of all, signs of life. Another is that our fly has simply not been noticed. A dead drift presentation means we must depend on the visual

The DHE has proven to be an excellent searching fly when there is no hatch

stimuli in our fly's design. Setting aside my presentationist excuses for the moment, I prefer to describe what appears as suspicion and discrimination in terms of much simpler stimulus-response behaviour – the search-image concept. For opportunistic, generalised predators such as trout, even when keyed to a particular food-form, their search-image must necessarily be a broad one, with 'fuzzy boundaries' if you will, and the number of successful fly designs in existence supports this argument.

Maybe I am making too much out of nothing here, but the idea that trout on hard-fished waters have wised up to artificial flies to the point that they reject the fly because they see the hook, remember and associate certain patterns with being hooked, or reject the PMD spinner because of an incorrect number of tails, is surprisingly prevalent among fly-fishers today. As if fly-fishing wasn't difficult enough, anglers commonly speak of educated, or even 'PhD' trout. This kind of thing must be pretty intimidating to a newbie presumptuous enough to square off with a spring creek rainbow for the first time, and they could hardly be blamed if they decided to take up golf at their first refusal. Having no neocortex in the physical make-up of its brain, necessary for such cognitive judgements, how the trout can understand the function of a hook remains to be explained, at least to my satisfaction, but we can allow that the hook might sometimes conflict with an established search-image. In principle, at least, this makes some sense.

What doesn't make sense is the implication that the selective trout will scrutinise and pass up our fake dun because it doesn't achieve the footprint of the ideal dun, and then proceed to choose *only* perfectly formed natural duns, or an artificial that more closely imitates a perfect dun. It may happen occasionally, but stretches the general usefulness of the selective trout concept too far for my lights, especially when Roberts himself explains that the effectiveness of the no-hackle duns is due to the fact that a trout preoccupied with duns will almost never pass up the vulnerable natural emerger, still-born dun or cripple. If he believes this to be the case, why damn the no-hackle dun with such faint praise? There is a conflict here, and I think it's the result of what researchers call theory perseverance.

To dry fly purists, a truly convincing imitation of the ephemerid dun is a kind of holy grail. There's nothing wrong with that, but we're really talking about a matter of preference. It is one's own business if he chooses to narrow the objectives to that extent, to make the pursuit more interesting and challenging. However, if we take the pragmatic approach, whether or not trout take duns, even if they occasionally become preoccupied with them, is immaterial if you want to catch them on a surface fly. Given an acceptable presentation, the thing that makes a truly difficult trout possible for the fly-fisher is its hardwired susceptibility to the vulnerable emerging, crippled or spent insect.

It's not that trout don't take the natural duns – they obviously do – it's just that trout will almost always eat the imperfect and helpless insect if it's available. A predator's behaviour, however inscrutable to us, must be adaptive if the animal is to survive. If the selective trout concept has validity it must surely rest squarely on this biological axiom. A trout that has developed feeding habits so narrow that it eats *only* fully emerged subimagos when emergers are available has to be the exception that proves the rule. This will only be the case where the dun is on the water in such numbers, and for such an extended period of time, that the trout has narrowed its search-image to accommodate only those triggers presented by the dun (such its footprint). This singular behaviour is not enough to base one's approach to dry fly fishing. In fact, I've wasted so much effort in presenting dun imitations to trout that only *appeared* to be taking duns that I've begun to question the extent they actually do eat them.

LaFontaine mentions a study that found twenty emerging nymphs for each dun taken during a hatch. This ratio improved in favour of the duns as the hatch progressed, to a point where the trout were taking 40% duns to 60% emergers. The increase in the percentage of duns eaten is logical. The emergers become scarcer as the emergent phase of the hatch approaches its end, so it is possible that some trout may switch to the most available food source – the remaining duns. It stands to reason that switching to a good dun imitation in the later stages of a hatch will sometimes catch some extra fish, but it is also true that as the food gets scarcer and harder to catch the larger fish will likely have ceased feeding – the law of diminishing returns. Big trout may stay on the fin where the dun remains on the water in large numbers, but I've seen big rafts of duns totally ignored on countless occasions. For a preferred food-form this is curious to say the least.

Moreover, a trout's search-image might shift from the emerger to the dun, but once preoccupied with a specific food-form they often take considerable time to adjust to another. One explanation for all those ignored duns is that the trout, keyed to the emerger, has not adjusted to regarding them as food – the duns do not fit its established search-image. The same applies to a fall of spent spinners, where trout often appear to be at their most selective. The trout's search-image centres on the size, and the distinctive body and wing profile of the spinner in the meniscus. Fishing a high-floating hackled dry fly is usually hopeless. Even on spring

Mike Wyatt bends a rod on an Alberta rainbow

creeks and chalkstreams up to 90% of the trout's food will be subsurface, which means emergers, duns and terrestrials combined represent the remaining 10%. There is a place for some special imitations with perfect footprints, for the occasional situation where a trout has become exclusively preoccupied with duns, but I think of it as a minor tactic for special occasions.

To develop a working schema for fly-fishing it is not necessary, or possible, to have all the answers to why a trout takes a fly. In the absence of a full-blown theory, you can at least adopt a few working rules of thumb that allow you to go forth and fish with confidence. My rule of thumb for trout fly design is that trout do not take our dry flies because they mimic accurately the appearance or footprint of the perfect insect, but precisely because they don't. Traditional dry flies work probably because they look enough like incomplete, damaged and above all, vulnerable insects.

The Grey Duster is a simple British hackle pattern that many old hands reach for when the trout start to rise to a hatch of Mayfly. Fifty years ago, Courtney Williams wrote in *A Dictionary of Trout Flies* that he regarded it as better than any specific mayfly imitation. His appraisal was based on empirical evidence, not a fly-tier's theory. Williams admitted that he did not understand why the Duster worked so well in a hatch situation, echoing Halford's annoyance with the dry

Gold Ribbed Hare's Ear. John Roberts acknowledges the Duster's effectiveness in his *Guide to River Trout Flies*, although he admits a preference for a parachute-hackled version. Parachute hackles have largely displaced the conventional collar hackle in North American dry flies, even on old American favourites like the Adams. The parachute-hackled dry fly presents the body of the fly in the surface, like a partially-emerged dun or nymph, a crippled dun, or a spent spinner. Incidentally, in *River Trout Flies*, Roberts also treats the parachute hackle with faint praise. You get the feeling that he relegates it to second-class status, again for not being a good imitation of the perfect dun, although he allows that it does a good job of suggesting the emerger.

In 1947, W.H. Lawrie, a particularly good observer of trout behaviour, produced *The Book of the Rough Stream Nymph*. In it he says, there is 'an important distinction between the manner the hatching dun floats and the way the dun floats after discarding the nymphal shuck. However superficial the distinction may seem to the angler, it is almost certainly appreciated by the trout, and the hatching dun, partly emerged from the shuck, floats with only the head and shoulder parts through the surface film, the remainder of the nymphal casing being below or in the surface film…No doubt many a badly cocked dry fly has been accepted by trout as a dun emerging from the shuck, although the deliverer of the fly may not have suspected it.' It appears that old Lawrie was on to the search-image idea twenty years before Tinbergen himself. This idea also occupied the lively mind of Skues, who described the act of ecdysis as 'without form… an awkward and fumbling occasion, affording the fish a much longer and better chance than is given by the dun.' We've got a pretty good idea today why the old Grey Duster works so well. The posture of the tail-less Duster is such that the dubbed fur body is usually riding in or penetrating the surface, presenting the prey-image of an emerging dun. A parachute or clipped hackle version just does it better.

Since *The Trout and the Fly* was published, John Goddard has concentrated more on the emergent phase, and I'd be surprised if Roberts hasn't done the same since he wrote *To Rise A Trout*. Goddard's Poly May, based on the revolutionary design of van Klinken's sunk-abdomen Klinkhåmer Special, is a good example, one that Goddard says he fishes *throughout* a hatch of duns. Goddard says the Poly May has accounted for most of his fish over recent seasons. Recently he has improved the Poly May by splitting the upright wing, which he considers a significant trigger, and he calls the new version the JG Emerger. All this thinking is tending in one direction, but we're back on the same old road.

From inspection of stomach contents, Mottram observed almost a century ago that even sophisticated chalkstream trout would eat bits of stream debris: seeds, bits of straw, etc. Where that fits into the selective trout concept is hard to say, but despite what we like to believe about the intelligence of our quarry, when a trout rejects a fly it is certainly not out of suspicion. As Brian Clarke points out, a trout doesn't reason, it simply recognises a fly as food or not. So, even the notoriously fussy trout of the Idaho's Henry's Fork are not really being selective in the way we anglers have described it, they are just so preoccupied with a specific phase of an abundant hatch that they don't recognise anything that is out of its narrow search-image context. Think of it this way; doughnut… doughnut… doughnut… doughnut… enchilada?

If a fish rejects what appears to be a reasonably good artificial, I tend to think it's because I've caused the fly to behave unnaturally in some way. If it behaves naturally, a fly that incorporates the three essential aspects of size, shape and posture is likely to be eaten. For the trout to recognise it as food, presentation of the fly has to mimic the behaviour of the natural. A big factor in refusals, often attributed to some defect in the fly, is unseen 'micro-drag' (unseen by the angler, that is). A suggestion of life is one thing but, if you think about it, seeing your burger suddenly start moving off your plate would probably make you hesitate too (Um…cheque please!). Another factor in what appears to be refusals is that the trout, situated high in the water column with an extremely narrow perceptual window, just hasn't seen the fly. Rene Harrop, doyen of Henry's Fork trout hunters, has said as much. Even at the height of trout selectivity during the summer PMD hatch, Harrop advises Henry's Fork anglers to not immediately blame their fly when a trout refuses it. Presuming it is of roughly the right size and basic shape, they should have confidence in it and make repeated and better presentations.

4. Tying for vulnerability
I: The Deer Hair Emerger
The Compara-Dun and no-hackle variations on that design have been an integral part of my main surface trout battery for many years. In fact, when heading for strange waters I've always made sure my boxes were stuffed with them and no-hackle Deer Hair Sedges in different sizes and shades. Just to round things out, I throw in some simple hackle dries like the Blue Upright, Grey Duster and Red Quill (for duns and making clipped hackle spinners); and a few good all-rounders like the CDC & Elk, Grizzly Palmer, Red Tag or Rob's Dry, clipped semi-palmered variants of the Brown Hackle Peacock. These fly styles will cover practically any surface situation and I know I'll catch fish anywhere with these flies. The only gap in this otherwise foolproof selection was a rugged, reliable, all-round emerger design that could be tied easily and cheaply and would make a difference in a hatch.

The Compara-Dun, Swisher and Richards' no-hackle flies, and for that matter all parachute-hackled duns, represent emergers and stillborn duns, not the perfect duns for which they are generally used. I wondered if the Compara-Dun could be improved, enhancing the aspect of vulnerability by getting its abdomen to penetrate the surface, Klinkhåmer style. The Klinkhåmer Special, originated by Dutch tier Hans van Klinken, took European fly-fishing by surprise in the late eighties. Conventional wisdom had it that big grayling and wary, selective trout tended toward small flies and tiny nymphs. Van Klinken discovered that his strange looking fly pulled fish in almost any situation, in startlingly large sizes. The special ingredient was no mystery; it was obviously the fly's sunk abdomen. What van Klinken describes as the fly's 'iceberg effect' represents the insect at its most vulnerable, floating just beneath the surface, about to begin the process of *ecdysis*.

Maybe just as importantly, the submerged abdomen enables the trout to see the fly sooner, and from further off. Behavioural ecologists have demonstrated that animals will respond more vigorously to artificial stimuli than they do to natural ones. Young gulls, for example, instinctively peck at a red spot on the adult's beak to obtain food. If you present a red pencil to the chicks, they will peck much more aggressively at the pencil than at the natural beak. It's possible that the deeply sunk, over-sized abdomen, including its clearly visible hook, acts as such a supernormal stimulus. Klinken originally tied his fly on the deeply curved Yorkshire grub hook, but hook manufacturers have since produced shapes specifically for the Klinkhåmer. The enthusiasm shown by fish for this design prompted some good anglers to claim that the parachute hackled Klinkhåmer Special is the best dry fly ever designed. Praise indeed, but make no mistake, the Klinker is a great fly.

Practically speaking, it's not important that a fly do more than present an indistinct and roughly generalised impression. After all, an emerging mayfly or caddis is something of a mess and presents a wide variety of forms during ecdysis. Reflecting this diversity of form, among the thousands of fly patterns there are hundreds of extremely good catchers of supposedly selective trout. On any given day, during a hatch on any great trout river, a survey would find a surprising range of flies that had caught trout. During a specific hatch on difficult water like Henry's Fork, there will be dozens of successful flies. Every time one of these flies does well, the angler believes the particulars of that fly to hold the secrets of his success. Although the best of them will probably share some essential features, many successful flies will be quite different in detail. This suggests that beyond some essential triggers, especially size and posture, the particulars of any fly are relatively unimportant. As long as the fly presents a reasonable prey-image, the difference in success rate is primarily due to the angler's presentation skills. In fact, when you look at the design of the flies recommended in *Selective Trout*, they too are simplified caricatures of the natural rather than slavish attempts at perfect mimicry.

Frederick Halford, the original colour and pattern guy, was responsible for the hackle fetish that today has become a multi-million chicken industry. Like today's cult of the Catskill style, Halford simply varied the hues of hackles and bodies on his rigidly codified dry fly model, to the extent that he relegated even that great trout catcher, the Gold Ribbed Hare's Ear, to non-U status because it didn't have a nice stiff hackle. He admitted that he couldn't explain why the trout showed such enthusiasm for the GRHE during a hatch of duns, so he just ignored it. Now, that's theory perseverance for you.

Over the latter half of the twentieth century some good anglers, and in some cases teams of good anglers, started thinking about the design of flies rather than pattern. Vincent Marinaro, W.H. Lawrie, Swisher and Richards, Caucci and Nastasi, John Goddard, Gary LaFontaine, Rene Harrop, and Hans van Klinken stand out as innovative dry fly designers. There are excellent and creative designers in France, Spain and Scandinavia, where there are remarkable divergences in

Drag is possibly the biggest factor for what we regard, mistakenly, as 'selective' behaviour

tradition, but whose books are not available in English. All these people have a common concern with form rather than metaphysics – in other words, an approach based on observation and reason, rather than convention, chauvinism and art.

Doing some concentrated seeing, putting in more river time than is usually possible while working up his 'general theory of attraction', LaFontaine brought further clarity and many questions to our thoughts on fly design in *The Dry Fly – New Angles*. He neatly reduced the sequence of a trout's response to a fly to *recognition*, *confirmation* and *acceptance*, claiming that recognition requires one primary aspect such as the wing for the trout to become interested in a fly. Marinaro had already proven that the wing was a primary trigger in extensive on-stream testing, findings backed up by Swisher and Richards. LaFontaine then looked for a secondary trigger to *confirm* the artificial as food to the trout. He studied the surface effects caused by the fly's hackle and body in the surface film (its footprint). He was well aware of the potential of having the body hang below the film, although, curiously, he did not make much of this feature when putting together his go-to selection.

My criteria for a great fly are that it is made of cheap, abundant and easily acquired materials, is easy to tie, and above all, catches a lot of fish in a wide range of circumstances. I regard flies to be just as important and just as expendable as ammunition to a shooter, but a great fly should have some durability built in. Excellent flies as they are, most parachute hackled, or CDC emergers just don't meet all of these criteria. For me, parachute flies are fragile, relatively complex, and fairly tricky to tie. Good hackle is expensive, and I don't like the blunt profile of those shaving brush polypropylene wing-posts, a fly-tier's trope that, to my eye at least, spoils an otherwise good prey-image. CDC is kind of fussy stuff, it's quite expensive and hard to get in any quantity, at least compared to deer hair and hare's masks. Hans Weilenmann says there are appropriate types of CDC feathers for different applications, and there are damn few CDC feathers on a duck's bum. Not least, it slimes up after only a fish or two and needs work to get it floating again. Anyway, for the price of a couple of top quality capes and a big bag of CDC feathers, you can buy enough deer hair and hare's masks to re-upholster your living room.

My rather prosaically named Deer Hair Emerger (DHE), incorporates the significant triggers of two proven designs, combining the high vulnerability posture of the Klinkhåmer Special's sunk abdomen with the ruggedness and ease of tying of Fran Betters' Haystack and his snowshoe hare Usual. It's not a pretty fly, but my fondness for its pedestrian homeliness grows with each trout that tries to eat it. To anglers who believe a fly just doesn't look right without a hackle, the DHE is plug ugly, but my idea of what constitutes a good looking trout fly has changed.

Where the DHE strays from the basic Compara-Dun/Haystack formula is in the tail-less, curved abdomen and the rather spiky hare's mask thorax. Like John Roberts, I've never been entirely happy with the way the Compara-Dun presents its body to the trout, but for different reasons. The Compara-Dun sits flush in the surface, propped by the fan-shaped wing and widely flared tail filaments. Al Caucci claims the Compara-Dun looks especially vulnerable to a trout because of the absence of a hackle, and I agree. The DHE's sunk abdomen does a better simulation of the most vulnerable phase of the insect's metamorphosis, the moment of ecdysis. I prefer to keep it as simple as possible. Getting floatant on to a tail or shuck might interfere with the way the abdomen sinks and hangs, so I leave those off. The fish don't seem to care about such niceties as much as we do, although I'm still considering whether the DHE can be improved by the addition of a secondary trigger. John Goddard incorporates a trailing translucent shuck in his JG Emerger and regards it as an important secondary stimulus. To my

There is usually no trout activity if there is no insect activity

mind, the sparkling material used for these shucks is at least as distracting as an exposed hook. On the other hand, old J.C. Mottram opined back in 1921 that the best way to represent the transparent parts of the natural was to omit them altogether – let the trout fill in the blanks, so to speak.

The DHE is effective despite the visibility of the hook, and it is possible that the glinting hook point looks to the trout like part of the insect's shuck, maybe a stray leg. By the way, for a good idea of what an emerging mayfly or caddis actually looks like, *Selective Trout* has some excellent photographs. We should keep in mind that the emergence from nymph to adult is a process, and throughout its metamorphosis a single insect presents a variety of shapes and postures. The DHE and Klinkhåmer Special are effective in unusually large sizes for trout and grayling. The natural emerger's sunken abdomen with its attached shuck is a very strong trigger to a predatory attack. The exaggerated sunk abdomen on these big flies probably acts as a supernormal stimulus and the clearly visible hook may even enhance this effect. For me, this explains the age-old mystery of why a trout will accept an artificial fly when there are plenty of perfectly good naturals on the water. The case for more realistic imitation isn't exactly watertight.

I use natural fur for the abdomen of the DHE. Some furs are pretty oily and tend to float, but hare underfur, seal, or a combination of those two materials tends to soak up water pretty quickly. I tie a full seal's fur abdomen for chunky caddis emergers, and soft hare or muskrat underfur for the slimmer *ephemerids*. LaFontaine believed that the halo effect created by an emerging nymph is an important secondary or confirming trigger, and the translucent seal's fur provides a good simulation of that distinctive feature. For added ruggedness, I use the tag end of the tying thread as a counter-wound rib on the dubbed abdomen.

The DHE's wing is more like that of Betters' Haystack than the flared arc wing of the Compara-Dun. The deer hair permits good light transmission while nicely breaking up the outline, as opposed to the blunt and solid shaving brush wing-post on many parachutes and emerger patterns, or the opaque feather wing-slips of Swisher and Richards Para-duns. The high wing is certainly noticeable by the trout, but just as importantly, it gives my aging eyes something to track on the water. I often use a white deer hair wing for fast water on sunny days, a dark one in overcast or dusk conditions on smooth water. LaFontaine observed that a white wing reflects the ambient light on any given day and almost always does well, whatever fly is on the water. For small sizes, fur from the foot of a snowshoe hare ties in nicely and floats beautifully (the SHE?). I like to think that the DHE has *two* primary triggers going for it, the sunk abdomen of the emerger and the upright wing of the dun, so, like the Compara-Dun, it doesn't specifically imitate either phase. The sunk abdomen, a primary trigger and probably a supernormal stimulus, announces itself to the trout long before the wing comes into view. When the upright wing enters the window, it confirms 'prey', stimulating the trout's predatory 'functional response'. The fish zeroes-in, locks-on and attacks – selects if you prefer – the artificial fly among the naturals.

The primary role of a dry fly hackle is floatation, so the hare's mask thorax means the no-hackle DHE usually requires some floatant, especially in fast water. To get the DHE to fish correctly, I apply the floatant only to the wing and thorax, carefully avoiding the abdomen and hook, which must penetrate the surface. Like old W.H. Lawrie, I want the DHE to float with only its wing and shoulder parts above the surface film. To make sure the thorax rides hull-down in the film, I apply floatant to only the topside of the thorax.

Once you have worked out your hypothesis of why a fly should work, following Swisher and Richards' scientific model, to generate a working theory and draw some conclusions you should achieve some 'replicable findings'. The DHE has been road-tested in western Canada, New

Zealand, Scotland, and the USA. This simple fly not only works – plenty of good flies work – but it has edged some excellent flies in almost every situation, and it has been fished in very good company. Everyone says this kind of thing about a favourite go-to fly, but the DHE has repeatedly made the difference for me, even during a fall of spinners. During an emergence, in appropriate sizes and colours, I'd confidently put it against any pattern. In the absence of a hatch it has so much built-in fish appeal that I don't hesitate to stick with it throughout the day.

Durability is a concern in a good design. I'm not a production tier and usually have only a handful of the fly that's working, especially once my pals cotton on to it and start raiding my fly box. On an extended trip to distant waters you don't want your hot flies unravelling. Several years ago, on New Zealand's Mataura, I took twelve biggish trout in a row, all over two pounds, on one size sixteen DHE, and it still went back in the box. I've never seen a parachute hackled fly withstand that kind of punishment, none I've tied at any rate. On a recent trip to British Columbia's Elk Valley, I got the number of big toothy cutthroat trout up to over a dozen on several occasions, only to lose the fly before I could go any further with the experiment. In every case, the fly was in perfect working order when it was popped off, tough as old boots. With a snowshoe hare wing the fly is, for practical purposes, indestructible.

The DHE with a plain hare's ear abdomen is deadly on the west-slope cutthroats, beginning to lose their normal air-head enthusiasm for anything that floats and ignoring flies that didn't look right – that is, an insect of the appropriate size, shape and behaviour. Over two five week trips in 2001 and again in 2003, I had the chance to put the DHE against some good flies, fished by some very good anglers. The sunk-abdomen no-hackle emerger certainly had an edge over other surface patterns I saw fished. Parachute hackled emerger patterns might have worked as well, but I doubt if they could have worked better than the no-hackle jobs, and it is unlikely that they would not have withstood all that punishment.

This no-hackle business will not be music to the ears of producers of fine dry fly hackle, but we're talking fish catching here, not fly-tying as an art. Hackles are important, but the conventions of style will undoubtedly continue to influence fly design anyway, keeping the big farms in business no matter how popular no-hackle designs become. The DHE falls into line with Fran Betters' concept of rugged simplicity and Al Caucci's views on vulnerability in fly design. I haven't used a conventionally hackled dry fly for many seasons, and I'm catching more fish than ever. Nothing has changed in my approach other than the flies I'm using, so the increase in my catch rate has got to be due to the flies, not some sudden leap in fishing skill that I can really brag about. A few (sometimes a lot) more fish can be accounted for in several ways, but I really believe the little extra vulnerability built into the prey-image of the DHE has made a difference for me. I think the half-submerged fly triggers the predator's hard-wired functional response to helpless prey. For me, since getting serious about designing for vulnerability, dry fly fishing has got simpler and better.

DHE (Deer Hair Emerger)
Hook: Kamasan B-100, or similar light wire, down-eyed, curved shank, emerger style hook.
Wing: medium to fine deer hair. Colour and shade according to naturals and light conditions (white or black for hi-viz versions). Snowshoe hare foot fur for small sizes (16-20).
Abdomen: natural fur; fine underfur for *ephemerids*, bulky hare's mask and/or seal's fur for sedge pupae. Colour mix as appropriate.
Rib: tag-end of tying thread.
Thorax: spiky hare's mask, from the front of the face.

1.Tie in a bunch of fine to medium deer hair, well back from the eye of the hook. Wrap down the hair butts and take the thread around the hook bend, leaving a long tag-end of thread for the rib.

2. Dub the tying thread and wrap to the wing. Bring the tag-end of tying thread up in a counter-wrapped rib, tied in ahead of the wing. For better floatation in fast water, flare the deer hair Compara-Dun style.

3. Take the tying thread to the hook eye and dub with spiky hare's mask (wax helps). Wind the dubbing *back* to the wing base, forcing the wing into an upright attitude, then return the thread to the eye with two snug turns through the dubbing, binding and flaring the guard hair fibres. Whip finish.

II: The no-hackle Deer Hair Sedge

In *What The Trout Said*, Datus Proper rates the no-hackle hair-wing sedge as one of his two indispensable designs. Tied with an elk or deer hair wing, it is one of the most widely used flies on earth. The deer-hair caddis (or sedge to Europeans) is not really a specific pattern, since it has many variations in colour and body material. Some variations sport hackles, both collar style and palmered. The deer-hair caddis design needs no introduction to British fly-fishers; Troth's Elk Hair Caddis is the best known of several such patterns. Because of the sharper outline of the abdomen, and its tendency to fish half-submerged in the surface film, I rate the no-hackle version higher than Al Troth's palmered design. The no-hackle DH Sedge is my sheet anchor on Scottish brown trout lochs, and pretty well anywhere that I expect trout with opportunistic feeding habits, which is pretty well everywhere. While the DHE is intended primarily as a static imitation for the emergent phase of a hatch, the Deer Hair Sedge fulfils more of an attractor role. It has a broader remit and does excellent duty in a variety of situations. For me, there is no better fly for the bob position in loch-style fishing for wild brown trout, bar none.

I grew up with this fly, or something very like it. There is an account by my Uncle Hornets of the genesis of a favourite trout fly for the south-western Alberta streams. His name is actually Ernest, but after being nearly stung to death by yellowjackets as a child, for the rest of his life even his mother called him Hornets. His story is set on the upper reaches of the Oldman, at the confluence of several freestone streams in the Gap, a notch in the Livingston Range that funnels the combined waters onto the grassy south flank of the Porcupine Hills. We called this area the North Fork. In the early fifties, the roads into that country were just tracks, with grass and mountain wild flowers growing between the ruts. And the fishing? Well, 'unspoiled' does not really convey a true picture, and implies an awareness of even the possibility of loss. In the limitless dream that was western Canada at that time, this was trout fishing at its most innocent and sublime.

One thing I can say about south-western Alberta before fly-fishing attained its current popular cachet is that an angler had plenty of scope for solitary contemplation. From 1956, for twenty years, it seemed to me I had the eastern slope of the Rockies to myself. That's an exaggeration, of course, there were certainly some other fishermen sneaking around, but I'm sure I was on speaking terms with most of them. Many were members of Calgary's venerable Hook and Hackle Club, which I joined around 1960. Orville Griffith, Archie Malcolm, and Dave Leeman were influential guys from the club that I never once met while fishing. They were more your north-central watershed types, I guess. The men I actually fished with were my father and my uncles, Jack, Ernie and Wilf from the Crowsnest Pass, and a few of their pals, Fred Cox, Willie Gregory, Matty Parker, and Jerry Avoledo.

Bob Morton unhooks a west-slope cutthroat

I can remember my Uncle Jack, admittedly at the tail-out of a long night of drunken rhetoric, stating categorically that the female Jock Scott was *useless* on the North Fork. The Jock Scott, as you know, is an old Scottish Atlantic Salmon fly, named after a famous gillie and which bears no relation to anything that ever flew or swam, male or female. According to Jack, you could tell the female Jock Scott from the male by the white wing tips.

'The trout on the North Fork, you know what I mean, Bobby, won't even *look* at the female'.

We assumed it was the male that had the white, you know what I mean, tips. Uncle Jack had an infectious way of speaking, and by the end of a fishing trip we'd all be going 'you know what I mean' about three times a sentence. It drove my mother crazy.

The first deer hair caddis I ever saw, in 1958, was tied by Jerry Avoledo. He had been tying it for several years by then, and although there are several claims to authorship of the style, I don't know of an earlier version. Like many things, it is likely the case that a couple of guys came up with the same basic idea at roughly the same time. I do know that Avoledo came up with his in isolation, during the early fifties. It was, I assure you, a startling innovation to guys who thought in terms of female Jock Scotts. Avoledo was the fishing pal of my uncle Hornets. They fished all the south-west Alberta streams together or alone and what they didn't know about those watersheds wasn't worth knowing. Something I'll always regret is not finding out about the Chain Lakes, a series of big beaver ponds that existed before they dammed Willow Creek. Hornets knew and kept it to himself for forty years. Even in his eighties, he'd go all suspicious and circumspect when I'd mention it. I wanted to say, 'It's okay Hornets, you can tell me about the fishing in Chain Lakes now. They've been under two fathoms of water since 1966'.

Jerry's tying for what he called the 'Bucktail' was a simple fat body of orange wool – later he used chenille – a thick wing of mule deer body hair, and a brown hackle collar. Uncle Hornets had a hand in it. According to Hornets, he and Fred Cox were on the North Fork of the Oldman for an extended period of fishing and drinking. One afternoon, the fish were rising but unusually hard to catch. Hornets insists that the trout were taking tufts of thistle-down, being blown onto the water, although it's more likely to have been something that would sustain life. You are possibly beginning to appreciate the poetic turn of mind common to these characters, although you should probably factor in the hallucinogenic effect of serial campfire piss-ups.

By Hornets' account, Fred Cox considered a raw deer hide that Hornets had found nailed to the wall of a cabin, and in an inspired moment decided to match the hatch. Employing yellow wool and thread from his sweater, Fred whipped up what must have been a pretty crude imitation of a tuft of thistledown. It worked, so the legend goes, and they proceeded to make heap meat with that fly. Avoledo began producing his Bucktail on Hornets' request to tie a tidier, more durable version from Fred's prototype. Now, Uncle Hornets is no stranger to the embellished truth and would not let a good story suffer for lack of art, but for crude historical purposes precisely how and why the fly was conceived is probably of less importance than who first tied it with serious intent, and when.

Avoledo started to supply the fly to the local boys in the early fifties. By the time I first saw it, on the Crowsnest River in 1958, Jerry's fly was already a big hit on the Oldman and Castle watersheds. Jerry always called it a Bucktail, rather than an Elk Hair Caddis or Deer Hair Sedge, which lends some credence to my claim that he came up with it by himself. There may have been a similar fly in use out west at that time, but if it weren't original Avoledo would have undoubtedly used its proper name, like he did the Blue Upright and the Royal Coachman, or the Jock Scott for that matter. On the Crowsnest River in the fifties, a fly's provenance was not the issue it is now, and no one I knew would have even understood the concept of intellectual property.

It may just be another case, familiar to Canadians, of an American idea arriving by a kind of cultural osmosis, essentially the same process that results in bushmen wearing hubcaps as hats, but I don't recall seeing a deer or elk hair caddis pattern in the big fishing magazines for almost two decades. Nothing like it is featured in the revised edition of Ray Bergman's *Trout*, which admittedly has an eastern bias, and I don't remember seeing Troth's Elk Hair Caddis in those parts until the late seventies, at the earliest. However he came up with the pattern, Avoledo was certainly a couple of decades ahead of any Canadian commercial tier.

Al Troth claims he based his Elk Hair Caddis on Skues' Little Red Sedge, and as a stockist of English tied flies Jerry was maybe aware of that design too. At that time, nearly everybody in those parts was a deer hunter, so the sheer availability of deer hair would suggest it as a winging material without much prompting. I don't recall Jerry ever claiming the fly as his own invention, to which, if there's more than whisky fumes to that thistledown story, even Fred Cox and Uncle Hornets have a partial claim. Some old boys in the Crowsnest Pass still call Avoledo's deer hair fly a bucktail, with the certain exception of the folks at the fly shop just down the road from Jerry's old store. Back then, on those rivers, nobody ever fished a proper fish-imitating bucktail. Jerry's Bucktail was a dry fly.It was Jerry's Bucktail that got me started as a serious fly tier, in preparation to our annual visits to fish with my uncles in the Crowsnest Pass. I used to dread the first words I'd hear as we arrived at my granddad's house in Bellevue, Alberta, for our annual two-week fishing trip.

'Roll me a couple dozen Bucktails there, Bobby. Orange. And give 'em plenty of, you know what I mean, *wing*.'

In anticipation of these demands, I'd stock up in the weeks before each trip, but it was never enough. Once my uncles realised I was capable of significant production they began to supply their pals with the generosity of a Haida chief at the annual potlatch. I used to sit for whole afternoons at one end of my grandmother's kitchen table, rolling Bucktails. Granddad sat at the other end, with a tumbler of whisky and milk and a big can of Sportsman tobacco, rolling cigarettes. That experience was enough for me to eliminate fly-tying as a commercial enterprise, but I'm certain that tying flies has made me a better fly-fisherman. Jerry Avoledo's Bucktail provided something like a conceptual framework for my approach to fly-tying and fishing, working with general characteristics rather than slavish imitation of the natural. Fishing Jerry's Bucktail, I learned to love the surface fly, seeing a trout appear from nowhere and turn down with it, in water as clear as air.

Although I don't use it in its original form any more, Jerry's Bucktail is still a good fish catcher. The version I prefer these days doesn't employ a hackle and is more effective without it. Although Gary LaFontaine believed that no-hackle designs imitate the actual body profile of the natural maybe too closely, and preferred hackled flies for his waters, I have found otherwise, throwing in with the likes of Al Caucci and Datus Proper. I think the well-defined body silhouette, combined with one or more outstanding triggers like a wing or sunk abdomen, makes for a much more compelling design. The differences between my tying and that of several other deer-hair caddis patterns are small, and it's really just another variant of a standard pattern, identical in almost every respect to Datus Proper's version. To differentiate it from many others I just call my tying the Deer Hair Sedge, or DHS.

The wing does not vary much, except in the shade of deer hair employed and its degree of bulk or sparseness. I tie it longer than the wing on Troth's Elk Hair Caddis, in keeping with the actual proportions of the wings on a natural caddis, overhanging the abdomen. Unapologetically crude, the only part of this fly that requires thinking about is the body, and even that doesn't take much. The DHS fishes well in a wide range of circumstances depending on the colour and body profile. Over the years I've narrowed the colour variations down to about four. They all work, on their day, but I can't really say why for sure. The interesting thing is that a certain colour should make a difference at all, particularly when it doesn't seem to bear any relation to the colour of a natural fly on the water. Since anything below the surface gets a good look from the trout, my guess is that the body penetrates the meniscus to the extent that colour becomes significant. The all-round favourite for the northern Scottish lochs is unarguably the robust body of dark claret/black seal's fur dubbing.

Among the gang I fish with, this fly is inevitably in the bob position and goes simply by 'the sedge'. We just assume that means the dark claret seal's fur body and accept the undeniable fact that, in most conditions, the black/claret seal's fur mix works better than anything else. For my annual week in Sutherland, I fill a box with only the dark claret fly in a couple of sizes and another box full of colour variations: dark hare's mask, grass green, dirty mustard, and silver. Except for the dirty mustard, a mix of hare's mask and golden olive seal's fur, the other colours are straight seal's fur. Seal is the finest dubbing for this fly, combining bulk with a translucency not found in any other material, producing a nice 'halo' effect. It also soaks up water like a mop and sinks the body, probably the most important factor in the effectiveness of the Deer Hair Sedge.

The grass-green body is a true, intense Green Highlander hue, and why it works is beyond me. It has made the day on bright afternoons, for reasons known only to the trout. The Irish Green Peter makes use of a green body, but I really can't say that it's because of a similarity to the natural Green Peter sedge. In fact, a hot fly on the Irish loughs is a Red-Arsed Green Peter. LaFontaine's theory of attraction might have an explanation. He says that mid-day light has a lot of green in it, making a green body appear more intense. This doesn't really explain why a trout should be attracted to intense green in the first place, but he says that it's simply because they take notice of it in greenish mid-day light. He backs up this claim with the example of the lime-bodied Trude, which does so well on western streams at mid-day, and it's hard to argue against thousands of hours of river time. I haven't yet got around to giving a lime green seal's fur body a thorough try-out, but sooner or later I will. The Mottled Sedge, a popular Scottish caddis pattern tied with a chartreuse wool body and a palmered grizzly hackle, makes me think there might be something in it.

The hare's mask 'dirty mustard' mix makes more imitative sense, sort of, but in normal conditions on the Scottish lochs it doesn't work as well as the dark claret. The exception is a day when there is a lot of light, unfortunately few in the far north, when the brighter colours seem to make a difference. The plain hare's mask body is a good choice for clear water streams in western Canada, but for some reason is not as reliable on the peaty waters of Sutherland. Although it makes no sense to me, light clarets, reds, oranges and yellows, effectively half of the visible light spectrum, are comparatively ineffective on moorland lochs, which for me keeps the whole colour question open. I vary the degree of bulk in this fly. Sometimes I fish it very sparsely tied with only a few strands of deer hair over a skinny body of hare's ear. In a big wave on a lake, I'll use a robust body of seal's fur and a good thick shock of deer hair, for maximum disturbance.

Jerry Avoledo died a few years ago, and I understand that Jerry's Sportshop has lately been turned into a *faux* country-style Cappuccino bar. Old Uncle Hornets passed away recently too. Wherever they are now, maybe the trout are rising to thistledown.

The No-hackle Deer Hair Sedge:

Hook: Kamasan B-400, or similar light wire emerger style.

Body: seal's fur and/or hare's mask, mixed to the desired colour and shade. Suggestions: for Scottish and Irish lochs: 70-30% mix of black to dark claret; or 70% hare's mask to 30% golden olive SLF. On brighter days, a silver tinsel body can be excellent, sometimes with a fluorescent green tag. For western North American freestone streams, straight dubbed hare's mask is deadly.

Rib: tag end of tying thread, wound counter-wise through body from hook bend.

Wing: deer hair, bunched (stacked if desired). I usually use hair of a relatively light tone because it is easier to see on the water.

Head (or thorax): butts of deer hair, clipped to semi-muddler style.

Robbie McPhee about to release a bragging size South Island brownie   *photo: Bruce Masson*

South Island angler Robbie McPhee ties the Wee Muddler, a very good fly with some close similarities to the no-hackle Deer Hair Sedge. Bruce Masson and Keith Mitchell use this simple fly to great effect on the large wary browns of New Zealand's South Island, particularly during the summer Cicada hatch. An excellent, hi-visibility floater with a low-riding posture and clear body profile, this fly projects an excellent prey-image. Bruce thins his out pretty drastically before fishing and says it improves the fly significantly. He reckons it's because the trout on his rivers have seen the full version of the Wee Muddler too often. I'd suggest that by pruning the wing he's giving the Wee Muddler a more distinct body profile, for a more convincing prey-image.

McPhee's Wee Muddler (Cicada)
Hook: size 14 – 10, light wire dry fly.
Abdomen (1): dubbed seal's fur and possum mixture, shades of green, or to mixed to match a particular Cicada. Tied in at the bend to build up a thick rear portion of the abdomen, to themiddle of the hook shank.
First Wing: clump of medium deer hair, tied in at the middle of the shank, tips extending to just beyond the bend, butts trimmed and lashed down.
Abdomen (2): finish building abdomen, taking dubbing to near the hook eye, leaving enough space to tie in the over-wing.
Over-wing: another clump of deer hair, tied in to lay over the first wing. Butts trimmed to form a muddler style head.

III: the CDC & Elk

All dry flies have a signature or footprint, the disturbance pattern that the fly makes in the surface film of the water. The no-hackle DHE and DH Sedge are designed to exploit the fact that the bodies of most dry flies contact or penetrate the film and present to the trout an impression of an insect at its most vulnerable. The CDC & Elk is an excellent design by Hans Weilenmann incorporating the built-in floatability of cul de canard feathers and deer hair for a killing combination of visual triggers and a vulnerable posture. Its footprint is similar to that of the Compara-Dun and no-hackle Deer Hair Sedge, flush in the surface, but is supported and enhanced by the soft, mobile tendrils of CDC feather used as a body material rather than for the wing. Hans is a stickler for correctness, so pay attention, or else.

CDC & Elk Recipe (Hans Weilenmann)
Hook: tiemco 102Y #11 – #17 (or equivalent dry fly hook).
Thread: brown 6/0.
Body/hackle: CDC feather (Type 1).
Wing/head: Fine tipped deer hair.

1. Select a properly sized (Type 1) CDC feather. The longest barbs should be approximately two times the hook shank length. Hold the butt of the CDC feather with the fingers/thumb of your left hand, and draw the feather between thumb and index finger of your right hand toward the tip, bunching the tips together.

   Tie in the bunch, butt pointing backwards over the hook bend. Tie the feather down with two tight turns of thread, then slip a third turn under the tips to force them upward and follow with a fourth turn over the tips, just forward of the third turn, to lock the CDC barbs in place. Spiral-wrap the thread forward to eye, then wrap back one touching turn away from the hook eye.
2. Clamp the feather butt with hackle pliers and wind the CDC feather toward the eye in

touching turns. The rear half of the body resembles a dubbed body, but as you progress toward the eye more and more free barbs will stand out. Stroke these back with each turn. With a little practise, you will learn to arrive at the hook eye with only the bare part of the stem left.

Tie off the CDC feather with one or two tight turns of thread and unclip the hackle pliers. Do not trim yet. Tighten with another two turns of thread. The CDC butt will move with the thread, tightening further at the tie-off point. Trim the CDC butt.

3. Take a small amount of straight, fine-tipped mule deer hair. Look for undamaged tips with distinct colouration (dark tips with a lighter coloured band further down the hair) and a fairly steep taper to the hair, which makes for the distinct, rounded head on the CDC & Elk.

Even the hair tips in a stacker. Position the bunch of hair on top of the hook parallel to the hook shank. Measure the tips so the wing will be long enough to just reach the back of the hook.

Trim the butts square (perpendicular to the strands) with the front of the hook eye prior to tying in the wing.

Tie down the wing with two tight wraps of thread over the hair stubs. Make a third wrap with the thread, through the stubs, at a 45 degree angle. A fourth wrap goes under the stubs. Complete the fly with a whip-finish under the stubs and a little varnish. Aim for a neatly rounded head.

As the old saying goes, the man with one gun probably knows how to use it. Hans is not what you would call a strictly one-gun guy, but he tends to start and finish with this fly more often than not. The CDC & ELK is another impressionistic design that suggests no particular insect and incorporates some strong primary triggers and the lifelike mobility of CDC fibres. Anyone who has used the CDC & Elk regards it as a killer, and that includes some very expert anglers worldwide. I'd use it more often myself but for my laziness as a fly tier, and the not so freely available CDC feathers in its construction. Anyway, I've pretty well established the Deer Hair Sedge and the DHE as my main go-to flies. It's hard to change habits that have been reinforced by success, and I'm sure it's the same way with Hans.

Hans has some other deadly flies that should go into any angler's 'vulnerability' box. The CDC & Elk provides the basis of a 'concept' group that includes a cripple variant designed by Bruce Salzberg, and spent and diving versions by Hans. His Itty Bitty and Partridge and Olive Emergers both present an excellent prey image.

CDC & Elk Cripple (Bruce Salzberg)

Bruce Salzberg's variant of Hans' CDC & Elk is an excellent example of the extra stimulus of the sunk abdomen. He gives an account of its conception on the river one day. 'I was fishing a local stream a couple of summers ago, and having good success with the original CDC & Elk, but lost the last size 16 I had. I returned to the truck, where I keep a tying kit, only to find I had no size 16 dry fly hooks in the kit. I began to tie the fly using a light wire scud hook, which I believed would permit the body of the fly to suspend more under the film than the original. After wrapping the CDC feather, it occurred to me that I could get the body under the surface even more by reversing the wing. The result was a fly that enticed the fish to literally rocket off the bottom of the stream to take the fly, often coming completely out of the water. This rise form is usually associated with the take of a caddis pupa, which the fly suggests nicely; however, in smaller sizes, it has accounted for a number of fish during mayfly hatches. Because the body is intended to fish subsurface, a type 4 feather creates the desired effect, and small sizes can be tied using a few CDC fibers and the split thread technique.'

*The 'iceberg effect' –
photo: Hans van
Klinken*

IV: The Klinkhåmer Special

The reputation of this fly has spread rapidly and North American anglers have received it warmly. However, many so-called Klinkhåmers are just flies with sunk abdomens, and some that really are Klinkhåmers are being promoted under new names without credit. Hans van Klinken acknowledges several others who arrived at similar designs around the same time. Unknown to van Klinken, the 'Paratilt', by American tier Mike Monroe, was published in 1979, four years before the Klinkhåmer Special.

The Klinkhåmer Special (Hans van Klinken)

Hook: Partridge GRS15ST, size 8-18 for grayling and trout.
Thread: uni-thread, 8/0, grey or tan for body. Spiderweb for tying in the parachute hackle.
Body: Poly 2 dubbing, any colour of preference. (Hans' favourite recipe has a dark biot abdomen with a wire rib – possibly enhancing its 'supernormal' aspect).
Wing: white poly-yarn.
Thorax: three strands of peacock herl.
Hackle: blue dun, dark dun, light dun, chestnut, in good combination with body colour.
Wind the hackle around the base of the wing post. Start at the top of your wing base, taking each successive turn closer to the hook shank. Take as many turns as the type of hook requires. Small flies about 5 windings and bigger flies at least 7 or 8 windings. Remember that the fly has to float mainly on the parachute. A lot of people wind their hackle in the opposite way, working up the wing. The hackle is less durable and may still come off. Working from top downwards ensures a compact, well-compressed hackle and a most durable construction. Pull the hackle tip in the opposite direction to the wing and secure with a few turns of spiderweb. Secure well around the base of the wing, between the wound hackle and body. Use your whip finisher. Trim away the waste hackle tip and hackle barbs that are pointed down. Apply some varnish to the windings just under the parachute.

Hans van Klinken is constantly working up new designs, which can be found on his website, along with those of other innovative continental tiers; www.hansvanklinken.com

A superbly conditioned cutthroat trout from a wilderness stream

V: The clipped-hackle dun and spinner

Good news to hackle growers is the fact that there will always be a place for good quality dry fly hackles. The simple hackle fly is a venerable and indispensable design. If we stick to our criteria that a good fly should be simple to tie and rugged, the hackle dry fly meets both. When the hackle is clipped below the hook shank, it often does a better job than the winged patterns designed specifically for imitating both duns and spinners. The hard thing to swallow is our resistance to chopping up those beautiful and expensive hackles, but once we get over that it's a whole new ball game.

Since anything above the surface is more or less indistinct to the trout, an accurate wing silhouette is necessary primarily on the glass smooth water of spring creeks and chalkstreams. The wing is undoubtedly a primary trigger, but a feather wing is too opaque and solid for my taste. Feather slips, as used on Marinaro's thorax duns are bad for leader twist when new, but fray quickly anyway. I have a hunch the feather slip wings are partly to blame for John Roberts' disaffection with no-hackle duns, rather than the fly's posture. When frayed, duck quill makes for very tough wings, but still resemble messy emergers more than any dun. Hackle, hair, or CDC better suggests the translucency of most ephemerid wings. Besides, the surface distorts anything above the surface, and all we really need is enough.

Old Halford probably spins in his grave every time I butcher a nicely tied dry fly hackle, but I keep a couple of boxfuls of hackle dries just for that purpose. My best patterns are old standards: the Blue Upright, Grey Duster, Red or Ginger Quill, and Grey Hackle – with variations on this basic theme with quill or dubbed bodies in a complete range of sizes. For a spinner fall, a quick snip of the bottom hackle gives a cleaner profile. For those occasions when you have convinced yourself that the trout are selecting only the perfect dun, you have plenty with a full hackle ready to fish. If it helps you fish more confidently, by all means tie on some wings.

For a fall of spinners, clipping the hackle above and below the hook, leaving barbs only at the sides, is about as good a representation of the transparent wings of a spent spinner as you can devise, something that has been noticed by many excellent anglers, notably W.H.Lawrie. The natural translucency of good glassy dry fly hackle is actually more appropriate for this job than it is for imitating an insect's legs, which are of minor significance anyway. The colour can be chosen accurately for any species of fly expected. Four capes; one blue dun, one grizzly or cree, one badger and one ginger, will cover pretty well everything. All have a high degree of translucency. Good stiff hackle is a joy, but it's important to know that the best grade hackles aren't really necessary for this pragmatic approach. Second and third class necks, even so-called wet fly capes, are great for clipped hackles because they don't have to support the body clear of the surface. Treated with floatant, webby cock and hen hackle barbs make a very convincing impression of the wings of a spent or crippled insect.

Clipping only the underside hackle and leaving the dorsal hackle intact gives you something to track out there on the water, especially in low light, and doesn't seem to put the trout off at all. For purely aesthetic reasons, we can delay the clipping until we are on the water, so our fly boxes are acceptable in polite company. My regular hackle dries have the hackle wound through the thorax area, rather than simply as a collar at the shoulder, to provide a convincing silhouette.

Grey Duster

Hook: fine wire, dry fly, straight shank or curved emerger style.
Tail: none.

Body: dubbed grey fur, mole, muskrat, or hare. I wind the tag end of the tying thread along the body as a rib.

Hackle: Badger, wound two turns back and forward through thorax section; clipped underside when appropriate.

(* One of the best all-rounders ever, and particularly deadly in a hatch of lake olives. My latest version of this old never-fail, the Dirty Duster, is tied on a curved emerger hook for the extra stimulus of the sunk abdomen. As usual, I clip the hackle on the underside to ensure the desired posture.)

Blue Upright

Hook: fine wire dry fly, all sizes.

Tail: stiff hackle barbs from good quality cape, splayed with a couple of turns of thread at bend of hook. Webby hackle from a hen cape makes for a nice 'cripple' effect.

Body: slim dubbed dun fur, or stripped peacock herl or turkey biot, varnished lightly for strength.

Thorax: slender dubbed blue dun fur

Hackle: good quality blue dun hackle, light or dark, wound two turns back and forward through thorax; clipped on underside so the fly sits flush with the surface.

(*This pattern can be tied in a range of colours to suit the prevailing hatch,, e.g.; red spinner, etc. I like the dark Blue Upright for low light situations, and the Red Quill for a spinner fall in sunlight.)

Grey Hackle

Hook: fine wire, dry fly.

Tail: red wool tag, or dyed red hackle barbs (optional).

Body: bronze peacock herl, ribbed with tag end of tying thread.

Hackle: grizzly, wound through thorax section; clipped when appropriate.

(* A reliable midge pattern in small sizes. The Red Tag is the same fly with a brown hackle. Tied in a full palmer style in small sizes, it is known in America as Griffith's Gnat.)

Badger and Black

Hook: fine wire dry fly.

Tail: none.

Body: black ostrich herl, ribbed with tag-end of tying thread.

Hackle: Badger, clipped when appropriate.

(*An excellent hatching midge imitation out of the same kennel as the Grey Duster. The ostrich herl slims down to a very buggy profile.)

* * * * *

8. New Arts and Old Mysteries

Of all sportsmen probably the angler knows the habits of his quarry least: possibly because a great gulf separates hunter from hunted, their worlds are different... the solution, instead of coming nearer, seems, like the mirage, to keep ever receding before him as time passes by, until at last he must leave the problem unsolved, fortunately for the everlasting pleasure of those who follow.

J. C. Mottram
Fly Fishing – Some New Arts and Mysteries

Homewater, in the Alberta foothills

1. The contemporary wet fly

As a kid in western Canada, until I saw Jerry Avoledo's Bucktail, fly-fishing meant the wet fly. In those days, in that neck of the woods, and in every mom and pop hardware store in North America, wet flies were sold on little perforated cards of three. The flies were pre-snelled on a short looped dropper of monofilament that must have tested a ten-pound pull. We used these on the point and dropper, often three at a time. Crude indeed, but those mountain trout had no reason to think the flies were anything but something edible worth trying out.

My brothers and I knew nothing of the great northern English and Scottish wet fly tradition, despite our grandfather being a trout fishing Yorkshireman. He undoubtedly knew everything about it, but was such a mean old bastard he couldn't bring himself to give even advice away for free. I have a clear memory of the old man on the Crowsnest one afternoon, the only time I ever saw him fish. He was fishing a rod's length of line in a quartering upstream cast, and he followed the flies' drift with the rod tip held high, playing the bob fly on the surface. I'd never seen anything like it before, nor did I again, until I found the description of it in W.C. Stewart's *The Practical Angler*. The old man was fishing the classic north country upstream wet fly. If he hadn't put the rod away forever that day, to husband his remaining time for drinking and starting arguments, I might have been a different angler entirely, maybe even a traditional wet fly man.

The flies we used were classic down-wing wets; Royal Coachman, Blue Upright, Black Gnat, all the old North American favourites, and some strange ones to boot. One was called a Stone Fly but resembled no stonefly we ever saw. A dry fly that we fished wet, it had a pinky-orange hackle and divided hen pheasant wings. It was a killer on the Crowsnest, for reasons known only to the fish, and in retrospect my first hint that colour was worth investigating for its own sake. Interestingly, there was also another version of the Stone Fly on the shelves, identical but for a dark dyed olive hackle that we referred to as the 'female', which didn't work at all. There were also a trout versions of old Scottish Atlantic salmon flies, the Jock Scott and Silver Doctor, in reduced dressings to be sure, but fancy enough. Old Uncle Jack was adamant that if the Jock Scott didn't have white wing tips it was, 'you know what I mean, *useless* for the North Fork cutthroats'. You can see that, for us, fly selection was voodoo, pure and simple.

I started catching bigger fish when I began tying my own flies. Avoledo's so-called Bucktail was the only dry fly we used, the only fly not intended to be fished downstream and sunk. Tying wings was a bit of a chore for a while, so my early wets were wingless hackle wets, similar to what W.C. Stewart called wet 'spiders' back in 1857, and what American anglers now call 'soft hackle' flies. At first, the hackles I used were from webby hen capes, really just the head and upper neck of dinner chickens, chopped off by Doodles Melvain, who ran a cattle ranch on Todd Creek. An early favourite of mine throughout the fifties and early sixties was the Grey Hackle, a simple peacock body with a grizzly hackle, collar or palmered, that had more of the proportions of a horse fly rather than any spider, but which accounted for hundreds of trout. Later in life, I discovered that the palmered version went by the name of Griffith's Gnat. Simple hackle versions of old standards such as the Blue Upright are still among my first-line dry flies.

Wet flies have been somewhat neglected. They've always been with us of course, but somewhat unfashionable. The Americans have generally preferred the nymph, at least since the Second World War. The W.C. Stewart style, soft-hackle wet spider has life and translucency provided by the mobile game bird hackles and the use of dubbed fur in the bodies. Sylvester Nemes sort of re-heated the wet spider for North American anglers with a book on soft hackle flies, although they were still alive and kicking on the rivers of Yorkshire and central Scotland. These old-time patterns are excellent catchers of trout, fished dead-drift or on the lift. I generally rely on a few basic patterns, all of which can be varied in terms of colour and bulk, with an eye toward some resemblance to the prevailing hatch:

Woodcock and Hare Lug (hare's ear) Spider
Body and thorax: hare's mask or ear fur, colour as appropriate.
Hackle: partridge, woodcock, or webby cree hen hackle.
Rib: fine gold wire or yellow tying thread wound through hackle.

Partridge (or Woodcock) and Orange Spider
Body: yellow/orange silk.
Hackle: partridge or woodcock shoulder, or cree hen.

Black and Peacock Spider
Body: peacock herl.
Hackle: black hen, Stewart style.
Rib: tying thread or fine gold wire wound through hackle.

Blue Dun Spider
Body: dark dun dubbing.
Hackle: starling covert or dark blue dun hen, Stewart style.
Rib: tying thread wound through hackle.

Snipe and Purple (or Woodcock and Claret)
Body: royal purple or claret silk.
Hackle: dark snipe (or woodcock) shoulder feather.

Greenwell Spider
Body: dun yellow fur dubbing, sparse.
Hackle: dark badger or greenwell hen, Stewart style.
Rib: fine gold wire or tan tying thread, wound through hackle.

Hackled very sparsely in the Stewart style, with the webby game bird or hen hackle tied in at the hook eye and wound back through the thorax of the fly in open turns, these are very fishy flies. By winding the wire or tying thread-tag rib forward from the bend of the hook, through the hackle, you reinforce the hackle stem and get a very rugged fly. When fished, the soft hackles envelope the body of the fly, presenting the shape of a rising nymph or pupa with translucency and life.

The literature on the wet fly is thin but long. *The Art of the Wet Fly*, an excellent book by W.S. Roger Fogg, Magee's, *Fly Fishing: the North Country Tradition*, and Dave Hughes' *Wet Flies* are the best of the few relatively recent books that deal with the wet fly at any depth, and they place the early classics of Pritt, Edmonds and Lee into a contemporary context. Fogg bases his approach on Stewart's somewhat prescriptive one, although his preference for the sparse soft-hackle spider dressings is not a result of conventional thinking but the result of a close personal study of the habits of trout and their prey. In *The Art of the Wet Fly* and *Fishing the Flymph*, V.S. Hidy promoted the use of nymph-like soft hackled wet flies. He called them 'flymphs' with a straight face, but I can't.

W.H. Lawrie gave us a very fishy group of wet flies that are sadly neglected these days. His Rough Stream Nymphs are based on the phases of specific hatches, conforming pretty closely to the style I've just described, but with the soft hackle clipped on the top and underside of the fly. Lawrie designed his flies to be fished barely submerged in the surface, more like modern emergers than classic nymphs. His nymphs led directly to his hatching dun series. On the same principle V.S. Hidy designed impressionistic, soft-hackled flies that he rather unfortunately named 'flymphs', a name that never really caught on, mostly because you feel so stupid when you say it. Lawrie's designs are a bit complex for my taste, but this is the kind of thinking I like in trout fly design, clearly the result of years on the river, watching the behaviour of trout and their prey, as opposed to speculating at the tying bench or in front of a word processor.

It's important to know that these simple wet fly designs are usually all one needs, the rest is down to the way they behave when fished. Most nymphs and pupae are pretty simple in form, and except for some colour variations they are very similar. Size, colour, and basic shape are the main things. Some simple Hare's Ear or Pheasant Tail variations and a few skinny, spider style wets are enough to approach any water with confidence. Although I always go forth in the hope that the trout will rise to a surface fly, I'm prepared for this not to be the case. Even on prime dry fly water at the prime time, I've often found the trout ignoring surface flies. I always hope this means that they are feeding subsurface, and sometimes it is the case. The trout are at times preoccupied with the pre-emergence movements of a hatch, and the good old wet fly is still good medicine.

A nice brown trout to the emerger   *photo: Margaret Mitchell*

2. The modern Irish lough fly

It is a short hop across the Irish Sea from the United Kingdom, insignificant in terms of destination fly-fishing today, but a long distance culturally. If any persuasion is needed regarding the cultural nature of fly-fishing, a day on one of the western loughs will dispel the idea that it is simply a technical matter. The Irish have a characteristic way of doing things, and fly-fishing there has a distinctive flavour.

When we speak of the traditional Irish wet fly we usually mean the 'Bumble' style dressings popularised by T.C. Kingsmill-Moore in his wonderful book, *A Man May Fish*. Kingsmill-Moore based his patterns on the old English 'buzz' style of tying a palmered hackle along the body of the fly. This tying style has been around the Irish loughs since the days of Francis Francis, and has appeared in several sub-styles like the Gosling. For all their beauty, Kingsmill-Moore's Bumbles are extremely rugged flies, tied with a reinforcing rib of wire up the body of the fly and through the palmered hackle. He added a collar hackle of barred jay to finish these very attractive and artful flies. The bodies are rather fulsome, of well picked out seal's fur, the whole thing a symphony of colour, translucence and life.

What is notable about the Irish fly-fishing tradition these days is that it doesn't look so traditional. A perusal of Peter O'Reilly's *Trout and Salmon Flies of Ireland* will illustrate that point. The classic Bumble style wets are in wide use, but the influence of recent competition angling is evident. The Dabbler has maybe usurped the classic Bumble to a certain extent. The Dabbler, a descendant of the Gosling style, has a heavier shoulder hackle or collar of bronze mallard, tied long so it shrouds the body hackles. There is also a stout tail of mallard. The Dabbler is what Kingsmill-Moore would probably call a 'shameless lure', but there is no denying its effectiveness on the big loughs. Primarily a pulling fly, it's hard to say just what it represents, but in several versions it is used to imitate everything from fry to sedges. I think it presents a stimulating prey-image to trout that are beginning to switch from insects to fry feeding.

A recent twist on the traditional Bumble theme is the Octopus, a leggy, heavily dressed pulling fly tied with webby golden olive hackles and a fluorescent chartreuse floss tag. A lure for sure, normally fished on an intermediate line at a brisk pace this fly has a lot in common with the old Carey Special of the Pacific Northwest. I've seen this fly out fish everything, especially what I was using. I've spent whole days fishing the surface with classic Bumbles and drawn a blank, while others were stripping the Octopus for good catches. Stripping lures on a sunk line is not really to my taste, but a fish or two on the line is a great tonic against the funk of a blank day.

The Green Octopus

Hook: size eight to twelve.
Tag: fluorescent chartreuse synthetic yarn.
Body: golden olive seal's fur.
Body hackle: golden olive cock hackle, palmered from hook eye toward the tail.
Rib: gold wire, wound up though the body hackle.
Shoulder hackle: large, webby golden olive hackle.

The Dabbler (Donal McLoon)

Hook: size eight to twelve.
Shoulder hackle: bronze mallard (or oak turkey tail) barbs, tied in first round the hook shank as a collar hackle, tips left pointing outward from the eye until the rest of the fly is completed.
Tail: bunched bronze mallard (or oak turkey) barbs.
Body: mylar, silver or gold tinsel; or seal's fur in any colour.
Body hackle: any soft hackle wound palmer style.
Rib: silver wire.
(*stroke the mallard barbs backward as a full hackle 'cape' top and bottom, and tie off.)

Father Ronan (Murt Folan)

Hook: size ten or twelve.
Shoulder hackle: bunched bronze mallard, tied in first as a collar hackle, tips pointing outward from the hook eye.
Tail: golden pheasant crest, or fluorescent chartreuse yarn
Body: fiery red seal's fur.
Body Hackle: fiery red and golden olive cock hackle, palmered together from hook eye to tail.
Rib: silver wire wound through hackle to eye.
(*Stroke the bronze mallard barbs back to form the shoulder hackle and whip finish.)

In the old days, fly-fishing on the great western loughs meant a few weeks from the end of April to the middle of July. A very few anglers had a lot of prime trout fishing at their disposal. Now, on any weekend on Corrib, there are hundreds of boats out and the fly-fishing season has been extended from March to the end of September. The chironomid, or 'duck fly' hatch is first on the fly-fisher's calendar, bringing the trout to the fly as early as the beginning of March, so the majority of visiting anglers miss the hatch. The duck fly, known as the 'buzzer' to UK anglers, is probably the most important fish food on British stillwaters. The Irish loughs also have fabulous hatches of *Baetis* olives that appear in the slightly warmer weather of April.

The traditional Irish approach to the duck fly has been to use sparsely tied traditional wet flies, and there is no doubt that the wet fly does very well when the buzzer is up. Recently, Irish tiers have designed flies that suggest the chironomid more specifically, for conditions that don't suit the wet fly. The naturals are often pretty big, so some of the flies, the Grey Boy for instance, are often a size ten or even an eight. Long leaders, of up to twenty feet, and static presentations are increasingly the order of the day during the duck fly hatch on the quiet mud-bottomed bays of Corrib, Mask and other big western loughs, especially when there is no wave.

The simple Shipman type buzzer, really nothing more than a picked out body of seal's fur, is reliable for surface work in any buzzer hatch, and also serves as a general emerger. For subsurface, there a several very good buzzer patterns of varying density, depending on the depth the trout are found. The use of a long leader with a team of sunk epoxy buzzers is seen with increasing frequency, sometimes under an indicator, a deadly tactic imported from the English reservoir scene. It's not everyone's cup of tea, but there's no denying its effectiveness on the wild Irish brownies. Epoxy bodied buzzers fished with a slow hand twist retrieve are proving to be big medicine year round on the Irish loughs.

Grey Boy Buzzer

Hook: size 10 to 14, medium wire emerger style, weighted with lead wire if desired.
Abdomen: any dark grey fur such as hare, etc. Chris Reeves ties his very similar Grey Goose Buzzer with wild goose barbs wound as herl.
Rib: White or light blue tying thread.
Wing case: section of 'plumulaceous' grey goose secondary wing feather, from lower portion of the feather shaft, with soft plumes at end of the barbs, tied in before thorax is dubbed. The wing case is tied in so the soft plume extends beyond the hook eye.
Thorax: dark hare's ear.
(*Bring the goose feather over thorax and tie in so the plumulaceous 'breathers' extend beyond the eye. Pinch off the breathers to the appropriate length.)

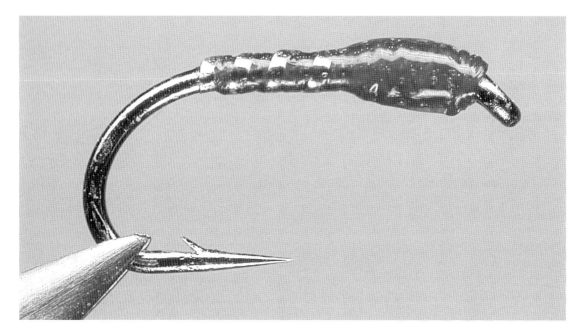

Epoxy Buzzer   *photo: Hans Weilenmann*

Epoxy Buzzer (Ron Oldroyd)
Hook: heavyweight, 12 - 18 buzzer or grub style.
Body: tying thread.
Ribbing: pearl mylar or lurex.
Thorax cover: pearl mylar or lurex.
Coating: epoxy or Hard as Nails varnish.
(*Half-dressed, a size14 hook effectively results in a size16 or 18 fly. English stillwater expert Chris Reeves acknowledges Ron 'The Pub' Oldroyd as creator of this fly. Chris says Oldroyd developed the minimalist epoxy buzzer after a successful year of catch and release fishing had made the fish wary of large more gaudy flies. The slim mylar thorax cover is an important factor in the effectiveness of this fly; that little flash seems to trigger the takes. Three coats of Sally Hanson's 'Hard as Nails' varnish is much easier to work with, and has the same effect as epoxy.

Shipman's Buzzer (Dave Shipman)
Hook: size 10 to 14, fine wire dry fly.
Breathers: optional, poly yarn, snowshoe hare foot fur or CDC tufts, tied in before body is dubbed.
Body: hare's ear, seal's fur, or any similar coloured dubbing, picked out.
(*Tie this fly slim and sparse, or thick and bushy, depending on conditions.)

3. The magical Smithy
I love the Irish style pulling flies, everything about them, especially the way they don't really imitate anything but still work. They must suggest something, but really, you have to admit

Early season in Scotland

they're pretty damned Irish. They're poetic, not flies so much as metaphors for flies. I fell under their Celtic spell soon upon arriving in Scotland. After thirty years of no-nonsense fly-tying, I was fascinated by the aesthetic approach to Irish fly design, exemplified by Kingsmill-Moore in *A Man May Fish*. Despite his inclination toward amateur science and logic, Kingsmill-Moore was as much a creature of the Irish romantic tradition as Jamsie, his archetypically wild Corrib boatman. For proof of this just read his analysis of the effectiveness of his own go-to point fly, the *Kingsmill*. It's only a short step away from leaving the fly out in the moonlight to increase its powers of enchantment. The same thing holds for his famous Bumbles, proven fish catchers that have in them as much sorcery as science. Compare his Golden Olive Bumble with a natural lake olive, at any stage of its development. What's with that barred jay collar hackle and golden pheasant crest tail? Or, try to figure out why his jewel-like Claret Bumble works so well later in the season. Well, it must be some kind of fairy deal.

Necromancy notwithstanding, the operative term there is 'fish catchers'. These flies work, are deadly in fact. They continue to evolve as good flies always do, and everyone who fishes the Scottish and Irish lochs has their favourites. Most of us have worked up some little variation of our own, which, to us, makes all the difference. My own two favourites do business when the northern brownies are on to a pulled wet fly. The Veyatie Black is a sort of deconstructed Connemara Black, tied in the Bumble style with a badger body hackle. The Veyatie Silver, the same fly with a silver tinsel body, does well on a really sunny day.

A variation of the Veyatie Silver, identical except for a long tail of dyed fluorescent red golden pheasant crest, is a fly named after the wife of my pal Bob Morton. Bob is married to Scottish celebrity Elaine C. Smith, so we called the fly the Smithy in a pathetic attempt to curry favour. The colour scheme is essentially that of the old Priest, except for the collar of pheasant covert for that extra Irish 'kick'. An out and out trigger fly, the Smithy is one of those magical patterns that find their way onto a cast in a wide range of circumstances for no reason other than it usually works, and only the fish know why.

The Smithy is a good estuary pattern, and there at least I can see some reason for it. It makes a passable impression of a small shrimp. It has caught many Scottish sea-trout and sea-run cutthroats off the west coast of Canada. It has a nice broken transparency in the water, and the long hen pheasant covert feathers in the shoulder hackle pulse seductively with each pull. The silver body mirrors the surrounding colour and light, adding to the 'pale and interesting' effect.

The Smithy is utterly reliable for sea-trout and night-feeding brownies on a summer river. It has all the features that made the great old flies great, so I have that confident feeling of working with a tried and true design, which helps when you're fishing at night. In fact, I am so confident in the Smithy for this purpose that when I'm tooling up for a late session I'll often tie on two, point and bob. With a big one on the point, up to a size six on a dark night, but normally an eight, I have more faith in the Smithy than Falkus' Medicine for sea-trout, at least in the waters we fish. For some reason, even at night, the dyed red tail fishes better than the natural yellow Golden Pheasant crest feather. I can't venture a reason for that which makes any sense, but on a warm summer night when the river is gleaming silver in the thick-scented darkness, the Smithy just looks right. It's got to be a fairy thing.

The Smithy
Hook: size 10 through 6, medium weight wire.
Tail: dyed fluorescent red, golden pheasant crest.
Rib: silver wire.
Body: silver tinsel.
Body hackle: silver badger saddle, wound 'Bumble-style' from shoulder toward tail. Trap hackle at tail with wire rib. Wind wire through hackle toward head.
Shoulder hackle: medium long, light coloured hen pheasant wing covert feather, wound as collar. Wind tying thread a couple of turns through shoulder hackle for strength.

Veyatie Black
Hook: medium wire wet fly.
Tail: golden pheasant crest.
Rib: silver wire.
Body: black ostrich herl, dyed black rabbit or seal's fur, slim.
Body hackle: golden badger, sparse, palmered toward the tail and trapped by the wire rib.
Shoulder hackle: long sparse hen pheasant wing covert feather, tied in by its tip.

4.The indispensable nymphs
The Hare's Ear and Sawyer's Pheasant Tail, in their many variations, will catch fish anywhere. All you need is a range of sizes, and few weighted with lead wire to fish a little deeper. If pushed, I'd even say I could live without the Pheasant Tail as long as I had some light and dark Hare's Ears, so universal is the HE's remit. In fact, a hare's ear bodied Deer Hair Sedge and a weighted Hare's Ear nymph would undoubtedly be my survival kit selection for that desert island with the trout stream.

Gary LaFontaine designed some simple caddis pupae imitations that are best tied with translucent dubbing. The Sparkle Caddis Pupa is an excellent fish catcher, and undoubtedly his most well known design. The sparkling dubbed body simulates the visual effect of sub-

Late season in New Zealand; no anglers, low water, spooky trout – perfect   photo: Margaret Mitchell

cutaneous gas, produced by the pharate adult to assist its ascent to the surface. Some biologists, who have found no basis for it in nature, have refuted the theory of the subcutaneous gas. Maybe it's another of those fly-fishing lacunae, that black-box thing, something yet to be explained. Despite the positivist counter-claim, thousands of fly-tiers have been happily designing flies based on the gas-bubble concept, and thousands more anglers have been catching trout on them, ever since *Caddis Flies* appeared. Many experts claim to have observed this phenomenon first hand, and there are plenty more who are convinced they have caught trout that were selecting *only* the pupa displaying the gas-bubble effect. My amateurish enquiries have failed to turn up any literature on it one way or the other. Aquatic entomologist and macro-photographer, Dr Dean Hansen of the University of Minnesota told me recently that although he has plenty of respect for LaFontaine's work, he has not observed the gas-bubble effect himself, nor does he know of an entomologist who has. Whether or not the science behind LaFontaine's design is sound, it is an excellent catcher of trout and something like it is worth having on lakes where sedges are prevalent. I've always used a simple, seal's fur 'flymph' style pupa myself, which seldom lets me down.

A stillwater fisherman should include a good damsel nymph imitation, but not the blousy type of thing referred to as a damsel nymph by British reservoir anglers, another shameless lure and kin to the Dog Knobbler and Woolly Bugger. A natural damsel nymph is a slim, delicate critter that is well represented by an elongated hare's ear nymph, with maybe a tuft of marabou or game bird filoplume for a tail. A few barbs of partridge suggesting legs help in providing some movement and look good, but the natural bug folds them back while swimming, so they are probably unnecessary. Kept sparse, such a fly will take fish on most lakes and you'll know the reason why.

As a kid, I used skinny, reduced versions of the old Doc Spratley and Carey Special to great effect on western lakes. The Doc Spratley is a kind of crude colonial version of the Connemara Black, usually tied with a cock pheasant tail fibre wing. Old Archie Malcolm, of Calgary's Hook and Hackle Club, reckoned it was the black wool body that pulled the fish, the rest of the dressing was decoration. The Cary Special is kissing cousin to the Dabbler, tied with a sweeping pheasant rump feather hackle instead of bronze mallard. Intended originally as a sedge pattern, the Cary serves well enough as a dragonfly imitation when tied long and sparse. I mention these lures among the nymphs only because they incorporate some essential nymphlike triggers, not because they bear specific resemblance to any natural bug.

I use nymphs primarily for fishing the bottom of the water column, so I usually incorporate a certain amount of lead wire for weight. The low light periods before daybreak and after sundown are the prime times for invertebrate drift, and consequently the best time for fishing the nymph. It's a good thing to remember, especially when the hoped-for evening rise doesn't transpire. When things get a little too quiet at dusk, a team of soft-hackle spiders or nymphs might kindle the spark of hope.

Pheasant Tail Nymph (McPhee variant)
Hook: grub/emerger style.
Bead head: black tungsten.
Tail: hackle barbs.
Body: cock pheasant tail feather barbs wound as herl.
Rib: copper wire.
Sighter: single strand black accent flash.
Thorax: hare's ear over built-up copper or lead wire.

Simple Hare's Ear Nymph
Hook: light wire; weighted with lead wire or tungsten bead for depth.
Tail: a few hare's mask guard hairs.
Body: hare's ear or mask, tapered and well picked out at thorax.
Rib: tag end of tying thread, wound counter to dubbing.
Legs: partridge (optional), or picked-out guard hairs.

Teeny Nymph (Jim Teeny, variant)
Hook: short shank, heavy wire, weighted with lead if desired.
Body: a bunch of cock pheasant tail barbs, measured for length against the hook and tied in by their butts. Wind forward to the shoulder, leaving the tips intact for the legs. Pheasant tails are used in several colours. I like oak turkey tail barbs.
Legs: tips of pheasant tail barbs, tied down below the shank. On large sizes, a separate bunch is tied in for the thorax and legs.
(*An extremely simple but effective caddis pupa design. Jim Teeny is a legendary figure in the Pacific Northwest and a leading exponent of the 'basic design' school of fly tying.)

Simple Damsel Nymph
Hook: light wire. Black bead head for weight, if desired.
Tail: a few barbs of dyed marabou or game bird filoplume, sparse.

Body: dyed olive or natural dark hare's ear, tied slim.
Rib: tag-end of tying thread.
Legs: sparse dyed olive partridge or hen pheasant covert, wound back once through thorax and trapped by thread rib.

Simple Caddis Pupa

Hook: appropriate size, medium wire, weighted with lead wire.
Abdomen: green, tan, or golden yellow/orange seal's fur, well picked out and quite robust.
Thorax: seal's fur.
Legs: game bird (grouse, woodcock or partridge) wing covert feather.

Simple Grannom Pupa

Hook: medium wire, weighted with lead wire.
Head: black tungsten bead.
Abdomen: dubbed dark hare's ear and black seal's fur mix.
Rib: tag end of tying thread (olive) counter-wound.
Wing case and legs: picked out dubbing.

5. Baitfish imitations for big trout

We can be sure that any trout over two or three pounds is a cannibal to some extent. Early writings attributed a moral aspect to what is the natural behaviour of trout by this epithet. Once spotted, the keeper usually removed these brutes by any means. The reality is that, unless a stream has extraordinary amounts of insects and crustaceans available, a big fish simply has to switch over to feeding on fish in order to survive. This is especially the case on rain-fed streams, and even on fertile reservoirs and moorland lochs. To a big trout, in terms of units of nutrition per unit of energy expended, baitfish and small trout offer more payoff for effort. This is the principal reason why big trout so seldom rise to flies, except that is in a heavy and sustained hatch situation. In addition is the reason we should always have a few streamers and bucktails in our fly boxes.

Baitfish imitation has a long and deep tradition in America. The Eastern Brook Trout, as it used to be called, is a char and an enthusiastic fish eater, like its cousins the Lake Trout and the western Bull Trout. The lake fishing tradition of upper New York state and Maine is a streamer fly tradition; exemplified by the beautiful hackle-winged smelt impressions of Carrie Stevens. These elegant, long shank lures are still trolled behind a boat or canoe for brookies, and another eastern American game fish, the landlocked Atlantic salmon. They are trolled because these lake fish tend to follow for a long time before they take, much like the Pacific Coho salmon, often failing to take hold before a cast and retrieved fly reaches the boat, and spooking at the last moment. Also, the long hackle 'wings' on these streamers tend to wrap the hook shank when cast.

On a review of the literature, one might be forgiven for believing that British streams had no big trout in them. The reason for this mistaken belief is that they are not seriously fished for. In Britain, the fly-caught river trout is normally under a pound in weight. That is your free-rising fish and the prime quarry for river fly-fishing. On lakes, it is different. Fry imitations are standard issue for late season work on the big UK reservoirs. Seasonal surges in perch and roach fry populations make for major feeding opportunities once the aquatic insects have had their day. Big trout, capable of herding and attacking massed shoals of bait, become preoccupied with

An early brownie to the DHE during a Baetis *emergence*

them just as smaller fish do during fly hatches. The number of big brown trout that are taken by salmon anglers on the rivers I fish has surprised me. These fish are usually taken during the normal salmon fisher's hours, between nine in the morning and five in the afternoon. This coincides with Kelly Galloup's experience on North American rivers. In their inspiring book, *Modern Streamers for Trophy Trout*, Galloup and Bob Linsenman catch eighty percent of their big trout during mid-day. Although a big trout's feeding activity is normally at dawn and dusk, their big baitfish designs seem to trigger an aggressive predatory or territorial response, despite the trout not being in a feeding mode.

Some anglers maintain that leeches are a significant prey for trout, but I can't remember ever finding one in a trout's stomach. I have read reports of trout full of leeches, but assumed that I just wasn't seeing the evidence that others were. The fact remains, however, that so-called leech patterns are good medicine for big trout, and on some waters, such as England's Roadford reservoir, leeches are considered to be significant trout prey. That said, many of the marabou leech patterns in use today on western rivers, like the ubiquitous Woolly Bugger, are better impressions of baitfish than they are of leeches. The way they are usually fished confirms this. Leeches are weak swimmers and move slowly with an undulating action, while these lures are normally fished on a swinging across-and-down line, or stripped back fast on an upstream cast. No leech under the sun ever moved like that. Again, it may be a combination of a stimulating prey-image and the trout's hard-wired chase response working for these tactics.

Some recent and radical baitfish designs are excellent for river trout, especially after dark. Mark Bowler, publishing editor of *Fly Fishing and Fly Tying* magazine, has been using foam bodied poppers for sea-run brown trout to great effect on Scottish rivers, taking fish to over nine pounds. His pattern is just a short length of cylindrical foam run lengthwise down a hook shank, with a bit of bucktail or something for a tail. The popper is plug-cut for maximum surface disturbance, and fished down and across in the dark. Hugh Falkus whittled fly rod plugs out of balsa wood and painted them with aluminum paint. Rob Sloane likes a cork-bodied lure that is otherwise similar. A.K. Best's Butt Faced Lemming is similar in design for traditionalists who prefer to use stacked and clipped deer hair for the plug portion of the fly. Bowler says that the

Original Fur Fly (Tony Sloane) – photo: courtesy of Australia's Best Trout Flies

cylindrical foam works better than deer hair, at least as well as cork or balsa. It also takes no time to tie, which appeals to me, being a very successful hooker of bank-side trees myself. Just where this lure ranks on the fly-fishing purity scale is hard to say. Like most things, it depends on one's taste, even in the dark.

There are many excellent baitfish designs from New Zealand and Tasmania that deserve a good soaking in northern hemisphere waters. Tony Sloane's simple Fur Fly, tied with rabbit, possum or kangaroo, is a standard down under. I haven't seen kangaroo fur on the shelves yet, but expect to sooner or later. The bigger Tasmanian and Kiwi trout are inveterate fish eaters, and they have big runs of smelt and whitebait that make baitfish designs essential. Chris Beech's transparent whitebait designs would certainly convince fry feeders anywhere. For the Irish loughs and English reservoirs, where perch and roach fry make explosive seasonal appearances and the trout go on fry feeding sprees, these Aussie baitfish designs really look the business.

Since I prefer to catch trout on the surface, I have never really developed my own line of lures. One exception that has saved many a cold day in the early season or dour days in August is the Bullethead Bugger, simply a Woolly Bugger with a weighted head similar to that old British reservoir favourite, the Dog Knobbler. I use pierced lead air-gun pellets because they are small, heavy, and dirt cheap. I trim off the soft conical flange at the base of the pellet and run a heavy dubbing needle through the lead bullet. The weight at the front end of the fly gives a tantalising action to the marabou tail. It was tied as a lazy substitute to the old Ace of Spades, a Matuka-style lure that was a standard for Scottish loch brownies for a decade or so. Stripped on a high-density line, a black one will usually pull trout from deep water in cold spring weather, or when they are hunting minnows in late summer.

Tasman Whitebait (Chris Beech)
Hook: 2x long shank wet fly.
Body: silver mylar or tinsel.
Wing: pale grey polar bear, or similar translucent synthetic.
Eyes: stick on epoxy eyes. Epoxy the entire head and forward portion of the fly.

Matuka Muddler (Dave Whitlock, variant)
Hook: loop-eyed salmon iron, 2-2/0.
Body: dubbed possum fur.
Dorsal 'wing': strip of mobile skin with fur, tied Matuka style.
Collar (pectoral fins): flared tips of deer hair.
Head: clipped deer hair, muddler style, shaped wide and flat.

Foam Lure (Mark Bowler)
Hook: wide gape wet fly.
Tail: bucktail or other material.
Body: 1 to 1.5 inch section of cylindrical foam, run lengthwise onto the hook shank and glued.

Bullethead Bugger
Hook: medium-long shank wet fly hook.
Head: pierced .177, or .22 caliber lead air-gun pellet, conical flange removed with a knife.
Tail: marabou, with a few strands of sparkly material like Flashabou, if desired.
Body: seal, possum or other fur, picked out after hackle is tied in.
Body hackle: Chinese cock, wound palmer-wise from shoulder to tail.
Rib: silver or gold wire, wound through the hackle from tail to shoulder.

Fur Fly (Tony Sloane variant)
Hook: medium-long shank wet fly hook.
Tail: clump of fur or peacock herl.

*Tasman Whitebait
(Beech) – photo: Rob
Sloane*

Body: a strip of rabbit fur, or soft mobile fur of any kind, folded double over the hook shank and tied in at the head.

Eyes: (optional) dumb-bell, epoxy, or jungle cock. The original had a head of peacock herl.

(*The fur strip is not wound on to the shank, but folded over it lengthwise. This is a variation, among many, of Tony Sloane's simple Rabbit Fur Fly. Sloane's son Rob says the original, or his Modified Fur Fly, similar to the one described, is still the best.)

6. On the beach

The west coast of British Columbia is a difficult proposition for a visiting angler. Not because it is frightfully expensive or hard to get to, at least in comparison to places like Chile or New Zealand, but because you are faced with thousands of miles of coastline. When you think about all that water you feel defeated before you start. This is a common reaction to fly-fishing the salt anyway and is the reason that it has not been pursued much until recently. I'm talking about trout fishing here, but really, when you think about it for a minute, there should be no more mystery to finding a trout in the sea than there is to finding a mullet.

The sea-trout of British Columbia are to be found all along the coast in water more or less adjacent to rivers entering the salt. The native Pacific sea-trout is not a brown trout but a cutthroat. The cutthroat fills, more or less, the same niche on the Pacific coast that the sea-run brown trout does in Europe. For the fly-fisher, the one important difference between the European sea-trout and the sea-run cutthroat is that the cutthroat does not tolerate the proximity to human population that the sea-run brown trout might. So, to find fishable populations of sea-run cutthroats, the further north you go the better.

The way to hunt cutthroat is from a boat; the way to catch them is with a fly. Well, maybe it's not a fly so much as a lure, but there is no doubt that fly-fishing is the way to catch them, despite the prevalence of a lazy attitude that a spinner is more productive. This is absolutely the biggest mistake you can make after doing everything else right. The cutthroat is probably the shyest of trout, at least as shy as the European sea-trout, and should be approached with the same degree of stealth and cunning. These fish are boat shy, line shy – you name it and cutthroats are shy of it. A spinner flung into a pod of trout will bring a follow or two, maybe even a strike, but after that one fish you may as well start throwing stones at them, because your fun is done.

Your biggest problem is arranging a boat and a guide, or someone local who knows their way around coastal waters. With salmon and steelhead being the big ticket attractions, it is rare to find a guide who knows enough about fly fishing for cutthroat trout to make it part of his programme, but plenty of them will pretend to know all about it. A good boatman is probably more important. Luckily, if there is anything that is not scarce on the Pacific coast, it's boats. Beware of cousin Dwayne and his sailboat, no matter how eager he may be, since you will be in waters with some fascinating tidal effects. Besides, life is way too short to spend all day belaying the mizzen topgallants, or whatever. You want a fast, spacious, hard-chined boat that can be run up to the shore to allow you to fish from the beaches. If you know anyone who owns a vessel like this, get friendly.

The strategies and tackle for sea-run cutts are pretty similar to that of other saltwater fly-fishing. A fast-action rod of nine feet throwing a number seven, long-belly floating or intermediate line is perfect for this fishing. Waders aren't really necessary in the summer – I like to wade wet in jeans and wading boots. Felt soles with prominent studs, even caulked logger's boots, are a good idea and will help on slippery rocks and logs. Wearing shorts is great until the horseflies find you, and then you'll wish you had carried a baseball bat.

Flies are baitfish imitations for the most part, but a few shrimp patterns are good to have on hand. I use a baitfish pattern derived from Bob Popovic's generic Surf Candy family that has evolved over the last ten years or so of beach fishing. The main constituent is Polar Bear hair and I like the fly to have eyes on it – they definitely make a difference. Tie the hair long and slim when imitating needlefish. Stainless steel hooks give the fly some durability in the salt, and allow you to keep flies in use for several trips. Sharpen the hooks and crimp the barbs for easy hook-ups and fast releases. Now, go to a place known or suspected to contain cutthroat trout.

Right about here, I get all sly and circumspect about specific places. A good cutthroat beach is something that is whispered only to your best friend with your dying breath, maybe, but the general principles are enough that you should not burn up too much time or fuel before getting stuck into some fish. Such a place will usually have one or more of the following features (more is better): a clean river or creek entering the salt chuck; a stone or gravel (not sand) beach, preferably with oysters; a slough or estuarine marsh with an extensive tidal channel; no active logging or fish farms nearby; schools of needlefish (sandeel) or herring sild. Find a place like this at the right stage of the tide and you're almost home.

The best strategy is to cruise the shoreline well back from the beach and to watch for signs of baitfish being chased by trout. A flooding tide is the right time, but the ebb can also be good. Fish through the tide changes but eat lunch or snooze only during slack tide. The ability to see the bait in the water comes soon enough, and you learn to distinguish between the ripples caused by wind or tide from the 'nervous' water caused by a balled-up shoal of herring. Wheeling Black Headed Gulls are always a good indicator of bait at the surface, but deeper needlefish schools can be located by standing up on the bow and watching for the dark masses of moving bait. Don't be put off by the appearance of seals – they live on fish. When you find the bait and the seals, the trout will not be far away.

The tendency will be to put the vessel right on top of the bait, but you will have to impress upon your boat-person that the boat must stay well away from the target area. When the bait goes down, so do the trout. I've put down the fish so often in this way that I now like to get out on my legs if it is possible to reach the fish from shore. If you can stay twenty yards away from bait activity and can reach it with a cast (that's why you might need a long-belly line and a decent double-haul), you will be able to fish the area for a considerable length of time without spooking everything. Once the tide moves the bait onshore you should get out, wade the beach and wait for the fish to come into range. The trout will usually keep the bait in against the shore.

When there are no fish or bait showing, the river mouth is an obvious place to begin your search. If the place has most of the amenities listed earlier, and you have arrived at the turn of the tide, it would be unusual for no fish to show, but working along the beach down-current will put you into fish soon enough. Long casts from shore that cover the water where the bottom is just visible, and a long, smooth, stripping retrieve is the way to provoke a take. Sometimes these trout really like a chase, and you will find that you just can't strip the line too fast. At other times the trout want the fly sinking as if dead, making it difficult to detect the take unless you watch the line closely. I recently discovered that skating the long flies on the surface like a wounded baitfish is deadly, making me think that deer hair or foam-bodied poppers are something to investigate. With the big baitfish flies, a constant retrieve is the most reliable for solid hook-ups.

The trout will often move into the river channel as the tide floods, and you have to work quickly upstream to stay with them. You will get a few fish and then everything goes dead. This might not mean that the bite is over, only that the fish have moved on. Slack tide is the time to stop for a coffee or lunch, and watch for eagles and killer whales while waiting for the ebb to begin. On a blue west-coast day while the bite is on, this definitely qualifies as a form of happiness. Time spent doing this will not be deducted from your allotted span.

Desolation Baitfish

Hook: stainless steel saltwater, size 4 to 2/0.
Thread: white 3/0. Tie in mylar tubing first, hanging forward from hook eye.
Tail: white or pale grey polar bear hair.
Body: silver coffee bag mylar, or white thread.
Dorsal 'wing': polar bear, white or coloured according to baitfish.
Under-wing: white polar bear.
Varnish all thread wraps. Roll the mylar back over the bear hair toward the bend and fray the ends to mix with the hair. Add stick-on epoxy eyes, varnish or epoxy body and head.
(*This lure was developed for the saltwater cutthroats of the BC coast in the mid-eighties. My pal John Dixon and I hunted the creek mouths and inlets of Desolation Sound in my old Texas-built death trap, the absurdly named King Commander, later in John's much safer, welded-aluminum Apple River. Great days.)

* * * * *

9. The Experience is the Thing

It is not essential to the hunt that it be successful.

Jose Ortega y Gasset
Meditations on Hunting

What would fishing be without fishing pals?

1. The big fish-off

He started it. Just wouldn't let it lie. Threw down the gauntlet one night on *Fly Fisherman Magazine's* Virtual Fly Shop Chat Room. As we were discussing our plan to hook up on the Elk later that year, Lance Filimek of Elko, BC, said something to the effect that it would be interesting to watch Hans Weilenmann and me fish together, each with his favourite fly. Hans, a Swiss resident of Holland and a regular on the fly-fishing Internet boards has a great trout fly, his CDC & Elk. Hans isn't shy about extolling its elegance, simplicity and effectiveness. Nor should he be, his fly's a killer. I've been banging on about my own DHE for a few years now to anyone who will listen, and to some who won't. These days, like Hans with his CDC & Elk, I don't use much else and I'm catching more fish than I ever did. I'll put it this way; you don't *have* to use the DHE, but you should.

Anyway, old Hans was feeling frisky that night. He picks up on the implication in Lance's remark and says, 'May the best fly win, Wyatt'. You know, right there for everyone to see. Now, of course, being male, there's no going back for him and no way out for me. Okay, I should say here that I don't really think competition has any place in fishing. It turns one of life's best experiences into a pissing contest and spoils everything, and I know Hans feels the same. Even friendly contests have a way of putting an uncomfortable edge on one of the purest forms of pleasure and happiness. Besides, this is the kind of pathetic male posturing that makes us so pitiful in the eyes of women. I thought about this as we chatted amiably on the chatroom that night and tried to think of a way to allow both of us to climb down gracefully, avoid silly contests, and just fish together like the mature and sophisticated adults we are.

Well, that's what I was thinking. What came out of my mouth was, 'OK, Hans...*bring it on*'.

So, two months later, there we were, rigging up on the banks of British Columbia's Elk River on a sultry August morning. Hans was over for the big fly-tier's conclave in Livingstone, Montana. Hans had been driving around the western states for two weeks straight and was excited at the prospect of finally putting in some serious river time with Fran Friesan, out from Vancouver.

Just as we were slapping each other on the back, starting toward the water, Fran chirped... 'So, this is the day of the big fish-off, huh, guys?' It was at that point I wondered if the reason men are such idiots is because women make us that way. Hans didn't respond to that, but I saw a wee smile cross his lips as he turned toward the river. Confidence? Superiority? Oh no, I thought, what if he really *does* have a better fly than me? I remembered grimly the old time gunfighter's maxim; 'Beware the man with one gun'.

The worm of competition had begun to turn. I looked down at the scrap of fur and deer hair hung in the keeper ring of my scruffy old RPL. Hans noticed this and said, in what I regarded as a tone pregnant with meaning, 'So, Bob, you're a keeper ring guy, I see'. I thought, what's this, Hans psyching me out here? With cool deliberation, Hans hooked his little CDC & Elk in the stripping guide of his GLX, tightened up on his rare and spectacular Lawrence Waldron fly reel, and fell in behind Fran and me. Surely, he's not doing anything, I thought, it's just me. *I'm* the one who's feeling competitive here. C'mon, Wyatt, shut up and fish.

The Elk River, British Columbia

Just to show everybody that a fish-off was the furthest thing from my mind, and that I was, you know, *definitely* not competing, I went into my chilled-out guide mode. I positioned myself casually downstream, pointing out riffles and slots with my rod tip as Fran and Hans limbered up. Fran hooked a fish immediately. 'One for the CDC & Elk', she shouted, in case we might have somehow forgotten this was a shoot-out. 'Of *course*!' shouted Hans, who then hooked a fish from the same riffle. With some relief, I saw that they were both ten-inchers, small fish on this river. Still…

Trapped in my phoney laid-back guide impersonation I couldn't just tear off downstream and begin frantically thrashing the water, like I wanted to, so I pointed out another particularly nice patch alongside a log jam. Hans ambled over, waded into position and went to work, fishing downstream dry…expertly, I noticed with growing alarm. I watched him lay out a beautifully controlled loop, presenting the little fly perfectly with his hand-plaited furled thread leader, mending, fishing through the eye of the pool with an impeccably drag-free drift.

Nope.

Five more casts…still nope.

I was well downstream of the sweet-spot. I flipped out my leader and a few feet of line, limbering up with as much *nonchalance* as I could muster. The leader was lying on the surface like a frozen garden hose, the tippet doubled back in a sloppy, embarrassing, tangle. Out of nowhere, a fifteen-inch cutt pounced on my DHE in a slam-dunk rise only two feet off the bank. He was on, and in a couple of minutes was unhooked and back where he came from. 'Nice fish', I heard Hans say from upstream. Outwardly impassive, on the inside I was doing a clenched-fist, Jim Carrie, 'A-W-W-W-RIGHT!' But, then I thought… hey, these are guests here, on my home waters; that's no way to feel. Then again, I was ahead on size, and I have to admit, that felt *good*.

It wasn't hot fishing. We fished down the big river for a quarter-mile. Fran took another fish, a nice one, on the CDC & Elk. Hans had no more action, but, still doing my guide impersonation, I managed to nail two more chunky trout before we had to meet Lance back at the bridge. We all headed downriver to join Lance Filimek at a run I had reconnoitred the afternoon before, where I had taken a cracking twenty-two inch cutt, the best trout of my summer so far (on a hare's ear bodied, white wing DHE – just for the record). I quit after that fish, not wanting to spoil it for the next day. I put Hans in the spot where a couple of good fish had shown. He worked the run carefully and expertly. Nope.

Hans fished up the run and I stepped in forty yards downstream of him. No more fooling around, I said to myself. I really wanted Hans to hook up with some fish now. However, at this juncture, the planets swam into alignment and the trout gods shared a wink. The air was right, the light was right, the water was right, and the fly was right…everything. I'd been out for five weeks, after a week in New Zealand and another in northern Scotland, quite frankly fishing myself stupid, and right then couldn't give a hoot whether I caught another trout all day. You know what I'm talking about, right? You've been there. I couldn't miss. I was in the zone.

All I had to do was toss that DHE down somewhere, anywhere – middle of the river, near the bank – and…*chug*! Five fish hooked in a row, all over fifteen inches. Three of them I managed to bring to hand and release. While this is going on, I noticed with concern that Hans had not hooked a fish. Uh, oh. I reeled up and climbed out of the river, walked up to Hans and told him to come downstream. I knew there were more trout in that stretch, and began to feel some real anxiety and guilt, sincerely regretting that we'd ever mentioned a stupid contest. 'I'm rising a few,' Hans said, 'but I'm missing them. Lipped a couple is all'.

'Well, your timing's probably a bit off,' I said, 'You'll get 'em, Hans. There are some nice fish down here. Don't be too fast on the old trigger. Let 'em take it.' I didn't need to tell him that, and I certainly didn't want him to think I was being patronising, but I wanted him to know that I was genuinely feeling for him and that the fish-off was now officially off. I meant it too, but that kind of solicitude just makes things worse. He hadn't been doing much trout fishing that season, didn't have his eye in yet, and this stupid fish-off thing was maybe putting him off his game.

The only difference I could see in our approaches, apart from our flies, was that Hans was using a bright green furled thread leader. It's possible that these hard-fished cutthroats were line-shy, or maybe the straight turn-over of that furled leader was causing unseen drag, but there's no way to be sure. As we know, other things being equal, sometimes it's the fly that makes the difference and this appeared to be one of those cases, but with all the variables in play there's no way to really ascertain that. Well, you know how this one goes, right? Hans worked hard the rest of the day. I fished behind him and continued to raise fish after fish. He got some fish, one a cracking twenty-incher but, let's face it, I should have cleaned out my bank account and headed for Las Vegas.

In the late afternoon, I put on one of Lance's big, beautifully tied foam grasshoppers, just to get away from the increasingly oppressive one-fly theme of the day. As we were winding things down, wading across the river together, I casually tossed the fly toward shore. Chug! Another thumping trout from an insignificant pocket, tight against the bank. There was a collective groan from the group, including me. I've been on the other end of that kind of experience enough times, so I know what it's like. Hans was just in the wrong end of the boat. Lance, of course, was delighted. He hadn't yet fished that grasshopper pattern of his, and he just beamed. I'm sure I caught that glint in his eyes that said we'd be hearing more about that hopper, confirming that we're a bunch of hopeless loonies.

The best fishing is usually hard to reach

Later in the trip, after I'd headed back to Scotland, Hans and Fran had some great fishing on the CDC & Elk, on the same water we fished that day and a couple of other streams in the area. I just wish we hadn't started that ridiculous one-fly fish-off on the only day we had to fish together. It certainly didn't prove anything with respect to the flies. Hans is a superb fly tier and angler, and as sure of his favourite fly as I am of mine, maybe more so and with good reason. We'll never settle which fly is *best*. First, because it doesn't matter. Second, because it's impossible anyway. All that dumb shoot-out demonstrated was that fly-fishing just has too many variables and imponderables, and is way too subjective an experience for such a positivist approach. The main thing is, I'd fish with Hans anywhere and I'm sure he feels the same way as I do about competing in something we love. He certainly isn't the slightest bit interested in a stand-up rematch, you know, just to settle this best fly thing once and for all.

2. Line dances with wolves

There is a type of angler who can be characterised as the perennial duffer. I really don't mean to sound harsh there and I'll try to explain. Waddy Dawson, a dear friend of my father, was my first experience of the type. He had all the gear, including a nice bamboo rod and a beautiful wood and canvas canoe. He loved canoeing and camping and fished intermittently with my father. Old Waddy loved fly-fishing but just couldn't catch fish. Even at fourteen years old I was aware of this and would leave a pool to him, pointing out where I knew a trout lay in wait to nail the first fly cast to it. Waddy would then proceed to fish what was always, for him, a fishless pool. I would follow up or down the water he had just worked, taking trout after trout on identical flies. Waddy would just laugh. It was clear that Waddy was a passionate outdoorsman but not a 'serious' angler, at least in terms of the intensity and purpose we associate with that term, and certainly not in terms of the others in our family circle. His death was deeply felt by my father, who never made another fishing friend.

Forty years later, I see this type of angler as a source of relief in the face of the unrelenting pressures shaping what I regard as a condition of mind and a state of happiness into just another competitive leisure activity, with a hierarchy of expertise ranging from 'entry-level' to 'pro-guide'. At its worst, it's a dumbed-down, pay-for-it entertainment, arranged like the services of a hotel hooker. Okay, *now* I'm being harsh.

I fish several times a season with a group of guys we call 'the club', but which is in fact just a gang. The few times on which we fish as a group formalises what is primarily a social relationship, and we do this on some local stocked water. Among this bunch there is little or no enthusiasm for the inducements of stockie bashing, which, it has to be said, represents a big part of contemporary British fly-fishing. To keep things in perspective, and for laughs, we stage a competition once a year on some local stocked water, fishing for a bottle of whisky. It's a hoot, but we know where we are coming from. If it needs to be stated, there is nothing wrong with just wanting to get out with the bubs and bend a rod, without the high seriousness and intensity we sometimes attach to it.

The same gang gets together for a week at a lodge in northern Scotland every summer. Though it doesn't involve handholding and drums, by the end of the week everyone has had an insight into how and why they fish, and a reminder of who their friends are. There is really no way to disguise one's character in such a situation. We are exposed to one another for what we are; the body-counters, the closet competitors, the existentialists, the romantics, the Pollyannas, the Cassandras, the gear-heads, fly spongers, braggarts, folk singers, and clowns; the poets, the priests, and the simply drunk. The angling rules of combination permit the embodiment of two or more of these characteristics in any single persona, any of which may hatch at different times over the week.

One of the guys, Davy Taylor, exemplifies the angler who has arrived at a kind of philosophical destination in his journey, striking an early bargain with fly-fishing's Wu-Li masters. In the ten years I have fished with him, it is fair to say that I have seen no quantifiable change in technique. Since Davy is an intellectual and an aesthete, I have decided that this may be purposeful. Unlike old Waddy Dawson, Davy catches fish, but I suspect that he has arranged it so every trout comes as a delightful surprise, a blank day is no more than one should expect, a big trout proof against the testicular preening of the experts.

Davy is a man for whom the adjective laconic might have been invented. To me, everything he says sounds ironic, although I know it can't be. He has the somewhat lunar and impassive face of one of those American Indian chiefs gazing in sepia inscrutability from a William Curtis print, an attribution that is reinforced by his habit of raising one flat hand in the air when he is about to speak. Not usually a big drinker, it is deep into a long night of it, when he is well gooned, that we see the inner Davy emerge like a caddis pupa. One memorable session several years ago provided us with Davy's spirit name, *Line Dances With Wolves*.

Sometimes Davy just seems to be tuned onto a different wave-length, one not necessarily of this world. One spring day, a couple of us watched while, as if in a slow motion segment on one of those television near-death encounters, Davy decided to calmly wade around the end of a stone croy in the river Tay, something you should never do. The current deepens and accelerates around the end of these things, impossible to withstand, and you are suddenly gripped and swept into the middle of the river. He didn't hear my shout to go back until he couldn't, and we were mightily relieved when he finally grounded on a gravel bar downstream, holding on to his rod and losing only his net. Later, of course, it was hilarious. Another time, Davy inexplicably let go of his rod – while casting – and watched it disappear like Excalibur into the depths of a trout loch. This rounded off a relatively unusual sequence of events in which Davy caught an eight-pound pike on a nymph.

I recently shared a boat with Davy on a rather good little northern brownie loch, and my appraisal of what makes him tick underwent an adjustment. The conditions were bad for fly fishing; a hard light and a cold north-east wind, which had been blowing hard for days, what they call in these parts a 'scourie' wind, flattening the waves in contrary iron grey gusts. The trout were dour and were coming short, when they came at all.

A stiff and variable wind at your back is not the helping hand one might expect for casting a fly line from a drifting boat. If you don't put enough speed and elevation into the back loop, and proper timing into the forward throw, you get a fly line and a two-fly leader in the back of the head. Doing this to yourself is annoying enough; having your partner do it to you twenty times in an afternoon is a severe test of patience and social skills. This kind of thing usually impresses me as a lack of appropriate seriousness and dedication, and brings out a really insufferable side of my personality, the ornery high school football coach.

By the time I had heard Davy's utterance of 'sorry' repeated with every third cast for several hours, like a respondent in some monastic litany, I was ready to send him to the showers. When he changed a fly, for reasons that to me seemed completely arbitrary, his rod would swing across mine, fouling my line mid-cast, striking the septum of my nose or knocking off my polaroids. To cap it off, he began to complain about being cold. The fact that he had as many fish in the boat as I did, one bigger than any of mine, was a reminder to keep things in perspective, to just go with it.

My cantankerousness is based in the cold realisation that I am on short time; each day on the water, even a bad one, is increasingly precious to me. Anyway, I take the view that pleasure in a thing deepens in direct proportion to one's skill in it. Once casting and line handling reaches the level where it becomes transparent, action merges with thought, your eyes, ears and touch are tuned to both a wider and more specific world of detail. This is the kind of thing described by practitioners of Tai Chi, and it applies perfectly to fly-fishing. Admittedly, it's also the kind of thing that prompts non-practitioners to suggest that one should get a life.

On our last northern trip, Davy fished with a new seriousness; he didn't hook me even once, didn't complain about the cold on some really nasty days, and got some remarkable bags of trout. He was a real pleasure to fish with, and it was plain to see the satisfaction he took in every aspect of his own performance. It was fun for both of us. Whether Davy becomes another fly-fishing expert remains to be seen. I rather hope not. What is clearly evident is the love he has, if not for the clean brilliant flame of experience when everything goes impeccably, then certainly for the pleasures of just stepping out of daily life and into the world of water, wind, wild trout and the company of old friends. Who's to say that isn't enough?

3. Liars

The popular construction of the angler, formed by centuries of deprecating jokes, cartoons and literary slurs, is of a simple-minded geek in a goofy hat who happily sits for hours in the rain, drowning worms and reeling in old rubber boots, and to round it off, is a liar. Upon hearing an explanation of angling as pitting one's wits against that of the fish, Ezra Pound is credited by Ernest Hemingway to have said it was certainly the way he had always regarded it.

Maybe that sort of thing produced the tendency to lie about one's catch. The socio-biological imperative to be perceived as a good hunter is imbedded in our genes; to be regarded as a time-wasting fool with no quantifiable results is too much for most of us. We had to invent the big one that got away, the fish story. Now, anyone who has done enough fishing to hook a few big ones knows that they do tend to get away, more often than not. This prepares the ground of credibility among our fellows, with the tacit agreement that we will respect each other's long distance releases.

The new ethos of catch and release has been a boon to those who nurse some real anxieties about how they are regarded as hunters. For the more insecure among us, success rates have spiralled, with a concurrent rise in attributed expertise. However, having big ones get away every time becomes unsupportable, even among a group of liars, so, with the advent of the catch and release ethos we now have a situation where, not only do we get to report on our own expertise, but we get the credit for being selfless, socially correct *and* environmentally friendly. Good for us, good for the fish – win-win.

Although it no longer involves pistols at dawn, custom prohibits an overt challenge of another angler's fish story, so, except when dealing with a really intolerable bullshitter any such doubts are normally expressed beyond earshot. In exceptional cases, lying becomes a problem and spoils things irretrievably. I have occasionally fished with guys who, for reasons we can only guess at, just have to lie about their fish although they are actually pretty good anglers. The worm of competition and social comparison gnaws away at them to such a degree that they invariably report success in the face of general failure and impossible conditions; they *always* catch more and bigger fish than anyone. The effect of this, intentionally or not, is to brand everyone else as incompetent, as if in our ignorance and insensitivity we hadn't noticed the subtle indicators in the environment, or possessed sufficient skill to exploit them.

Maybe not as reprehensible as cheating at cards or dropping golf balls in a money game, lying about fish drags angling into the domain of competitive games and the laying of bets. Fishing overlaps the penumbra of gaming – put two anglers together and they can't help competing to some extent – but fly-fishing has pretensions toward status as an art, which is supposed to preclude such base impulses. By the way, those who subscribe to the idea of fly-fishing as art obviously haven't been to an uptown art gallery opening. For a glimpse into a Darwinian arena of ruthless competition, just hang with some artists for a while.

Another thing maybe more important, the trading of useful information, is an essential and pleasurable part of any fishing conversation, a real guy-thing, rooted in the ancient male codes of group hunting. A liar in those days probably got a hot tomahawk where the sun don't shine. Nobody minds a little boasting or imaginative embellishment, but if the going has been hard and you haven't been connecting, the last thing you want to hear is bullshit. If someone is getting fish in a special place, on some particular fly or method, it's great to hear how they did it. If, however, they haven't been doing any better than you have and they *lie* about it, you just might waste valuable fishing time and effort, travelling to some new spot or following their advice, especially if you are on unfamiliar water or just a beginner.

On any group fishing trip some friendly competition will occur, the side bet, or the cash pool for the biggest fish. Incidentally, the guy who suggests this, just to keep things 'interesting', is usually the one with the relentless jokes and the weed-eater back casts, the guy who finds the wait between 'bites' unendurable, is not above sneaking a tin of worms into his pocket as a little insurance, and because he catches relatively few fish, considers a fishing trip just an opportunity for a wall-to-wall beer fest. But once the action is taken up by the others the nature of the trip changes a little, sometimes a lot. If it stays fun, that's great, but it has been known to turn bitter and can take the fun out of everything.

And that's the thing, isn't it? Spoiling the fun. Shattering the transparent sphere of quietude, simplicity and intense clarity, which at its best, fly-fishing will afford, if that's not getting too

The witching hour. Evening on a western Canadian trout river

pious about it. It's okay when one of the boys says he lost a big fish, maybe the biggest yet, or exaggerates the size of those he did catch, rounding them up to the next half pound. Good on you, pal. Rock on. Only when fish are being lost, caught and released at a rate or of a size that is apparently intended to turn a fishing trip into some kind of pissing contest does it inspire resentment. Maybe, in those situations, such a contest might actually settle things, and then maybe we could all just go fishing.

4. The deep end

When you have begun measuring your life by the number of fishing seasons left in it, a poor one provokes the worst sort of anxiety. Non-fisherpersons and those born yesterday don't understand this, as if a poor season could be made up in some other way, like 'next year'. People say, 'Oh well, there's always next year' when the future stretches out before them like a freeway, with amusing stops of interest along the way. Well, sorry friend, but I already have *plans* for next year.

Fishing is like some other pursuits that take on the aspect of an obsession in men's lives. I say 'men' knowing that many women are becoming almost as crazed, but I have yet to meet the female equivalent of the extreme trout or steelhead bum. They may be out there, ruining their lives, but so far they seem to be relatively scarce. Most of the women anglers I have met seem to be pretty well balanced types, while serious enough, and seem to be fishing for pleasure, displaying little of the white-eyed fervour of the far-gone fish bum.

Near-bums manage to stick together enough of the requisites of civilised life to carry their weight in polite company and regular employment. Some even manage to deceive women into something that has the appearance of a normal relationship, at least for a season or two. But you should know you're in trouble if you can argue that the Ted Jurascik saltwater reel is a better deal than the family holiday and think you're making sense. Her lawyer will make a pretty good case that those sensibilities are of a piece with turning every dinner conversation into a fishing report and spending so much time in the garage. Another good indicator of social dysfunction is the proven relationship between fishing tackle and sex. The number of high-end fly reels is in inverse proportion to the quality of your sex life. My collection, by the way, is the envy of all my pals.

My own hard-core period followed the break-up with my second major domestic relationship, and lasted only a year and a half. I look back on this part of my life fondly, but consider myself lucky. It was, let me tell you, a near thing. As I remember it, there really was a moment when I took stock of my life and made a choice. Out on the street, in front of what was no longer *our* house, loading the last of the duffle bags, guns, tackle, books and Emmylou Harris LPs into my pick-up, I realised that this was a juncture of existential purity. My loaded pickup truck was a concrete metaphor for my Nietzschean will-to-overcome. Life was pure potential. I would now re-invent myself. Buff, my Labrador retriever, unimpressed by the headiness of the moment, trotted pragmatically back into the house without so much as a guilty tail-wag.

I headed west to Vancouver Island. I had a few art school and hippie friends on the coast, some of whom were by then dealing in real-estate instead of controlled substances, albeit with the same degree of *sang froid*. More importantly, it was where the steelhead lived. Upon the selfless advice of an erstwhile real-estate friend, now languishing in a Mexican prison, I fetched up on a couple acres south of Campbell River at a place ironically named Fanny Bay. I had a nicely appointed (realtors' jargon for Wally World baroque) mobile home, a sort of plush culvert on wheels, and a new dog.

I also got myself a boat, a snappy fifteen-foot aluminium death trap made in Texas in 1952 (the previous owner described her knife-like prow and tendency to porpoise as 'sea-kindly'). I quickly got down to business as an existential steelhead warrior and sporting artist. I painted in the morning and fished in the afternoon, mooching for salmon off Denman and Hornby islands or prowling the rivers and estuaries for steelhead and cutthroat. There was a great oyster beach right out front of my trailer. My rods were never taken down, just canted against the porch rail every evening, a salutation to myself of my new warrior status. This was also a way of signifying to passers-by and casual acquaintances that this was the no-frills base of operations for your dedicated Steelhead Bum, not simply the weed-infested redoubt of your Common Bum, which to the inexpert eye it may have resembled.

Prepared for a period of adjustment to the warrior's life, what spooked me was the shocking realisation that it was actually possible. Worse, after a few months of quiet evenings staring into the fake fireplace, I found myself hanging around the local 'meat holes'. These are the spots on any west coast river that hold disproportionate concentrations of fish and attract fishermen in numbers usually associated with organised sports. In European terms, the Ridge Pool on the Irish river Moy is the kind of thing I'm talking about. In this case, the local meat holes were on the Big Qualicum and Stamp rivers, and each had a bunch of regulars, just like a Glasgow pub. The regulars were those who lived near the respective rivers, the Homeboys. Visitors from the other river were known as Bastards. The Stamp had more and larger fish than we did, so there was a patronising air of superiority to the Stamp Falls Bastards. Tourists and out of town anglers were all called Mainlanders, which was somehow worse than being a Bastard.

Protocol required that you showed up at these places as if you were just checking on the current run of fish, trying out a new rod, or testing some new fly pattern. The idea was that, for you, this was just a day off from the *real* fishing on those legendary wilderness rivers. This act was for the Mainlanders, and especially the Bastards from the other rivers. The regulars, of course, were there for the same reason you were – human company. The thing about those wilderness rivers is, sure, they have lots of fish in them, but at that time at least, they were such *lonely* places.

I put the picture together pretty quickly. First, there were no women out there. The few that had accompanied their man out to big fish country lasted a winter, maybe two, then high-tailed it for the nearest mall. There was a local race of women who for economic or ideological reasons did live in the region, but they seemed to be a flinty-eyed and practical bunch. They also lived at a pretty high standard, provided by the comparatively enormous incomes of their men, commercial fishermen, loggers, chopper pilots and real-estate agents. Many of these women worked at these jobs themselves. Not the kind to be impressed by some idiot living like Robinson Crusoe.

Secondly, it was pretty clear that, for the most part, the meat hole gang was made up of lonely guys on low incomes. If it had been a bowling alley, we would be the guys in the satin team jackets with the personalised bowling balls. The really sad cases did in fact adopt a kind of uniform; big floppy hats, beards, aviator polaroids, Willie Nelson bandanas – the full video outlaw. The look, I guess, was supposed to mimic that of the contemporary fishing guide, who in turn is affecting the style of the Hollywood version of an old-west gunfighter. Talk about your simulacra; old Beaudrillard would have had a picnic with this crowd. It was a conscious effort to separate ourselves from the Mainlanders, who apart from the bandido *chic*, were doing exactly the same thing we were, fishing.

Finally, for all the talk of fishing the great wild rivers, we were always there, at the meat hole. The guys fishing 'out there' were mostly rich businessmen who flew in to the best spots by chopper or float plane, often accompanied by sleek women who fished as well as the men without so much as chipping a fingernail. By the way, through the occasional sale of a painting, I've fished with some of those expensive people and I found that they were just as serious and competent as any deep-end, outlaw fish bum I ever met. I suspect it comes from spending a lot of prime time on the best water in the world.

And sometimes, when you get things right, this happens

By mid-autumn, when things got *really* quiet at Fanny Bay, I was showing up at these places pretty regularly myself. Just like the guys who get together to shoot muzzle-loaders or practise Kung Foo, I would look forward to seeing old Mike or old Dave every afternoon down at the meat hole. We would show each other some idiosyncratic improvement on the traditional rigs, compare reels, swap fish gossip and try hard to look like battle weary veterans for the Mainlanders and Bastards. There was always some new report on the fabled big-time rivers, and we would make plans to put together a trip up to the Queen Charlotte Islands or the Nass – this, while twenty-pound Chinooks wallowed like hippos in the pool at our feet. Occasionally we took a turn down the pool, often hooking a fish, which we released with a studied nonchalance – just to prove to the Mainlanders and Stamp Falls Bastards that it was no big deal.

'Yeah Mike, that rig oughta work just fine up on the BABINE this year'.

Now, on the other hand, being within striking range of some world-class rivers, I did get in some pretty spectacular fishing in that year and a half, so it quickly becomes a matter of relativity. I mean, to whom could I brag... Mike and Dave? We'd get pissed in the camper, grin like idiots at each other, give rebel yells and punch each other on the shoulder, followed by a goofy silence. I think we realised that our social loop was maybe a teensy bit small.

Several times over that period, I would be visited by Mainlander friends and their wives who were making the Big Fishing Trip, and who would invariably express their envy at my audacious and selfish, if monastic, lifestyle. I would, of course, play the role for them. We'd spend a few days out on the salt chuck, bucktailing for coho, a few more hunting steelhead or wading a beach for cutthroat, then wrap it up with a big barbecue and oyster roast. I would pose heroically at the gate and wave them off as they went home to their real life, taking their wives with them. It seemed to me that they maybe had it right; a fishing trip should be a rare and magical event. These visits made me lonelier than ever, so within hours of my friends' departure I would show up down at the meat hole. There would be some awkwardness as my pals would give me the old 'Well, look who's back!' treatment, as if I'd been cheating on them.

It ended when a group of friends from Vancouver arrived for a long weekend. Among them was Margaret, a rehabilitation psychologist who got me straightened out in several ways and shut down my fledgling steelhead bum operation pretty quickly. I made the *faux pas* of proudly taking her down to the meat hole to show her off to my pals. I may as well have arrived wearing a tuxedo. The boys closed ranks with an exaggerated politeness usually reserved for the game warden and excused themselves, making a big show of examining the contents of their fly boxes. It may have been the look on Margaret's face; the one that asked, 'Are you guys *serious?*'

5. The big sleep

Evidently, upon reviewing the sporting journals over the past few years, some British anglers still think catch and release is morally wrong, an example of imported American political correctness. They believe that fish, if caught, should be killed. This, they reason, will keep us from playing into the hands of the anti-angling lobby. Those who don't want to kill the fish they catch, but would like to go fishing all the same, are described as the type of person who would play football with a live hedgehog (and worse, presumably, once that moral line has been crossed). And, despite the growing opinion that a wild trout is maybe too precious to be put to death the first time it makes the mistake of eating a Royal Wulff, those who fish for reasons other than food are just a bunch of nasty hedgehog-kickers at heart.

Well, if that's the argument, I say horsefeathers. I fish for pleasure, first and last, and like to

Brief encounters. A beautiful brown goes back, maybe for someone else to meet again   photo: Bruce Masson

argue that fly-fishing is what wild trout and salmon are *for*. But, even if you think that's playing off-side, it seems to me that the whole fishing for food argument is just a little disingenuous, and more than a tad self-righteous. I kill plenty of fish on waters that will support or are even improved by an appropriate cull, so I am not arguing against killing, *per se*. In fact, if we go on the evidence, you'd be forced to concur that killing makes the world go round. The hedgehog and anti-fishing lobby argument sounds rather like a straw man set up to distract attention from a fundamental fact. What makes everyone go all puritanical and solemn is the fact that fishing, like sex, is deeply and naturally pleasurable.

I spent the last couple of summers fishing a region where fishing pressure has a whole new meaning for anyone used to the ordinarily sedate British experience. Five straight weeks in southern Alberta and British Columbia, and a lot of pondering, confirmed for me the rather counter-intuitive realisation that, with some reservations, fishing pressure is ultimately good for fish. I fished some of the old places, most of which are now catch and release fisheries to some extent, and what I encountered is interesting.

The rivers in Alberta and British Columbia are being intensively managed on a limited-kill, or strictly no-kill basis. This is because the fishing pressure from a tooled-up and outwardly-mobile public is just too great for a wild eco-system to support. The rivers are 'slot managed' on a sustained, wild-fishery, basis. They have kill sections and no-kill sections. The kill sections have rather severe daily limits on the size and number of fish one can kill - normally one or two fish in a certain size kill-slot. Fish that fit that kill-slot, as you can imagine, are pretty scarce. A clear outcome of this kind of management is that there are more and bigger fish on the no-kill sections and the fishing is better, if more 'technical', because the large fish are definitely wide awake. There are undoubtedly a few big trout on the kill sections, but they are likely immune to sporting methods. There is just no comparison between kill and no-kill rivers. Days on the limited-kill waters are seldom better than fair, while on no-kill rivers I now catch wild trout of a size and number that I haven't seen for over forty years.

Recently, my brother Bill suggested a trip to a secret river, one that was designated limited access, wilderness, barbless hook, fly-fishing only, and strictly no-kill. I expected to find well-trodden trails, plenty of sophisticated company, and some spooky trout with sore lips and pet names. It was simply one of the best day's fly-fishing I have ever had. To have a day like that and not have to fly to New Zealand for it is a balm for the soul. The trout were big, wild, and free rising, just like it's supposed to be. They were spooky enough to be challenging, so it was real fly-fishing. The combination of limited access, strict tackle restrictions and an absolute no-kill policy, resulted in a superb day's fishing. At the end of the day we all felt terrific, absolutely as high as kites. We didn't kill a single trout and no one even mentioned it. It just didn't matter. I should mention here that the only trails were grizzly trails, and they appeared to have a fast lane.

The western rivers are busy places these days, but the fishing is holding up

The famous western trout waters are fished relentlessly, from ice-out to freeze-up. A small army of professional guides, plying the larger rivers like the Bow and the Elk in a steady procession of Mackenzie style drift-boats, provides much of this constant attention (there are currently something like fifty trout guides operating out of Fernie, BC, alone). A commonplace these days is to be nearly run down by a drift-boat, then glared at contemptuously by some hired gun, as if to say, 'Look, friend, you may be just out for fun but, goddammit, I'm *workin'* here!' Sometimes they do say it.

If we add to this the thousands of local recreational anglers, many of whom are now pretty good fly-fishers, you begin to get the picture. Intensity breeds expertise, and to a casual observer these rivers look like they are being loved to death. Up-close, this is something of a nightmare for anyone who regards fly-fishing as a contemplative activity, the quiet sport. Well, any holiday weekend on the Bow and Elk can give one the impression of fly-fishing as an *organised* sport. Every pool and run seems to have someone earnestly thrashing away under the polarised gaze of a coach.

At the height of the season, the Crowsnest, a river on which I spent countless solitary hours as a kid, seems like some kind of fly-fishing theme park, with impatient queues of Orvis-clad enthusiasts marking time on every riffle and run. The Bow flows right through the middle of a booming city of nearly a million avid and tooled-up fun-seekers, all of whom appear to own a fly rod and an SUV. One just can't ignore this level of intensity, which, one has to admit, might appear to the uninformed eye disturbingly like persecution.

The answer is maybe to leave the glamour rivers to the crowds, at least on the weekends, and seek out smaller, obscure, more intimate situations, in keeping with the reasons you fly-fish in the first place, usually for fewer and smaller trout. This approach has nothing to do with the opportunity to catch fish, but purely a matter of angling aesthetics. If you want to catch lots of big trout, the high profile rivers are the place to go, and for good reason. If you don't mind the company those wonderful rivers produce fly-fishing of a high order, season after season. Naturally, living with the constant attention of anglers, the really big fish are spooky and somewhat harder to catch, but that just seems the way it should be.

Over the years, the Bow and other rivers in the region have become more technical. A four-pound Bow River 'bullet' is really something to bark about, and believe me, after trundling a San Juan Worm under an indicator for twelve hours beneath a blazing sun, you've earned it. The Bow was one of the earlier Canadian experiments with no-kill angling. The policy has been extended to several other waters, especially since 1995 when devastating floods damaged several trout streams in Alberta and south-eastern BC. No-kill was established as a means of allowing the trout populations to recover, but has remained ever since as an effective tool for quality management. In some cases the recovery has been astounding. Anglers are asking themselves, just how good can the fishing get? Well, the answer seems to be: pretty good.

The slot-management of the North American streams is based on the understanding that killing and eating trout is not a bad thing in itself, in fact it is one of life's luxuries, you just have to reduce the level of attrition somehow. Even Alberta's Bow and Crowsnest rivers have a kill-slot for a lip-smacking rainbow between twelve and sixteen inches long (on the Bow, I believe this has recently been adjusted downwards to one fish under fourteen inches). Apart from that unfortunate slot-fish, everybody goes home happy, even the trout.

The results are conclusive. If you want great public fly-fishing, no-kill is the way to go. The rivers of southern Alberta and BC, Montana and Idaho have always been pretty good. Now, however, they are spectacular. Frankly, considering that I grew up on these rivers, the fishing

The Alberta Rose Café, Crowsnest River

has never been better in living memory. You can't have fishing this good without large and healthy populations of fish. The irreducible fact is that if you take a fish from the water it is no longer there to catch. You've created a hole, one that might take years to fill, and with today's pressure possibly never. Put that fish back and it is there to reproduce and live out its life, maybe for you or someone else to catch. Win – win.

This is the sticking point. Many people sincerely agonise over the *morality* of this situation. Should we allow a fish to live only to be caught again, an object of a mere game, for human pleasure rather than good old, down-home food gathering? Well, for starters, those who say they fly-fish for wild trout primarily as food should have their heads examined. Once you have seriously tackled up, organised, and paid for your trip, the cost of fly-caught trout must come in at roughly the same as Beluga caviar flown in by helicopter. If fish is that important to one's diet, it clearly makes more sense, in terms of edible product and financial outlay, to take a sea charter for some real freezer-fillers. On the other hand, since wild trout or salmon is considered a luxury food, how does one distinguish that from fishing for pleasure?

On the ecological account, the energy and resources expended to catch the calories contained in a trout are ridiculous, if not technically insane. Anyway, the element of pleasure is undeniable. Otherwise, why fly fish? The argument must be that the pleasure is unintentional, a *posteriori*, and therefore guilt free, an intellectual conceit presented most sincerely and elegantly in *Fishing and Thinking*, a fine book by religious scholar A.A. Luce. The 'innocent angler' position amounts to something like Brer Rabbit's briar patch. Once someone holes-up in there you ain't *ever* going to argue them out of it. Besides, splitting philosophical hairs still gets you fishing as pleasure. Philosophically and morally, the strongest argument for fly-fishing is as a form of happiness. Food for the belly is one thing; food for the spirit is something else. Forget the worthy Puritanism of the food argument. That dog won't hunt.

Some of us are worried about how this is regarded by the non-angling public, who clearly don't understand it and don't want to. I can't answer that one, only that the question of personal righteousness must be set against the greater question of steadily suppressing the natural population of a wild eco-system. This is a twenty-first century question, a 'post-modern' one if you like, but it certainly isn't going to go away. It's ironic that, of all the contemporary excesses and crimes against nature in the name of urban pleasure and comfort, the animal rights people should single out fishing for proscription. There is little point in even engaging in a debate with those who have already made up their minds and have no intention of considering another point of view. You'd have a better chance arguing with the Taliban to open a lap-dancing club in Kabul. The bigger issue, the pay-off for anyone who believes in the morality of no-kill fishing, is that it permits the best possible outcome for everyone, not least the fish.

Pragmatically, the current level of non-consumptive pressure is actually a good thing, as annoying as it is for cranky old bastards moaning about the good old days, before *A River Runs Through It* ruined everything. The rivers receive constant attention and protection, simply because they are worth something to anglers and the economy. The fish are allowed to live and grow. We are allowed to make contact with them and their environment in a meaningful way, and, as far as I can tell, the fish aren't really bothered that much. Because we only protect something we care for, on rivers and lakes where the fly-fishing is good the fish are doing just fine, thanks. You might say it's just a matter of changing roles.

The *meaning* of a fish changes, from potential fry-up to the object of something like a spiritual quest, which isn't diminished just because you catch a fish that has been caught before. In fact, catching an old veteran trout seems to increase the level of emotional attachment you have for these creatures and the places they are found. As John Gierach put it, what good is a sport if you can't get all mushy about it? It all depends on what *use* you are managing for: salmon or trout; quality or quantity; food for the belly or for the soul. Take your pick, but make no mistake, nature today is always managed, even when it's being preserved.

Those who argue for a kill fishery often complain about the holier than thou attitude of those who practise catch and release. In North America and New Zealand there is no longer even an argument, except among a few die-hards who, having pretty well fished out their kill fisheries, have begun to agitate for the right to kill fish on some of the recently re-populated rivers. No-kill is just considered an essential part of good management policy and is here to stay. In Germany it has been legislated that a dead fish is more morally correct than fishing for pleasure or spiritual contentment. Incredibly, the Green party have succeeded in making it illegal to let even an inedible fish live after catching it, putting human self-righteousness before all other ecological considerations. It goes without saying that these kind-hearted people presume to speak for the fish, which, we are to assume, would rather be dead than live as an angler's plaything. Surely, if we are sincerely going to consider the fish's point of view, it begs the question; isn't a short workout and a photo-op a better deal than the big sleep? Somebody should really find a way to ask the fish.

In Britain, there are anglers who also argue that killing for food is somehow more morally correct, as if it was not fishing primarily for pleasure. For them, catch and release is just playing with your food. These angling puritans are philosophically getting into bed with the 'antis', who clearly want to put an end to *all* recreational fishing. To my mind, we tend to take our eye off the ball here. This isn't a moral question, or even one of taste, but one of appropriate management policies for the intended use.

It's not that wild trout aren't great eating, I just think that if you want to eat trout there are waters, such as some northern Scottish lochs, that could support kill fisheries indefinitely, so by

There's more to fishing than catching fish. And sometimes less

all means take your frying pan with you. The best eating trout are those under a pound anyway. But since, as food, wild trout must fall into the dietary category of, say, lark's tongues, there is no good reason for killing a big trout other than predator management. If you haven't tried it, by the way, dining on a five-pound river trout can be compared unfavourably to eating a wet phonebook.

Whatever the fish experiences when caught, I'm satisfied that it isn't anything like what humans experience as 'pain' or 'fear'. A fish simply does not have the cognitive horsepower for complex sensations and emotions that have a psychological dimension for humans. Fish may have a degree of memory, but anyone with any angling experience has seen the trout that immediately resumes feeding, or is caught again, only minutes after being caught and released, or the salmon with the fresh cormorant wound or seal bite that takes a fly. There is nothing in their behaviour that indicates they contemplate these experiences.

I recall a big buck grayling one late summer day on the Tay. As I was releasing it, I noticed that its nose was raw and bloody, from grubbing for nymphs and caddis larvae among the stones of the riverbed, ground off at an angle like an old coal shovel. I mean, that nose looked *sore*. Nevertheless, it had risen confidently to my dry fly. Evidently, the tiny hook in its lip was not painful at all, and the hook's connection to a line and me was certainly beyond its comprehension. To all appearances, it swam away completely unaffected by the experience. How could it be otherwise? It had no knowledge or understanding of what had happened, no cognitive capacity to anticipate it, or sufficient memory worry about it later. I'm convinced that grayling will not remember much about that encounter, or make sense of it – it can't. But I will, for the rest of my conscious life.

Does being caught and killed, or caught and released, even matter to a fish? Morally speaking, just when does a fish's life, or the quality of a fish's life, begin to matter? The philosopher John Harris argues that, in order to value life, a being would have to be aware that it has a life to value, something like Locke's conception of self-consciousness, which requires an intelligence able to 'consider itself in different times and places', and is, he says, 'not simple awareness, but awareness of awareness. To value its own life, a being would have to be aware of itself as an independent centre of consciousness, existing over time with a future that it was capable of envisaging and wishing to experience.'

In other words, a fish cannot ask itself 'who am I?' With no capacity for apperception, the life of a fish matters more to you and me than it does to the fish itself. It has neither experience of itself as an individual, nor the cognitive equipment to envisage or wish anything. A widely reported experiment observed the response of trout to bee venom and acid injected into their lips. Dr L. Sneddon concluded that her experiment 'fulfilled the criteria for animal pain', ergo the trout experienced pain. Sneddon's research offers no explanation on how fish might interpret such noxious stimulation as pain. According to the American Pain Society, pain is not merely a physical sensation of a noxious stimulus, but is a conscious experience with sensory and emotional components, modulated by mental, emotional, and sensory mechanisms. Professor J.D. Rose argues that, while it is undeniable that fish react to noxious stimuli in ways that can be imputed to be pain or fear, by those who desire to see it so, the make-up of its brain and the existence that it leads means it is impossible for a trout to experience these sensations in anything like human terms. If it were otherwise, I might have a different attitude toward catch and release fishing, but I sincerely believe trout do not suffer post-traumatic stress disorder, a catfish cannot know love, hate or happiness, a herring does not dream, need counselling or sing the blues. A fish just is – a quality a Buddhist can respect without imagining them in little hats and jackets.

Too innocent for this century? The wild cutthroat trout

On the other hand, I need fish for my own happiness, love fishing for them, especially wild trout and salmon, and cannot imagine my life without them or the strange and beautiful environments they inhabit. That human psychic need, not food, is our true basis of value for a wild trout or salmon, and why it is essential that we preserve wild fish and their environment. That utterly selfish human desire to be involved with them – to care for their survival, consider our self in those different places, to wish our self into that experience – is why fishing is good for fish.

In *Meditations on Hunting*, Ortega says, 'to the sportsman, the death of the game is not what interests him; that is not his purpose. What interests him is everything he had to do to achieve that death – that is, the hunt'. Incidentally, Ortega also argues that hunting that does not end in the death of the animal is ridiculous. He argues that the 'British aberration of photographic hunting', in which the animal is not killed but merely 'collected' by camera, removes the essential reality and meaning from the hunt, its tactile drama and inevitable tragedy. While the death of the animal is not essential to the experience, the possibility of the death of the animal authenticates the hunt and grounds it in reality. His is a Spanish perspective, of course, an existentialist one written over sixty years ago, and there is clearly a qualitative as well as a quantitative difference between catching a fish and shooting a big warm-blooded animal like a deer (or, God forbid, an elephant), but there is certainly something to his argument. The great thing about fly-fishing is that, ideally, the death of the fish is not inevitable. The drama of the hunt is real, but the angler usually has the choice to kill or not. Except in Germany, that is.

So, can catch and release fly-fishing catch on in Britain? On many salmon waters, it already has. On certain heavily fished public rivers, where few trout live long enough to reach any size, it is evident that a slot-management policy would improve the quality significantly, and reduce the negative effects of artificial stocking. All we have to do is get off the defensive, stop beating ourselves up over how we are regarded by the implacable anti-angling people, forget the posturing on both sides of the catch and release argument, and remember that to have good wild trout fishing you have to leave some fish in the water.

6. Limits

It's a seven-mile walk from the upper end of the Spray Lakes, a muddy trudge and steady climb through thick timber, along a horse trail that follows Bryant Creek to its junction with Marvel Creek and finally Marvel Lake. Marvel Lake sits, marvellously, at the foot of Wonder Pass, which leads to Mount Assiniboine, the lesser Matterhorn of the Alberta Rockies. The first time I walked it there was a bad washout on the Spray road, so it was closer to twelve miles and a real heartbreaker with forty-pound packs. I swear half that weight was in the old wood and canvas pack frames we used, primarily for reasons of style.

With me were my pal Jim and my father, making his last big hike as it turned out. Dad was in the closing stages of his mid-life *been there - done that* phase, and the previous summer he and Jim had canoed the Bowron Lakes chain in British Columbia. On this walk he brought along five pounds of military surplus powdered egg, which had been such a big hit on the Bowron trip that he had twenty pounds of it left over. Still thinking of it as food, he was trying to use it up in camp meals. When we finally reached the lake and set up the tent, poor old Dad just crawled into it and stayed there. He never did see Marvel Lake, said he just didn't have enough strength left to care. All he could think about was the twelve-mile walk out, but decided that if he lay quietly in the tent for a couple of days he might just make it.

There was another camp at the outlet of the lake, two guys who had also learned of the big cutthroats that could be caught when the ice went out. They had packed in an inflatable rubber raft and I watched one of them hook up with a fish out in front of the big logjam at the head of the stream. He played this fish for over half an hour. It pulled the raft around in big circles while he shouted to his partner on the shore. The partner was anxious to get down the trail for home and was making a big deal about his pal taking too long to land the fish. I think the guy on shore was a little jealous over the obvious size of that trout, so he was berating his pal as if it was utterly inconsiderate of him to be wasting time and holding them back. 'Nice going,' he shouted with heavy-handed sarcasm as he paced the bank, 'Oh, nice going.'

When the guy beached his fish his buddy went real quiet. I saw the trout when it was held up for a photograph. It weighed twelve pounds and it is still biggest cutthroat trout I have ever seen. I stood on the logjam to watch this event and observed the schools of big trout that circled regularly, occasionally swimming under the logs at my feet. The trout seemed to travel in platoons, some composed entirely of trout the size of the one I'd just seen caught. These fish ignored my best efforts with the fly rod, but I'd seen enough to realise that Marvel Lake was something special.

The only other remarkable incident, which cut the trip short, was when for about twenty minutes my father regained consciousness and left the tent for a pee and a discouraging attempt to get his legs to work. He had stiffened up pretty badly but hobbled almost as far as the lakeshore, and in that short time a bear got into the tent and ate all the food. This was a bear with some experience at lightning raids and vandalism because, unbelievably, all that was left was one perforated and drool-covered can of baked beans. The roof of the tent was ripped and it was raining, our clothes, sleeping bags and other gear were all wet and torn and tangled up. There was, of course, a thick damp scum of powdered egg over everything, enough to make you want to set fire to the whole mess and just walk away.

It was too late in the day to walk out, and old Dad had a fixin' to die look on his face, so Jim and I walked around to an outfitter's horse camp on the lake's north shore. After hearing our story the camp cook gave us a big pot of boiled potatoes leftover from the previous evening. She also let us borrow her big yellow dog to chase that damned bear out of the valley. We repaired the roof with a layer of polythene, and for supper, our appetites whetted by a stimulating bear chase, we made a kind of sticky Spanish omelette from the potatoes, beans, and some salvaged powdered egg. This was fried with no butter or bacon until it was nicely scorched and then divided among the three of us. Dad poked at this muck with all the enthusiasm of a condemned man at his last meal. There was at least some coffee to wash it down with, and thankfully enough for the morning. I hoped this might give the old boy something to hold on to through the night. Evidently, the project for the next day was to get Dad down the trail without actually having to carry him.

It was another six years before I made that walk again, this time with my brother John and a pal. The washout had been repaired so it was just the seven-mile slog. The signs of change were everywhere and although there was still snow in the shaded spots, the season seemed a couple of weeks further on in terms of human activity. The horse packers had obviously been busy, as the trail was a sloppy seven-mile river of ankle deep brown mud and horseshit. The parks service had banned camping at the lakeside by then, in an effort to control rubbish and environmental damage by the burgeoning numbers of hikers, as well as a partial curb on the inevitable entanglements with bears.

They had erected a log chalet a mile back from the lake on the Bryant Creek meadow. The new rules posted on the door stated that campers had to bunk and cook in the building, with no open fires and no food or rubbish left outdoors. This new situation came as a shock to my party, and we grumbled mightily about the way things were going, the passing of the wild west and rugged individualism – not to mention the loss of freedom to camp anywhere we damn well pleased. To hear us gripe you might have thought we were the last of the Mohicans. My brother Johnny observed that, so far at least, there was no dress code. There were already several hikers in residence when we arrived, although we noted with satisfaction that none of them seemed to be anglers. A guy who looked like John Denver sat on a rock in front of the chalet, rather ostentatiously reading a book of poetry by E.E. Cummings.

On this trip we really got stuck into some trout. I found a small wooden pram that Floyd Smith's outfitters had packed in to the lake. While our friend worked around the shore, Johnny and I rowed out into the lake to enjoy one of the best day's fly-fishing I've ever had. The pram was too small for two to cast comfortably so we took only one rod out with us. We found the trout were feeding hard on small black Chironomid midges, emerging from the emerald green surface. I found a decent imitation in a sparse, size sixteen Grey Hackle, which the trout acknowledged with confident, porpoising, head-and-tail rises.

Johnny would hook a fish and, since we had no net, I would get it into the boat by hand or release it, then he would pass the rod to me and help with my fish. He tried to light up a smoke while I fished, but action was so fast he held an unlit cigarette in his mouth through three fish. We saw that a big catch was imminent, and quickly established the rule that no fish would be kept unless it was bigger than the previous one. We lost several fish at the boat and put back at least as many as we killed, but even with this limitation and sharing the rod, when we added our catch to those of our other pal we finished up the day with a heavy bag of trout from two to nearly five pounds. I think it was the realisation that we had to carry the fish out rather than any concern about numbers that caused us to stop, but the rise had also begun to tail off. At any rate, our thirst for action had been thoroughly slaked.

We were pretty well pumped up by the experience. I had enjoyed very few days fishing as good before that. Now, thirty years later, I see those few hours among the best in my lifetime. Sharing the rod and the fun with my brother, the straightforward enthusiasm of the trout combined with the spectacular beauty of the place, makes this one of my all-time great life events. We strung the fish onto a long peeled sapling and packed them up the hill to the new chalet.

We proudly laid the fish out on a patch of snow at the side of the chalet, feeling full of the solid good cheer that accompanies the bringing of heap meat into camp. A few of the hikers gathered around to express amazement at the catch. It obviously came as a surprise to them that such fine looking creatures were to be found in the lake. They really were handsome trout; thick bodied and heavy shouldered, profusely spotted, iridescent gold backs and flanks, tangerine bellies. The characteristic flame red chevron blazed under each jaw. They were the perfect type of the wild native trout of the alpine lakes. As we admired the fish, the guy with the poetry said, 'Why did you have to kill so many?»

To that point in my life, I had faced such a question. We had never really paid much attention to the idea of limits, other than as some vague goal, a reasonable point at which to stop fishing, like the number of rounds in a boxing match. It was accepted that one didn't purposefully exceed the statutory limit, but, if you reached it, you knew you'd had a good day. Our catch that day was well within the bag limit at that time, so numbers were of no concern. To us, if there was any moral consideration to the killing of fish it was only that accorded to the means employed. I mean, we didn't resort to nets, set lines, dynamite or live bait. We even

The old ways

sniffed at the use of spinning tackle. Presented with a seemingly limitless supply of fish and game, the restraints we imposed on ourselves were more a matter of aesthetics and style than a concern that we might be doing harm.

We knew we weren't fishing out of any kind of material necessity. This was sport. I hadn't yet worked out my 'fishing as a form of happiness' philosophy, but the idea that the pursuit of trout by fair sporting means was anything other than the righteous, red-blooded behaviour of an upstanding chap had never entered my mind. That day at Marvel Lake, I faced the real meaning of public ownership, and the distinct and uncomfortable idea that I had taken more than my share.

I wasn't the only one, because from that point the other hikers really gave us the cold shoulder. John Denver was obviously the alpha male in the group, so the others were pretty quick to line up and register their distaste for what was apparently to be regarded as a middle-sized crime against nature and the commonweal. We looked at each other and without a word started to pack up the fish and make ready for the walk out. At the time I wondered what these gentle folk would have done if we had dragged a moose into camp.

Our sullen departure was ameliorated somewhat by the sudden appearance of a park ranger on horseback. I figured him for a romantic, since he had the look and demeanour of a full-time cowboy rather than a park official. Young but cut from the old cloth, he was impressed by the catch of trout and actually quite congratulatory. He must have clocked the atmosphere around the chalet because he made a big show of hefting and admiring a couple of the bigger trout, and then he offered to carry them out for us on his packhorse.

This was too good an offer to even offer a polite protest and we jumped at it. The ranger was riding out that day so we had only to walk over to his line-cabin and wait while he packed his horses. We saw that he really was a romantic when we got to talking about hunting and bears and he showed us his big single-action Colt pistol, certainly against the prevailing laws. Even at that time the established park protocol was distinctly pro-bear. Defence strategies were limited to shouting, climbing trees and playing dead, all sure-fire ways to increase a bear's interest in you, by the way. There are few better baits for a hungry bear than a nice fat saddle-horse, but the parks service wouldn't allow him to carry a rifle. Our boy said he was goddammed if some grizzly was going to get him or his horse without a fight. He was clearly born too late.

By the time we were on the trail we were fully restored to high spirits. As we walked down behind the horses we laughed and joked about the fishing and what a great day we'd had. I think we knew even then that it was one of the best we could ever expect, and were delighted that we could say it was so good that we needed a horse to pack out the fish. The ranger was party to these high spirits and laughed when we remarked, over and over, on the two big sacks full of trout that hung from the packsaddle (I realise that I've been bragging a little here, so I guess I'm still only partly reconstructed).

That was my last hike into Marvel Lake and by now I'm sure that there have been even more developments to accommodate the increasing numbers of visitors and the changing use of the Canadian national parks. For all I know they are holding summer arts festivals up on Bryant Creek. That wasn't my last big catch of fish either, though for many years now I have taken very few fish home. I still like to eat a wild trout now and then, but they taste best when fried in butter over a campfire. Also, over time, I've come to accept that one man's meat is another's Bambi. Wild fish and game are definitely not in limitless supply, they do not belong to me, and are partly owned by everybody, including those who don't want to take their share.

Some people like to think that the rivers and lakes still have trout swimming around in them, even if, as non-anglers, they don't have a chance to get to know wild fish in their natural state. Just believing that the fish are there is enough. Others think of wild things as sacred. While I don't take that pantheistic attitude to nature, and like to argue that fishing is what fish are for, I'm in deep sympathy with those who just want some things to stay wild and healthy and undisturbed. A lot of fine country has disappeared forever through the frightening growth of population and use, some hauntingly beautiful hunting ground and achingly good angling water literally loved to death by enthusiastic sports just like me. I don't have any answer to that problem, other than to treat it all with ever more care and restraint, or just stay home and watch the outdoor channel. What I won't hear again, directed at me, is 'why did you have to kill so many?'

'We fish for pleasure, and fishing becomes pleasure from within ourselves in proportion to the skill and knowledge, to the imagination and flexibility of soul that we bring to it. Like the hunter, the hawker and the fowler, the fisherman takes life in finding his pleasure. It is reasonable to ask him that he make it as keen and thorough and satisfying, as productive of growth in himself as he reasonably can. For only then can it be the strong and sensitive pleasure of a civilised man.'

Roderick Haig-Brown
A River Never Sleeps

* * * * *

Bibliography

Borger, Gary A. *Designing Trout Flies* (1991) Tomorrow River Press, Wausau, Wisconsin

Brooks, Charles E. *Nymph Fishing For Larger Trout* (1976) Crown Publishers, New York

Clarke, Brian *The Pursuit of Stillwater Trout* (1975). A & C Black, London

Edmonds, Harfield H. and Norman N. Lee *Brook and River Trouting: A Manual of Modern North Country Methods* (1916) Smith Settle Otley

Edye, Huish 1941 *The Angler and the Trout* (1941) A & C Black, London

Fogg,W.S. Roger *The Art of the Wet Fly* (197)9 A & C Black, London

Galloup, Kelly, and Linsenman, Bob, *Modern Streamers for Trophy Trout*

Goddard, John and Brian Clarke *The Trout And The Fly* (1980) Ernest Benn, London & Tonbridge

Haig-Brown, Roderick L. *A River Never Sleeps* (1946) Collins, London

Halford, Frederick M. *Modern Development of the Dry Fly* (1910) Routledge, London

Harris, J.R. *An Anger's Entomology* (1952) Collins, New Naturalist Series

Moore, (T.C. Kingsmill) *A Man May Fish* (1960) Herbert Jenkins, London.

LaFontaine, Gary *Caddisflies* (1981) Nick Lyons Books, New York
   The Dry Fly: New Angles (1990) The Lyons Press, Guilford, Connecticut

Lawrie, W.H. *The Book of the Rough Stream Nymph* (1947) Oliver and Boyd, Edinburgh
   Scottish Trout Flies (1966) Frederick Muller, London

Leisenring, James E & V.S. Hidy *The Art Of Tying The Wet Fly And Fishing The Flymph* (1971) Crown Publishers, New York

Luce, A.A. *Fishing and Thinking* (1959) Hodder & Stoughton

Marinaro, Vincent C. *A Modern Dry Fly Code* (1950) 1997 The Lyons Press, New York
   In the Ring of the Rise (1976) 1995 Swan Hill Press, Shrewsbury, Shropshire

Mottram, James C. *Fly Fishing: Some New Arts and Mysteries (1915)* 1921 The Field Press, London

Murray, Sir John and Laurence Pullar *Bathymetrical Survey of the Freshwater Lochs of Scotland, Vol 1* (1910) Callenger Office, Edinburgh

O'Reilly, Peter *Trout and Salmon Flies of Ireland* (1995) 2002 Merlin Unwin Books, Ludlow

Ortega y Gasset *Meditations on Hunting* (1942) 1986 Scribners, New York

Proper, Datus C. *What The Trout Said* (1982) 1993 Swan Hill Press, Shrewsbury

Roberts, John *A Guide to River Trout Flies* (1989) 1995 The Crowood Press
To Rise A Trout: Dry Fly Fishing for Trout on Rivers and Streams (1988) 1994 The Crowood Press, Ramsbury, Marlborough

Rose, J.D. *The neurological behaviour of fishes and the question of awareness and pain* (2002) Reviews in Fisheries Science 10: 1-38 (http://uwadmnweb.uwyo.edu/Zoology/faculty/Rose/Critique%20of%20Sneddon%20article.pdf)

Russell, Franklin *The Hunting Animal* (1984) Harper and Row, New York

Schullery, Paul *Royal Coachman – the Lure and Legends of Fly-Fishing* (1999) Simon & Schuster, New York.

Schwiebert, Ernest G. *Matching the Hatch: A Practical Guide To Imitation Of Insects Found On Eastern and Western Trout* (1955) 1972 Macmillan, New York.

Scott, Jock *Greased Line fishing For Salmon: Compiled From The Fishing papers of the late A.H.E. Wood Of Glassel* (1936) 1937 Seeley, Service & Co., London

Skues, G.E.M. *The Way Of A Trout With A Fly* (1921) A & C Black, London

Sloane, Robert *The Truth About Trout (Revisited) – Observation, Presentation & the Functional Fly* (1983) 2002, FlyLife Publishing, Tasmania

Sneddon L.U. Braithwaite V.A. & Gentle M.J. (2003) *Do fish have nociceptors: evidence for the evolution of a vertebrate sensory system* Proc. Roy. Soc., London

Stewart, W.C. *The Practical Angler* (1857) 1958 A & C Black, London

Swisher, Doug and Carl Richards *Selective Trout* (1971) 2000, The Lyons Press, New York
Emergers (1991) The Lyons Press, New York

Taverner, Eric *Trout Fishing From All Angles* (1929) Lonsdale Library, Seeley, Service, London

Williams, A. Courtney *A Dictionary of Trout Flies* (1950) A & C Black, London

Wright, Leonard M. *Fishing the Dry Fly as a Living Insect* (1972) Dutton, New York

Index of fly tyings